FOR DUMMIES™

BESTSELLING BOOK SERIES

Access Forms & Reports For Dummies®

Cheat Sheet

Access Form and Report Toolbox

Tool	Name	Description
	Select objects	Selects objects that you've added to a form or report design.
	Control wizards	Enables wizards that help you add objects (such as combo boxes) to your forms and reports.
	Label	Adds a text label to your form or report.
	Text box	Adds a text box to your form or report.
	Option group	Creates a set of option buttons that function as a group so that only one option can be selected at a time.
	Toggle button	Adds a button that has two states — up for off and down for on.
	Option button	Adds an option button to your form or report.
	Checkbox	Adds a checkbox that can be selected or deselected.
	Combo box	Enables you to add a box where the user can select from a list of options or enter a new value.
	List box	Enables you to add a list box where a user can select from a set of pre-existing values.
	Command button	Adds a button that executes a macro or a VBA procedure.
	Image	Adds a digital image to a form or report.
	Unbound object frame	Enables you to add objects such as text or images that don't change when moving between records.
	Bound object frame	Enables you to add objects that change when moving between records.
	Page break	Enables you to add a page break to force multiple pages to appear on the form or report.
	Tab control	Enables you to create a form that has two or more tabs that group related objects.
	Subform/Subreport	Adds a subform or subreport that is tied to a different table than the main table used as the source of data for the form or report.
	Line	Adds lines to the form or report.
	Rectangle	Enables you to draw a rectangle on the form or report.
	More controls	Displays a listing of additional controls you have installed on your computer.

For Dummies: Bestselling Book Series for Beginners

BESTSELLING
BOOK SERIES

Access Forms & Reports
For Dummies®

JAN 2 5 2012

Cheat Sheet

Types of Access Queries

Type	Description
Append	Adds records to an existing table.
Crosstab	Calculates and displays summary results using a spreadsheet-like layout.
Delete	Permanently removes a specified set of records.
Make-table	Creates a new table and adds records to the new table.
Parameter	Prompts for the record selection criteria whenever the query is executed.
Select	Displays records that match a specified set of criteria.
SQL-specific	Queries that can only be created using SQL statements.
Update	Modifies existing records in a database.

Handy, Dandy Access Functions

Function	Description
Abs	Absolute value of a number
Avg	Arithmetic mean
Count	Number of records
Int	Integer value of a number
LCase	Converts a string to lowercase
Left	Returns a specified number of characters from the left side of a string
Len	Length of a string
LTrim	Removes extra spaces from the beginning of a string
Max	Maximum value
Min	Minimum value
Now	Current date and time
Replace	Replaces a string with a different string
Right	Returns a specified number of characters from the right side of a string
Rnd	Random number
Round	Rounds a number
RTrim	Removes extra spaces from the end of a string
Sum	The sum of values
Time	Current system time
Trim	Removes extra spaces from both ends of a string
UCase	Converts a string to uppercase

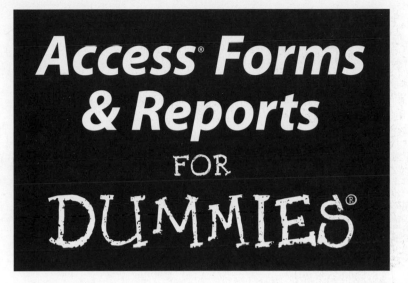

Access® Forms & Reports
FOR DUMMIES®

by Brian Underdahl

Author of iPAQ For Dummies

WILEY

Wiley Publishing, Inc.

Access® Forms & Reports For Dummies®

Published by
Wiley Publishing, Inc.
111 River Street
Hoboken, NJ 07030-5774

www.wiley.com

For general information on our other products and services, please contact our Customer Care Department within the U.S. at 800-762-2974, outside the U.S. at 317-572-3993, or fax 317-572-4002.

For technical support, please visit www.wiley.com/techsupport.

Wiley also publishes its books in a variety of electronic formats. Some content that appears in print may not be available in electronic books.

Library of Congress Control Number: 2005927725

ISBN-13: 978-0-7645-9965-1

ISBN-10: 0-7645-9965-8

Manufactured in the United States of America

10 9 8 7 6 5 4 3 2 1

1O/RZ/QZ/QU/IN

WILEY

About the Author

Brian Underdahl is the well-known, best selling author of over 70 computer books on a broad range of subjects. He has appeared on a number of TV shows, including the *Computer Chronicles,* and several *TechTV* programs, and is the subject of an hour-long interview on the syndicated *Computer Outlook* radio program. One of his titles was recently recommended to viewers by Scott Gurvey, Bureau Chief, on the *Nightly Business Report* on PBS, and his books have won awards including an Award of Merit from the Northern California Technical Communications Competition and the Referenceware Excellence Award for best title in the Graphic Design and Multimedia category.

Brian has been involved in personal computers from their beginning and has a background in electrical engineering. His last "real" job was as a Senior Programmer/Analyst for a large company, where he worked hard to bring the power and freedom of PCs to the desktops.

Brian figures that it's the author who should do the work so that readers can get their money's worth. That's why his books are different — he takes the time to explain what's going on so that readers can understand the subjects easily.

Author's Acknowledgments

No book is the product of one person, even if one person has the title of author and gets to have his or her name on the cover. I'm very lucky to have a lot of people I can thank for all the hard work and effort they put into this book. They include Terri Varveris, Nicole Haims, and Virginia Andersen.

I'd also like to thank the many people who provided me with the wonderful Access tools and add-ons so that I could give you an idea about how you can get even more from Access. Please do check out the Web sites I list for these great products — you owe it to yourself to see how much more productive you can be.

Finally, many thanks to Fred Holabird of Holabird Americana, `www.hola birdamericana.com,` for allowing me to use samples from the Holabird Americana databases in order to be able to show some real world examples in this book. Fred is a good friend and I'll always be grateful for his help!

Publisher's Acknowledgments

We're proud of this book; please send us your comments through our online registration form located at www.dummies.com/register/.

Some of the people who helped bring this book to market include the following:

Acquisitions, Editorial, and Media Development

Project Editor: Nicole Haims

Acquisitions Editor: Terri Varveris

Technical Editor: Virginia Andersen

Editorial Manager: Carol Sheehan

Media Development Manager: Laura VanWinkle

Media Development Supervisor: Richard Graves

Editorial Assistant: Amanda Foxworth

Cartoons: Rich Tennant (www.the5thwave.com)

Composition Services

Project Coordinator: Maridee Ennis

Layout and Graphics: Claudia Bell, Andrea Dahl, Lauren Goddard, Denny Hager, Joyce Haughey, Stephanie D. Jumper, Barry Offringa, Heather Ryan

Proofreaders: David Faust, Leeann Harney, Carl William Pierce, TECHBOOKS Production Services

Indexer: Sherry Massey

Publishing and Editorial for Technology Dummies

> **Richard Swadley,** Vice President and Executive Group Publisher
>
> **Andy Cummings,** Vice President and Publisher
>
> **Mary Bednarek,** Executive Acquisitions Director
>
> **Mary C. Corder,** Editorial Director

Publishing for Consumer Dummies

> **Diane Graves Steele,** Vice President and Publisher
>
> **Joyce Pepple,** Acquisitions Director

Composition Services

> **Gerry Fahey,** Vice President of Production Services
>
> **Debbie Stailey,** Director of Composition Services

Contents at a Glance

Table of Contents

● ●

Introduction

. . . .

Microsoft Access can be an incredibly useful application, but it can also be very frustrating if you don't know how to make it do what you want it to do. In a perfect world, you'd have a guru around, 24/7 — someone who knows Access inside and out and is willing to guide you along the way, showing you handy little tricks and useful techniques that help you to get the results you need.

Well, I may not be there with you, but this book is the next best thing. I've gathered the really useful pieces of information that you need to create powerful queries, very easy-to-use forms, and reports that actually tell the story of what is going on inside your data. Along the way, I make sure to show you the special tricks and techniques that I use.

About This Book

Access Forms & Reports For Dummies is a hands-on guide that uses real-world examples to show you just what you need to know about Access and why you need to know it. You won't find a bunch of buzzwords and jargon. Rather, you do find the solid information you really need and can't find elsewhere about creating queries, forms, and reports. Yes, I do give you good, solid information about queries in addition to forms and reports because queries are an essential element that will help you create better forms and reports.

Access Forms & Reports For Dummies is also a reference that you can use as you like. If you have a specific problem you need to solve right now, you can jump directly to the related topic and skip around as much as you want. But if you really want to make Access work for you, I suggest that you read through the entire book because you will discover many things you don't already know.

Finally, *Access Forms & Reports For Dummies* is for users of pretty much any version of Access from Access 97 onwards. The basics of queries, forms, and reports haven't changed much, so you'll find this book extremely helpful no matter which version of Access you use.

Conventions Used in This Book

We've used a few conventions in this book to make it easier for you to spot special information. Here are those conventions:

- New terms are identified by using *italic*.

- Web sites addresses (URLs) are designated by using a `monospace` font.

- Any command you enter at a command prompt is shown in bold and usually set on a separate line. Setoff text in italic represents a placeholder. For example, the text might read:

  Enter the following expression, using your own name and dynamic report title:

  = *"Report title"*&[CurrentProject].[Name]

- Command arrows, which are typeset as ⇨, are used in a list of menus and options. For example, Tools⇨Options means to choose the Tools menu and then choose the Options command.

- Key combinations are shown with a plus sign, such as Ctrl+F2. This means you should hold down the Ctrl key while you press the F2 key.

- All Access properties and fields are set apart in `monospace` font, as well, like this: Use the `Input Mask` property of the Data tab to create an input mask.

- Wherever I instruct you to use a snippet of code, I set it apart like this:

```
INSERT INTO LIVEWINBID
SELECT [Auction 67].*
FROM [Auction 67];
```

What You Don't Have to Read

I always have a hard time telling people that they don't have to read certain parts of a book if they don't care to. You can find some really useful information hidden away in things like the text next to Technical Stuff icons, but I understand if you feel that there isn't room in your brain for one more bit of technical information. Maybe the best thing that I can recommend is that if you don't want to read the whole book now, start by reading what looks the most interesting and then, after you've discovered how much really cool stuff I include, go back and have a look at what you missed the first time. You'll be glad you did!

Icons Used in This Book

Access Forms & Reports For Dummies includes icons that point out special information. Here are the icons I use and what they mean:

This icon makes you seem like a real Access expert in no time. It highlights special tricks and shortcuts that make using Access even easier. Don't miss any of these!

This icon reminds you of important information that can be far too easy to forget and which can cause a lot of frustration when you do forget.

Be careful when you see this icon. It points out an area where you'll want to be extra cautious so that you don't cause yourself problems. It also tells you how to avoid the problems.

Technical Stuff is information for folks who want to know all the geeky details.

Real World Examples tell you about actual ways to apply your new Access techniques. Don't miss any of these because they're sure to give you a lot of ideas you can adapt and use.

From time to time I may direct you to another book that can be a good resource for you as you become a master of all things Access. This icon highlights those moments.

Foolish Assumptions

Making assumptions is always a gamble because assumptions can quickly come back to haunt you. That said, in writing this book I made some assumptions about you. This book is for you if:

- You have Access and want to know how to use it more effectively.
- You don't yet have Access, but are wondering if getting Access can help you organize all of that data you're currently trying to manipulate with Excel or some other spreadsheet.

✔ You have a bunch of data that you want to turn into useful information.

✔ You want to see how you can create more efficient Access reports and quit wasting so many trees.

✔ You would like to know how to use data from an external database without having to get down on your knees to beg permission every time you need to run a report.

✔ You have finally realized that you are a *5th Wave* cartoon addict and simply can't pass up the chance to see what is hidden in these pages.

How This Book Is Organized

Access Forms & Reports For Dummies has six parts. Each part is self-contained, but all the content is somewhat interconnected. That way you'll see the most useful information without a lot of boring repetition.

Part 1: Accessing Both Ends: Getting Data in and Info Out

This part shows you the basics of queries, forms, and reports. You see how these pieces fit together and I make sure that you have the fundamentals down pat so that you have a good foundation for the rest of the topics.

Part II: Creating Effective Queries

Queries enable you to work with sets of data instead of simply dumping everything into the pot. This part shows you how to create effective queries that enable you to pick and choose what shows up in your forms and reports. You even see how you can step beyond simple queries by having a look underneath the fancy face that Access throws onto your queries.

Part III: Building Really Useful Forms

Forms make data entry and editing into a much easier task. This part shows you how to create forms that really are useful, and it tells you how to create forms that tackle data from more than one table at a time — for even greater efficiency.

Part IV: Designing Great Reports

With Access reports you can turn data into useful information. This part shows you how to create great reports that look good and that provide a wealth of understandable information.

Part V: Way Cool Advanced Queries, Forms, and Reports

Ordinary techniques are for ordinary people. This part takes you well beyond the ordinary and shows you how to get so much more from your queries, forms, and reports. This part also shows you some great tools you can use to make Access into an even more powerful partner for your database needs.

Part VI: The Part of Tens

This part tells you about some places on the Web where you can find even more information about Access. It concludes with some vital tips to remember as you work with Access.

Part I

Accessing Both Ends: Getting Data In and Info Out

The 5th Wave   By Rich Tennant

"Using the form to evaluate our software is simple. Just click 'Excellent', 'Good', 'Fair', or 'I'm Really Incapable of Appreciating Someone Else's Hard Work'."

In this part . . .

Y ou need a good foundation if you're going to build anything useful and long lasting. In this part, I make sure that you have a good foundation for the topics in rest of the book. Here you discover the basics of queries, forms, and reports that you really need but that you may have missed up until now.

Chapter 1

Getting to Know Forms and Reports

*W*ithout forms and reports an Access database is just a jumble of hard-to-use information. But with really good forms and reports that same database becomes both informative and a joy to use. Well-designed forms and reports make your Access databases into something that's far beyond the ordinary in utility, ease of use, and flexibility.

If you've been playing around with Access for a while, you have probably at least tried to create some forms and reports. Maybe some of your efforts didn't seem too bad, but you've probably had your share of frustration, too. Creating forms and reports that really do what you want them to do can be an awfully exasperating experience.

In this chapter, I show you a number of interesting things about forms, reports, and their sidekick queries so that you can see what each of them can do and why they're all important. You discover how queries can enhance the capabilities of forms and reports. I finish up the chapter by very briefly introducing you to some really cool tools that (find out even more about them in Chapter 20).

Finding a Fascination with Forms

In order to understand the importance of forms in an Access database, begin by looking at the alternative. Figure 1-1 shows the *Datasheet view* of a typical Access table (a *table* is the structure where Access stores information in your database). The Datasheet view looks an awful lot like an Excel worksheet. You are likely pretty familiar with this view of a database because it seems as though almost everyone's first attempt at a database is to just create a list in a spreadsheet. Welcome to the "if the only tool you have is a hammer, everything looks like a nail" club!

In Datasheet view each record is displayed in a single row with columns for each of the database fields. Even though this view of the data is probably pretty familiar, it's not very convenient. For one thing, unless you're only keeping track of a little information about each item, it's really hard to see an entire record in Datasheet view because everything has to fit into one row; that means you have to scroll back and forth to see all the fields. Depending on the length of each field, sometimes you can't even see all the entire contents of a single field on-screen. And don't even think about seeing a single record wrap around and take up multiple rows — making everything fit on-screen simply is not an option.

Each field is in a column

Records appear in rows

ItemID	State	County/Category	District/Sub-Ce	LotSize	Title	TypeID	
7	Arizona	Kingman			Map of the Bimetal Mine	Maps	Map p
8	Arizona	Yavapai	Big Bug	Lot of 24.	Leonita Development Company	Various	All of
9	California	San Francisco			57th Annual Session I.O.O.F Ribbon,	Ribbons	Portra
10	Nevada	Nye			Manhattan Higgins Mining Co.	Stocks	Cert.
11	Nevada	Storey	Gold Hill		Exchequer MC.	Stocks	Cert.#
12	Nevada	Storey	Virginia		Hale & Norcross MC	Stocks	Cert.#
13	Nevada	Nye	Bullfrog		Shoshone National Bank MC	Stocks	Cert.
14				Lot of 6.	Greenwater Copper Mines Smelter C	Stocks	Cert.
15	Nevada	Esmeralda	Gold Mountain		Oriental Gold Mining Co	Stocks	Cert.
16	Nevada	Esmeralda	Gold Mountain		Oriental GMC	Stocks	Cert.
17					Pioneer Cons. MC.	Stocks	Cert.
18	Nevada	Eureka	Prospect Moun	Lot of 2.	Ruby Hill Tunnel & Mining Co.	Stocks	Cert.
19	Nevada	Nye	Tonopah		West End Cons. MC	Stocks	Cert.
20	Nevada	Nye	Bullfrog	Lot of 2.	Tramps Cons. Extension MC.	Stocks	Cert.
21	New Mexico			Lot of 4 dif	New Mexico Embossed Port Wine B	Bottles	All Ar
22					Stillwater Token	Tokens	Stillw.
23	Nevada	Nevada.	Casino.		Palace Club Ashtray.	Ashtray	Blue a
24	Nevada	Nevada.	Casino.		Harold's Club Ashtray.	Ashtray	Black
25	N/A	General.		Lot of 16.	Prince Albert and Bond Street Tobac	Tins	Bond
26	N/A	Aviation.	General.		Polaroid Jet Flight Goggles.	Aviation	C.195
27	N/A	Mining.	General.	Lot of 2.	Drafting materials.	Mining	Draftin
28	N/A	Banking.	General.		Bank of America National Trust and S	Banking	

Record: |◄ ◄ | 1 | ► | ►| | ►* | of 11536

Figure 1-1:
The Access Datasheet view of the information in a table looks like an Excel spreadsheet.

Record navigation tools

There are, of course, some other factors that make the Datasheet view pretty inconvenient for most purposes. Can you imagine how little fun it would be to scroll through screen after screen trying to locate a specific record in Datasheet view? Now imagine that instead of finding a single record you want to find a dozen or so related records in a table containing 10,000 or more records. It's almost enough to make you want to go and live on a desert island where there aren't any computers, isn't it?

Fortunately, there's a good solution at hand in the guise of *forms*. Access forms provide a much more convenient way for you to interact with your database. Finding how to create great forms is certainly going to be a lot easier than packing up your stuff for that move to a desert island. The following sections give you a look at some of the ways forms can help you.

Using forms to streamline data input

No database has much value until it contains information. You wouldn't be able to get any useful data from an empty database, so a very important task in creating a database is inputting your data. Sure, you might have some existing data that you can import, but even that data required input at some point.

Entering data into a table by using the Datasheet view really isn't much fun. You first have to open the table and then locate the record where you want to enter your data. Maybe you're adding to an existing record or perhaps you're adding a new record right after the last existing one in the datasheet. When you've selected the correct record, you have to move the insertion point to each field in turn and type in the information. It's easy, of course, to accidentally start typing into the wrong field — especially if the layout of the table doesn't quite match the layout of the information you're entering (and when have you seen data on paper that did match the layout of the table?).

Forms can make inputting data much easier in several ways:

- Forms typically have labels that make seeing exactly which field you're filling in far easier.
- Forms can have drop-down lists so that you simply choose the proper information from the list without worrying about mistyping the data.
- Forms are usually laid out so that there's plenty of room to see all the fields in a record. That makes keeping track of which record you're entering a much easier task.

✔ You can easily create forms for special purposes such as entering data in specific sets of fields. In this case, the form might not need to include all the fields; when you only use what you need, you end up with a simpler, less confusing form.

✔ Forms don't have to be laid out by using the same field order as the table. This is an especially handy feature if you're inputting data that is laid out quite differently than your table.

✔ You can set up forms to validate the data so that users can't mess up your database by entering bogus information.

Even if some of these form features seem a little bit beyond your interests or immediate needs right now, don't worry — you'll find out about all of them and get many more great ideas in the chapters that follow.

Entering data with the Form Wizard

Entering data into an Access database by using a form is much easier than entering data directly into a table in Datasheet view. Figure 1-2 shows a simple form you might create, using the Form Wizard in Access. In this case the form was not optimized in any way — it's simply the way the wizard created it.

Enter data in the fields.

Field labels   Use drop-down list boxes to choose from a list.

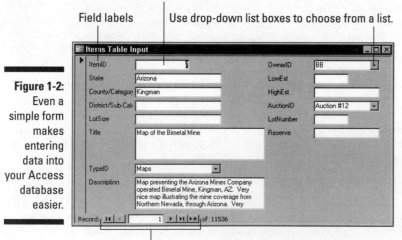

Figure 1-2:
Even a simple form makes entering data into your Access database easier.

Use these controls to navigate between records.

If you compare the form shown in Figure 1-2 with the Datasheet view shown in Figure 1-1, it's pretty easy to see how much more convenient the form is for entering data. Each of the fields is clearly labeled (even if the Form Wizard didn't quite figure out the proper size of a couple of the labels). Here are a couple of ways that the Form Wizard is easy to use:

- ✔ **Easy movement between fields:** You can move between the fields by clicking the field you want or by pressing the Tab key. Because the fields are labeled, you can easily to move to specific fields and skip the fields you don't want to use for now.

- ✔ **Easy movement between records:** You can use the navigation controls at the bottom of the form to navigate between records. In forms, pressing Page Down moves you to the next record and Page Up moves you to the previous record. In Datasheet view, Page Down and Page Up move you to a new screen page of records. (The number of records you jump depends on how many records are visible on the screen, and this can change depending on how you display the Datasheet window. Don't you just love the inconsistency?)

  In Datasheet view you can use the Up Arrow and Down Arrow to move a single record at a time, but in a form the arrow keys move the insertion point between fields.

- ✔ **Customizable drop-down lists:** Because you can modify the underlying table with *lookup fields* (fields that enable a user to select from a list of predefined values — see Chapter 17), you can make certain that the fields contain specific values that are found in related tables. For example, in Figure 1-2, the `TypeID`, `OwnerID`, and `AuctionID` fields can only contain specific values that are found in some related tables; the form includes three drop-down list boxes. Instead of typing an entry in these fields (and risking errors due to mistyping), you simply choose a value from the drop-down list.

- ✔ **Larger input areas:** To make entering longer values easier, the wizard provides larger input areas (in this case the `Title` and `Description` fields). In fact, if you type more information than can fit into the on-screen display of one of these fields, Access even automatically adds a scroll bar along the right side of the field so that you can view the entire value. How's that for handy?

The database I'm using in these examples contains some features such as lookup fields that you might not be using yet in your Access databases. All the special features are explained in later chapters as appropriate so that you will be able to incorporate them into your databases.

Editing information with forms

Forms are also much handier than the Datasheet view for editing existing database information. When you're editing information, forms retain all the advantages they offer when you're first entering data, of course, but there are some additional features that are especially useful for editing. As Figure 1-3 shows, if you right-click on a form field, Access pops up a very handy context menu that provides some really cool options.

Figure 1-3:
Right-click
on a form
field to
display this
menu of
options.

> Filter By Selection
> Filter Excluding Selection
> Filter For:
> Remove Filter/Sort
> Cut
> Copy
> Paste
> Sort Ascending
> Sort Descending
> Insert Object...
> Hyperlink
> Properties

For editing purposes, six of the pop-up menu commands are extremely helpful:

- **Filter By Selection:** This option limits the records that are displayed in the form to those with the same value in the selected field as the current record. For example, if you right-click on the State field and the current record shows Nevada, only records with Nevada in the State field are displayed as you move from record to record making your edits.

- **Filter Excluding Selection:** This option works in reverse compared to the first option. Only records that don't contain the currently selected value are displayed.

- **Filter For:** This option enables you to enter the value for the filter. You use this option to locate specific records that may be buried deep within your database and are therefore difficult to locate simply by scrolling through the records.

- **Remove Filter/Sort:** You use this option to reset the form so that all records are displayed in the default sort order that is used in the database.

- ✔ **Sort Ascending:** Choose this option to sort the records of a selected field in ascending alphabetical or numerical order. For example, if you choose to view the records in the `State` field and opt to sort the results in ascending alphabetical order, Alabama appears first. This and the next option are best used in a secondary field after you have applied a filter because they won't have any effect in a filtered field (unless you chose the Filter Excluding Selection option).

- ✔ **Sort Descending:** Choose this option to sort the records in descending order.

Be sure to use the Remove Filter/Sort command when you finish editing records. Otherwise you may find yourself confused later when the form doesn't display all the records that you know should be in your database.

Viewing data by using forms

You can use a form when you simply want to view the data without entering new information or editing existing records. You know that pop-up menu that appears when you right-click on a form field? Well, that same menu that makes forms so handy for editing data is just as handy when you simply want to view the records, too.

Recognizing Why Reports Rock

Okay, so forms are great, but what about reports? The following sections look at some of the ways that you can use reports; they're well worth the effort it takes to create them.

Using reports to show results

One very useful purpose for reports is to show results that aren't otherwise displayed in a table format. Create a report to see important details at a glance. Figure 1-4 shows an example of a report that summarizes results from an auction database created in Access. In this case, the report not only shows the individual records, but it also groups them according to the winning bidder and shows the subtotal, the buyer's premium, and the total amount owed for each winning bidder.

Figure 1-4:
Access
reports can
show
results
including
totals and
other types
of calcu-
lations.

The report shown in Figure 1-4 provides a good example of how a report can provide information that simply doesn't appear on its own in an Access table. Tables don't summarize the data from a collection of records, so unless you want to sit down with a calculator to figure out such details, you should create reports to get this kind of information from your database.

Using reports to present data in a professional format

Sometimes you may not need as much information as the report in Figure 1-4 includes. You may, for example, simply want a list that provides a snapshot of what's in your database. This is especially true if you want to distill complex information quickly and efficiently for your boss or client. If you just want to check things over for yourself, choose File➪Print. If you want to show off your data for others, going to the extra effort of creating a report makes sense for several good reasons:

✔ **Providing a professional layout:** Unless you are printing the data from a very small and simple table, the results of printing directly from a table's Datasheet view probably won't fit the width of your paper. Good luck trying to make sense of the resulting printout!

✔ **Easing report navigation:** You can easily include page numbers and dates on your reports — in fact, the Access Report Wizard adds this information automatically. Keeping track of a report that has dates and page numbers printed on it is much easier — especially if you have a limited amount of time to orally guide others through your exhaustive 100-page report.

✔ **Presenting data in a logical format:** You can use as much or as little room as necessary for the fields on a report to accommodate the amount of data that's in each record. Compared to the single line for each record on a printout of a table's Datasheet view, this feature alone is worth the effort.

✔ **Adding a title:** Including a title on a report is easy. With a title, you'll be able to remember the purpose of the report early on a Monday morning before your first cup of coffee kicks in.

Using reports to show data analysis

Of course, you can summarize data in an Access report, but that's just the tip of the iceberg in terms of the types of data analysis you can do. Here are just a few examples of some other ways you can use a report to analyze the information in an Access database:

✔ **Compare similar results:** You can produce a report that shows how each sales person's results compares to the average of all of your company's representatives.

✔ **Compare data over time:** You can use a report to determine which ice cream flavors to stock at each of your stands based on historical sales data.

✔ **Use data for prediction purposes:** You can use a report to show how temperature patterns affect the populations of various types of pests and use this information to predict the best time to send out flyers for your extermination business.

✔ **Determine the best course of action:** You can create a report that tells you whether it's worthwhile to set up a calling committee for your club's annual meeting based on an analysis of the results from several past meetings.

Using reports to preserve the moment

In most cases, an Access database is constantly changing as new data is entered, existing data is edited, or old data is deleted. Sometimes, though, you may have good reasons to preserve a record of exactly how things were at a particular moment in time. Consider these possibilities:

- ✔ If you keep the membership list for the local branch of your favorite club, you know that sometimes members can be a bit slow about renewing their memberships. I've seen instances where members have come back after several years away. Keeping all the past members in the database may not always be reasonable, but having an end-of-year membership report stored away is a useful way to keep the data in case you need it again in the future.

- ✔ If you run a small business, you probably want to keep track of your exact inventory at various times of the year. A dated report of your inventory stored offsite could be extremely valuable if you ever need to file an insurance claim after an untimely disaster.

- ✔ If you go into business with someone else, an Access report showing exactly which items you contributed to the business could save some arguments in the event you later split up. Sure, you both know now that the Babe Ruth baseball card is yours, but wouldn't it be nice to be able to prove it when your former partner tries to sell it for $10,000?

Even if you do keep the printouts, keeping backup copies of your database is always a good idea in case of an emergency. But be very careful. If you do need to open your old file, don't accidentally overwrite your current database file with the old copy. You can easily destroy months, or even years, of work if you're careless.

Seeing Why Both Forms and Reports Have a Place

Forms and reports seem somewhat similar in that they both provide ways to look at data that aren't available in the Datasheet view of a table. Do you really have to find out how to create both of them? Yes. Using forms and reports isn't an either/or proposition.

Even though forms and reports share some characteristics, they do have important differences, and your databases will lack a little something if you use one (and not both) of these tools.

Here's a list of things you should know about reports and forms:

- ✔ **If you want to add, remove, or change data in a table, use forms.** Sure, you can filter the data that appears in a report so that it appears as though some of the data has been removed from the database, but that's not the same as actually deleting data.

- ✔ **Use reports to view data in more than one record in a more permanent format.** In general, forms only display a single record at a time. In addition, because reports typically are meant to be printed and they often include the date, reports provide a somewhat permanent record of the information.

    It's not *strictly* true that forms can only display a single record at a time. As you will discover in later chapters (such as Chapter 10), some forms that are based on multiple tables can include a section called a *subform* that can display multiple records from the second table by using the Datasheet view.

- ✔ **Both forms and reports depend on a table (or a query as discussed in the next section) to provide the information that they display.** You can't create a form or a report unless you first have a table (or query) to use as a basis for the form or report. One important result of this fact is that Access forms and reports can only exist within an Access database file.

    Access forms and reports are usually tied to an Access table. When you create a form or a report, the name of the table is saved along with the form or report. If you (or someone else) delete the table you can't open the form or report associated with it unless you have associated the form or report with a different table.

Understanding the Value of Queries

I know, the title of this book doesn't mention *queries,* but queries are a fundamental and vital part of making your Access forms and reports really useful. Queries are nothing to be afraid of and they may end up being your favorite part of Access!

Introducing the query concept

So just what is a query? In its simplest form, a query acts like a filter; you can use a query to choose specific information that you want to see from a table. Figure 1-5 shows an example of this type of query, known as a *select query*.

The table that is the source of the data

The fields that will be included in the results

Figure 1-5:
A query enables you to choose records that meet specific criteria.

The criteria used to filter the results

When you run a query, Access displays the results in a Datasheet view, as shown in Figure 1-6. In the example I set the criteria value in the `State` field to Nevada, and this is reflected in the results shown in Figure 1-6.

Figure 1-6:
Running a query results in a filtered display that matches the specified criteria.

ItemID	State	Title	TypeID	
10	Nevada	Manhattan Higgins Mining Co.	Stocks	Cert. #22
11	Nevada	Exchequer MC.	Stocks	Cert.#21{
12	Nevada	Hale & Norcross MC	Stocks	Cert.#65
13	Nevada	Shoshone National Bank MC	Stocks	Cert. #72
15	Nevada	Oriental Gold Mining Co	Stocks	Cert. #A3
16	Nevada	Oriental GMC	Stocks	Cert. #A3
18	Nevada	Ruby Hill Tunnel & Mining Co.	Stocks	Cert. #21
19	Nevada	West End Cons. MC	Stocks	Cert. #N\
20	Nevada	Tramps Cons. Extension MC.	Stocks	Cert. #28
23	Nevada	Palace Club Ashtray.	Ashtray	Blue and
24	Nevada	Harold's Club Ashtray.	Ashtray	Black gla
30	Nevada	United Tungsten Mines of Lovelock, N	Mining	Very fine
31	Nevada	Brass Bullion seal for the Yellow Jacl	Mining	Nevada T
2325	Nevada	Carson City pictures	Postcar	2 white h

Record: 1 ▶ ▶| ▶* of 274

The query results in Figure 1-6 are shown in a Datasheet view that looks almost identical to the Datasheet view of an ordinary Access table, with only the title bar as a tip-off. You can, indeed, use a query as a substitute for a table as the basis for a form or a report.

Using queries to enhance forms and reports

Because you can use a query as the basis for an Access form or report, you now have a powerful tool that enables you to do otherwise impossible things with those forms and reports. Consider these possibilities:

- ✔ You can create a form that's based on a query that selects records that fall within specific date ranges. For example, say you want to follow up with customers who placed an order last year but who haven't ordered in several months. Use a query.

- ✔ You can create queries that combine data from several tables to produce information that is a composite of the information from those tables. You may want to use this data to create form letters that include new product information for products similar to those ordered in the past by specific customers.

- ✔ You can easily create a query that includes only the orders placed by a specific customer. This is a great tool if the customer wants a record of all its orders in the last several months or years.

Because queries are so important, you find information about them throughout the book. In fact, Chapter 2 digs right in to give you a solid basis in queries so that when you create forms or reports you know what your options are.

Queries, Forms, and Reports Basics You Must Endure

In Access, all of your data is stored in *tables*. You can create tables that are completely self-contained or you can create tables that are related. Databases that work from a single, self-contained table are often called *flat file* databases. Databases that have two or more related tables are called *relational* databases. Fortunately, you use the same tools in Access no matter which type of database you are using.

As I mention earlier in this chapter, forms and reports are usually based on either a table or on a query. Queries can be based on tables or even on other queries — although queries based on queries can be kind of confusing to work with at times.

Access provides two primary methods of creating queries, forms, and reports. You can start with a wizard, shown in Figure 1-7, or you can create the query, form, or report from scratch using *design mode*.

Figure 1-7:
Access has
wizards like
this one to
help you
create
queries,
forms, or
reports.

Whether you start with a wizard or in design mode, you begin the process of creating a query, form, or report by choosing the table (or tables) you want to use and then you choose which fields to include. Remember that you can also choose an existing query in place of a table.

In most cases, you can choose as many or as few fields as you like. You are likely to find some fields in a table (or query) that are simply unnecessary. For example, you might want to create a report that summarizes the values of the items in your collection and you have no need to include the field that tracks when you received each item.

After you have selected the fields you want to use, the next step depends on which task you're performing. If you're creating a query, you may want to specify criteria or a sort order. If you're creating a form or a report, specify the layout of the form or report. If you're using a wizard to create the form or the report, you simply choose from a set of predefined layouts. If you're working in design mode, you need to manually place the fields where you want them.

When your query, form, or report is finished, you name and save the final layout. If necessary, you can always return to the query, form, or report in design mode to make additional changes.

It's easy to become confused when you save objects in Access. Even though you use the standard File⇨Save command to save queries, forms, and reports, you aren't saving those items outside of Access. The objects are all saved within the Access database file and you can only view those objects from within Access.

Access Add-Ons and Extra Cool Tools

You may not realize this, but there are quite a few add-ons and extras that are available to help you work with Access. These tools aren't built into Access, but they do offer an awful lot of help when you're developing an Access database. Most of these add-ons come from third-party developers, although Microsoft does offer a few, too.

Just what can you do with these add-on tools? Here's a sampling:

- ✔ Easily document the various objects in your Access database so that you can maintain and correct the database with great ease.

- ✔ Compare Access databases to see how they differ. You'll find this opportunity invaluable when people building your database have used more than one computer.

- ✔ Repair database corruption so that you can recover from the problems that always seem to occur just before you plan on doing your backup.

- ✔ Locate and correct problems that are making your database run slower than you'd like.

- ✔ Create better forms by using options that you can automatically add to the forms without a bunch of programming.

- ✔ Turn existing paper forms into electronic ones that you can use to enter data into an Access database without having to master a whole new way of working.

- ✔ Share Access reports with someone who doesn't have Access installed on his or her PC.

- ✔ Send Access data to a PowerPoint slideshow.

I'm certain that at least one of these possibilities has you interested. If so, I'm sure you'll find Chapter 20 to be very useful.

Chapter 2

Getting Started with Queries

In This Chapter

▶ Knowing the different query types

▶ Using the Query Wizard

▶ Using Design view

▶ Making changes to queries

*U*nderstatement alert: Queries are important facets of forms and reports. In fact, queries are so important that we originally had a debate about whether to include them in the title of this book. Suffice it to say that they are important keys that can help you create the types of forms and reports that you want.

You use a query to control how Access actually functions. For example, you can specify which records will be displayed in a form or report, or which records will be modified by an *action* query. Queries put an awful lot of truly awesome power into your hands!

You can use several different types of queries in Access. The *select* query is by far the simplest and most common type of query, but Access also has many others. In this chapter, I explain each of these query types so that you can begin to utilize each of them in your databases. In addition, I show you how to create queries both by using a wizard and from scratch. Finally, you see how to modify queries so that you get even better results from them.

Understanding the Types of Queries

Let's face it — it can be downright confusing trying to figure out what type of query to use. Oh sure, the default type of query — the *select* query — is by far the one that most Access users choose the most. You use it when you want to select a specific set of records to display in a form or report.

When you get beyond the basics with Access, you will want to get a little more sophisticated; that's where things can seem about as clear as mud. Well, don't worry. In the next few pages you can gain a far better understanding of what the various types of queries do and how you can use them. Here's a list of the commonly used queries:

- ✔ Crosstab queries
- ✔ Make-table queries
- ✔ Update queries
- ✔ Append queries
- ✔ Delete queries
- ✔ Parameter queries
- ✔ SQL queries

A parameter query is actually just a normal query that is set up so that it asks for the criteria used in the query before the query is executed. Chapter 15 shows you how to create parameter queries. A SQL query is a query that you form by using *Structured Query Language* — SQL. Chapter 7 introduces you to SQL queries.

Introducing select queries

Select queries are the most basic and common type of query. A select query uses the criteria that you specify to choose a subset of the records to display in a Datasheet view. Figure 2-1 shows an example of a simple select query as it appears in the Query editor.

Although you can use the Query Wizard to create queries, you use the Query editor to edit any existing queries — even those created with the Query Wizard. You can also use the Query editor to create queries from scratch. Whenever you open a query in Design view, you're actually opening the Query editor.

In essence, the select query says to Access, "Show me these files." The specific criteria you set up specify what "these" means. For example, in Figure 2-1, the select query says, "include only files in Nevada and California."

From there, of course, you can make all sorts of specifications. For example, there are three fields, ItemID, State, and Title. These are the only fields that will have any effect on the results that are returned by the query. All three fields have their Show check box selected, so all three will appear in the datasheet after the query is run. In this case, the results will be sorted in ascending order according to the values in the `ItemID` field because I selected the Ascending option in that field's Sort row. Records with different values in the `State` field will not be included in the results. Figure 2-2 shows the result of running the query.

Tables in a query are listed here.

Figure 2-1:
This select
query has
two criteria
specified.

The query parameters are listed here.

Figure 2-2:
This select
query
returns the
records that
match the
specified
criteria.

In addition to simply returning a set of records, shown in Figure 2-2, you can also use the select query to provide additional information. You can set up a select query to group the records by using the values in the first field of the query, and then you can find the sum, average, minimum, maximum, or count of the records in each group.

> To use any of the grouping options in a select query, it's very important to make sure that you set the field that you want to use for the grouping as the first field in the query, because Access uses the first field as the primary grouping field.

Getting to know crosstab queries

Crosstab queries are probably the least understood of all the query types. A crosstab query groups data by using two types of information. One type of information is shown down the rows of the Datasheet view and the other type of information is viewed across the columns. Each intersecting row and column cell then displays a sum, an average, a count, or a similar type of analysis based on the values in the rows and columns.

This explanation actually sounds a lot more complicated than it is, and this is a case in which a picture really is worth a thousand words. Figure 2-3 shows an example of a crosstab query.

Figure 2-3:
A crosstab query is used to analyze data by using rows and columns.

LIVEWINBID_Crosstab : Crosstab Query

OWNER	Total Of ID	0	5	10	15
2	$2,399	$2,399			
3	$546,172	$372,276	$19,450	$16,986	$20,710
5	$4,840	$2,408			
7	$15,265	$15,265			
18	$39,156	$12,491		$2,823	
19	$2,791				
25	$2,804	$2,804			
33	$2,651	$2,651			
64	$30,006	$16,214			$5,074
75	$29,771	$7,983		$5,445	$8,210
111	$365,841	$152,786	$5,772	$11,300	$10,908
122	$24,554	$16,493	$2,463	$2,920	
127	$2,362				
141	$28,436	$22,549			
142	$2,933				
149	$21,954	$5,416			
152	$7,710	$7,710			
173	$20,101	$20,101			

Record: 1 of 47

The first column in Figure 2-3 (Owner) lists the owners for items in an auction database. The second column lists the total value of all items for each owner (Total of ID). The remaining columns to the right list the values of the items by bid amount. So, for example, Owner Number 3 has a total of $546,172 worth of items listed for auction. Of that amount, $372,276 has not yet had a bid. Moving farther to the right, $19,450 in bids was in the 0 to $5 category; and $16,986 in bids was in the $5 to $10 category. In the $10 to $15 category, Owner Number 3 has received $20,710 in bids.

Make-table queries

As the name implies, make-table queries create new tables by using data from one or more existing tables. The new table typically contains a specially selected set of information that matches criteria that you specify. For example, you might want to create a table that you use to create a catalog of items that will be included in a specific sale. Figure 2-4 shows an example of this type of query.

Figure 2-4:
A make-table query creates a new table that contains a specified set of records.

When you create a make-table query, you specify a name for the new table that Access creates when the query is executed. It's very important to make sure that the name you specify is actually a new table name and not the name of an existing table. If you don't create a unique name, Access will delete the original table when you run the make-table query and replace it with the new table you created. Access does warn you, as shown in Figure 2-5, but it's very easy to click that Yes button and do a lot of damage without giving much thought to what you're doing.

Figure 2-5:
A make-table query replaces any existing table that has the name you specify for the new table.

Even though make-table queries are useful for creating new tables, they're not very handy if you want to change information in an existing table or add new information to a table. See the following sections on update queries and append queries if you want query tools that will help you perform such tasks.

Using update queries

An update query modifies the values in an existing table. You specify how to modify the records by using *expressions*. These expressions are similar to the formulas you create in a spreadsheet and can consist of mathematical expressions, string manipulation expressions, or even specific values — depending on the field type. Figure 2-6 shows an example of an update query that increases the value in the LowEst field by 25 percent.

Figure 2-6:
Use an update query to modify existing values.

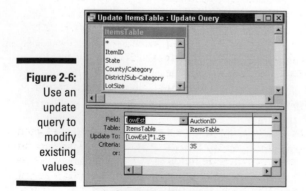

Using the asterisk to add fields without a fuss

To include all the fields from the source table in the query, you can choose the asterisk (*) at the top of the field list. This shortcut works with any query type, but is probably most useful for select queries and append queries because these two query types typically don't suffer any ill effects from accidentally including extra or unnecessary fields.

When you create an update query, it's important to understand which table the query will modify. Unlike a make-table query, an update query makes changes in the existing table — the one that is shown in the query. This can be a little confusing because a make-table query uses the records from the listed table (or tables) to create a new table, while an update query actually modifies the listed table.

When you create an update query you only need to include fields that you want to update and any fields that you use to select the records to update. In Figure 2-6 this meant that only two fields were required in the query. The LowEst field is the field that is updated and the AuctionID field is the field used to limit the update to records for Auction 35.

Introducing append queries

Append queries add new records to the end of an existing table. They're pretty similar to make-table queries because both types of queries add records to tables; the difference is that an append query doesn't delete the existing table before adding the records — those changes are made to the original table. Figure 2-7 shows an example of an append query. In this case, I added the items that were slated for Auction 36 to Auction 35, so the append query is set up to select records where the AuctionID value is 36 and then to add those records to the existing Auction 35 table. As such, append queries are aptly named.

If you look carefully at Figure 2-7, you may notice a subtle difference between the append query and the make-table query shown in Figure 2-4. The append query doesn't give you the option to include fields in the query that won't be included in the results of the query. The reason for this is simple but it might throw you for a loop until you understand it — only those fields that already exist in the destination table can actually be used when the query is run. If you include fields that aren't in the destination table, Access simply ignores those fields when it adds the records to the table.

Backing up your records just in case

If you're nervous about the permanence of the delete query, you might want to create a make-table query that uses the same criteria you intend to use for your delete query. Run the make-table query before you run your delete query. By doing so, you create a copy of the records that you're going to delete so that you can restore those records in case you later realize that you messed up in deleting the records and needed them all along.

You may also want to back up (or *archive*) the entire database file after you've made a backup table of the records you're deleting from the main table. Be sure to give your database file backup copy a different name so that you don't accidentally open it in the future instead of opening your working copy.

Figure 2-7:
You use an append query to add records to an existing table.

Add to Auction 35 table : Append Query

ItemsTable
*
ItemID
State
County/Category
District/Sub-Category
LotSize

Field:	State	Title	Description	LowEst	ItemID	AuctionID
Table:	ItemsTable	ItemsTable	ItemsTable	ItemsTable	ItemsTable	ItemsTable
Sort:						
Append To:	State	Title	Description	LowEst	ItemID	
Criteria:						36
or:						

Getting to know delete queries

Delete queries remove selected records from an existing table. They are most helpful when you use them to trim out records you no longer need in the table. Figure 2-8 shows an example of a delete query that reverses the effect of the append query shown in Figure 2-7. In this case, I decided that I didn't want to include the Auction 36 items in Auction 35 after all.

Figure 2-8:
You use a
delete query
to remove
records
from an
existing
table.

Field:	State	Title	Description	LowEst	ItemID	AuctionID
Table:	ItemsTable	ItemsTable	ItemsTable	ItemsTable	ItemsTable	ItemsTable
Delete:	Where	Where	Where	Where	Where	Where
Criteria:						36
or:						

Window title: Remove from Auction 35 table : Delete Query
*ItemsTable fields: *, ItemID, State, County/Category, District/Sub-Category, LotSize*

Creating Queries by Using a Wizard

There are two methods you can use to create queries. In this section you see how to use the Query Wizard to build a query. Later in this chapter, I show you how to start from scratch and create a query in Design view.

You can save yourself a lot of grief by creating a copy of your favorite Access database and using the copy to practice creating and running queries. By using the copy you can get as wild as you want in experimenting with different types of queries without worrying about destroying any live data. You might want to add something like `practice copy` to the filename of the copied file just to be sure you don't get confused.

Why you should be off to see the wizards

Access includes quite a broad range of wizards to help you with various tasks. If you're one of those macho users who thinks, "I don't need any stinking wizards," you're welcome to skip over this section, but be forewarned — even the experts sometimes find that the wizards can cut down on the drudgery of common Access operations. Letting a wizard do some of the work enables you to get more done with less effort (and fewer mistakes).

Some people always seem to have the answers right at their fingertips. Ask one of those people how to do something that he or she is expert on and you'll instantly hear the whole process rattled off to you. Most of us, though, have too many different interests to make it worth our time to become experts on everything. That's one reason why the Access query experts, or *wizards,* are so useful. When you create a query with a wizard, the wizard steps you through the process so that you don't have to remember everything upfront. As each new piece of information is required, you can depend on the wizard to ask for it. And, if along the way you need to change something, you can also back the process up, effectively telling the wizard, "Wait. I need to check something a few steps back."

Used correctly, a wizard is a useful learning tool. For example, when you create a query with a wizard, the wizard builds the query in the same Query editor you use to create a query in design view. So if you watch what the wizard does, you can easily create your own queries from scratch.

Understanding the limitations of the wizards

The Access Query wizards may be awfully handy, but they can't do everything. Access doesn't include wizards to build every type of query, so if you want to create a make-table query, an update query, an append query, or a delete query, you'll have to do at least part of the work yourself in Design view.

If you already know what you're doing, using a wizard to create a query can take a bit more time than creating the query manually. In real-world terms the difference is pretty small, but then some people just prefer to do things for themselves.

Creating your first query with a wizard

Creating a query with a wizard is pretty easy stuff. You simply answer a few prompts and in a very few moments you have a new query that's ready to use.

To create a query by using a wizard, follow these steps:

1. **Open the Access database in which you want to create a new query.**

2. **Click Queries in the Objects list.**

    The Objects list is along the left side of the database window. A list of queries appears, as shown in Figure 2-9.

    In this example I have several existing queries, but your list may be empty except for the two create query items at the top of the list.

Select Queries from the Objects list

Click New for more Query wizards.

Figure 2-9:
Open the
Queries list
to work with
queries.

3. **Click New.**

   The New Query dialog box appears, as shown in Figure 2-10.

   If you want to create a simple select query, you can bypass the New Query dialog box by clicking Create Query Using Wizard in the query list.

Figure 2-10:
Choose the
type of
query you
want to
create.

4. **Select the type of query you want to create and then click OK.**

   For this example, I chose Simple Query Wizard to display the Simple Query Wizard dialog box, as shown in Figure 2-11.

Simple Query Wizard

Which fields do you want in your query?

You can choose from more than one table or query.

Tables/Queries

Table: ItemsTable

Available Fields:

ItemID
State
County/Category
District/Sub-Category
LotSize
Title
TypeID
Description

Selected Fields:

>
>>
<
<<

Cancel   < Back   Next >   Finish

Figure 2-11:
Use the
Simple
Query
Wizard to
select the
table and
fields for
your query.

5. **Choose the table or query you want to use as the basis (record source) for the query from the drop-down Tables/Queries list box.**

   You must choose the table or query first before you select the fields because the list of fields depends on the table that you select.

6. **After you have selected the table, select the fields you want to include and then click the > button to move the field from the Available Fields list box to the Selected Fields list box.**

   You can select as many or as few fields as necessary. If you select fields individually, the fields will appear in the Selected Fields list in the order that you added them — an important point to remember if you decide to apply grouping to the records. You can also click the >> button to add all the fields to the query. You can use the left-pointing arrows to remove fields you don't need.

7. **Click the Next button to display the options shown in Figure 2-12.**

Simple Query Wizard

Would you like a detail or summary query?

○ Detail (shows every field of every record)

○ Summary

Summary Options ...

1 AAA XXX XXX
2 AAA XXX XXX
3 BBB XXX XXX
4 CCC XXX XXX
5 DDD XXX XXX
6 DDD XXX XXX

Cancel   < Back   Next >   Finish

Figure 2-12:
Choose the
detail or
summary
option for
your query.

8. **Select the Detail option to show all the records in the result or Summary to show just the summarization of the results.**

   If you choose Summary, you must also click the Summary Options button and then select the types of summary values you want to see. For this example, select Detail.

9. **Click the Next button to display the options shown in Figure 2-13.**

Figure 2-13:
Enter a
name for the
query and
choose an
option for
opening the
query.

10. **Enter a name for your query in the text box near the top of the dialog box.**

    Generally it's a good idea to enter a descriptive title so that you can easily identify the query later.

11. **Choose whether you want to open the query to view the results or to modify the query in the Query editor.**

    For this example, I selected the Modify the Query Design option to give you a bird's-eye view of what the Query Wizard created using your selections.

12. **Click the Finish button to close the wizard and create your query.**

    Figure 2-14 shows the query I created using the selections in this example.

After you finish creating the query, you can view the results of the query by choosing Query⇔Run from the Access menu or by clicking the Run button (it looks like a fat exclamation point) on the Access toolbar. In this case the results probably won't seem like much because you haven't yet specified any criteria for selecting specific records. You can find out how to modify your query to specify criteria in the section "Modifying Queries for Better Results," later in this chapter.

Figure 2-14:
The finished query as it appears in the Query editor.

Creating Queries in Design View

As handy as the Query Wizards may be, you eventually do have to use Design view to create truly effective queries. The reason for this is pretty straightforward — you need to be working in the Query editor (otherwise known as Query Design view) in order to specify criteria. Until you specify criteria, your queries don't really do any record selection; they return all the records from the source table.

Getting to know the Design view

You have already seen most of the important elements that you use in Design view, but now it's time for a more formal introduction. Figure 2-15 identifies the Query Design view objects that you will use most often.

The Query editor is a window that has two panes that you use to build a query. The upper pane shows any tables that you have added to the query. The lower pane shows any fields you are using in the query along with any parameters you have specified. As Figure 2-15 shows, the Query editor starts out empty after you select the Create Query in Design View option. You use the Show Table dialog box to add tables to the Query editor so that you can use the fields from those tables in the query.

Click here to display the Query editor.

Add tables here.   Query editor   Show table

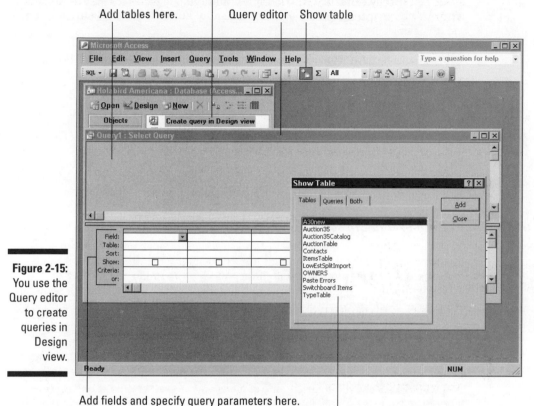

Figure 2-15:
You use the
Query editor
to create
queries in
Design
view.

Add fields and specify query parameters here.

Select tables for the query.

For the sake of simplicity, the query examples in this chapter use fields from a single table. Chapter 5 shows you how to use multiple tables in queries.

Getting your fields straight in Design view

When you add fields from a table to one of the columns in the lower pane of the Query editor, the fields appear in the same order that you placed them. Although the order of the fields isn't really important for many queries, it becomes important when you select a sort order or when you summarize the results by using grouping. Access sorts and groups starting with the fields farthest to the left in the query layout and then moves one column to the right after each sort or group operation. So, for example, if you place a State field first with a City field second and then select an ascending sort order for each field, your records will be sorted by state and then by city within each state. But if you place the `City` field first and the `State` field second, the sort would be by city and then by state — probably not a very useful sort order in most cases.

You can add fields to the columns, using any of several different methods:

- ✔ Drag and drop fields from a table in the upper pane of the Query editor.

- ✔ Click the down arrow at the right side of the Field list box to display a list of the fields and then select the field you want.

- ✔ If you like to do things the hard way, type the field name in the box. Even if you choose this method, Access tries to help by filling in the name that matches what you're typing. When you have added a field name, Access automatically enters the table name for you.

Getting everything sorted out correctly in Design view

The Sort list box provides three options. You can choose ascending, descending, or not sorted. The Show check box controls the display of the field in the final results. You might want to include a field in the query for sorting or grouping purposes but not have the field appear in the final results. If so, simply deselect the Show check box.

Getting your criteria set in Design view

The Criteria boxes enable you to specify conditions for selecting records. The conditions you enter must be appropriate for the field type. For example, if you want to specify a numeric value such as >500 to select only those records where the value is greater than 500, the field where you enter the criteria must be one of the numeric field types. You can enter additional conditions in the Or boxes. Access then selects records that match any of the criteria you specify.

Creating an example query in Design view

Creating a query in Design view is pretty easy, but it does require just a bit more thinking about the process because you don't have the wizard prompting you to make the correct choices. Here's how to create a simple select query in Design view:

1. **Open the Access database in which you want to create a new query.**

2. **Click Queries in the Objects list.**

3. **Double-click Create Query in Design View.**

   The Query editor and the Show Table dialog box (see Figure 2-16) both appear.

Figure 2-16:
Use the
Show Table
dialog box
to select the
tables to
use in your
query.

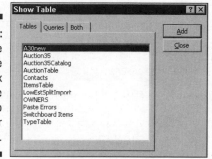

4. **Select the tables you want to use in your query and click the Add button.**

5. **Click the Close button to close the Show Table dialog box so that you can work in the Query editor.**

6. **Add the fields to the lower pane of the Query editor.**

   You can drag-and-drop them or choose them from the drop-down Field list box.

7. **Optionally, choose a sort order for any of the fields.**

8. **Leave the Show check box selected for any fields you want to display in the results and deselect it for any fields you don't want to see in the results.**

9. **Enter any criteria you want to use to select the records to include in the results.**

10. **Repeat Steps 6 through 9 until you have added all the fields and criteria that you want to include.**

    Figure 2-17 shows the completed query I created for this example.

11. **Click the Run button or choose Query⇨Run to run the query.**

    Figure 2-18 shows the results of running the query shown in Figure 2-17.

Figure 2-17:
The
completed
query is
now ready
to run.

Figure 2-18:
The
completed
query
displays the
results
when it is
run.

12. If you want to save your query for future use, click the Save button.

The Save As dialog box appears, where you can enter a filename and click OK to save the query. If you don't save the query, Access prompts you to do so when you attempt to close the query.

The query shown in this example is very simple, but you'll probably discover that most of the queries you create will be quite simple. In later chapters you find how to create queries that do a whole lot more.

Modifying Queries for Better Results

As you work with queries, you may soon find that the queries you create could probably use a bit of fine-tuning. Maybe you want to pare down the results so you don't have to wade through so many records, or maybe you've discovered that it really is a pain to slog through a whole bunch of unsorted data. Whatever the reason, being able to modify existing queries instead of starting from scratch can be a real timesaver.

When you're experimenting with modifying queries, be sure to heed any warning messages that Access displays when you attempt to run the modified query. Remember that select queries and crosstab queries are always safe because they don't modify any of your data, but the other types of queries can modify data.

Deleting a query

Sometimes, of course, the easiest, safest, and smartest thing to do with a query is to get rid of it entirely and start over. If something has gone wrong and you're not sure what it is, go ahead and delete the query. Just highlight it in the list of queries and press Delete.

Modifying an existing query

No matter which method you used to create a query, there's really only one option for modifying an existing query. That option is to open the query in Design view and make your changes in the Query editor. Access doesn't offer any wizards to help you modify existing queries.

To open an existing query in Design view, you select the query in the database window and then click the Design button. When you open a query this way, the Query editor looks exactly the way it does when you're creating a query in Design view. That is, there aren't separate creating and editing modes to confuse you.

In some cases, you may find that fields you added to a query don't appear in the Query editor when you edit the query. The reason for the mysterious disappearing fields can't be attributed to aliens or ghosts; it's simply that Access drops any unused fields when you save a query. If you had fields in the query that didn't serve any purpose in the query, those fields are gone when you reopen the query.

After you open the query in Design view, you can click the Show Table button on the toolbar or choose Query⇨Show Table. The Show Table dialog box appears so that you can add additional tables to the query. You can also add additional fields to the query by using the same methods you use when you're first creating a query in Design view. Likewise, you can add or modify any of the query criteria exactly the same way you do when creating a query.

Examples of query modifications you ought to know about

Just in case you need a few ideas about the types of query modifications you might want to try, consider these options:

✔ Add a sort order to make it easier to understand the data that appears when you run the query.

✔ Specify some criteria to limit the amount of data that results from the query.

✔ Rearrange the columns in the query to produce more logical groupings when you sort on more than one field.

✔ Add additional fields to the query to show data that didn't appear in the original query.

✔ Simplify your query by removing fields that don't add any value to the results.

✔ If you have already created table relationships, you can add fields from the related tables to the query.

✔ You can change the type of query by selecting a different type from the Query menu or by choosing a different type from the drop-down list that appears when you click the right side of the Query Type button on the toolbar.

Rearranging and deleting fields in a query

The one task in editing a query that you might find a little confusing at first is rearranging the fields in the query.

You can change the order of the fields by

✔ **Dragging and dropping new fields:** When you drag and drop a field onto the column of an existing field, the existing field (and any fields to its right) shifts to the right so that the new field is inserted before the existing field. To drag and drop a field, you need to drag the very small gray bar that's just above the Field row.

✔ **Deleting existing fields:** To delete a field, position the mouse pointer at the top of the field's column just above the Field row and then click when the pointer becomes a solid black down arrow. Choose Edit➪Delete or press the Delete key to remove the field. The remaining fields to the right shift to the left to fill the empty column.

You can also click in the Field box of a column and select a different field for the column to change the field order.

Chapter 3

Creating Simple Forms

In This Chapter

▶ Using the Form Wizard

▶ Building forms

▶ Modifying forms

You could argue that forms are an unnecessary luxury because you can, after all, enter information into a database table directly. In making that argument, though, you'd have to ignore the fact that if it weren't for forms, most people would probably think of databases as some strange and difficult application best left to some guys stuck away in a climate-controlled room with a bunch of mainframe computers. Forms really give PC database applications like Access their friendly face.

In this chapter you see how to create simple Access forms, using both the Form Wizard and Design view. After you have the basics mastered, I show you how to improve the forms that you've created by using some simple techniques to improve the layout of your forms and also to make your forms a bit more compact for easier use.

Creating Forms with the Help of a Wizard

Just as it does with queries, Access provides you with two primary methods of creating forms. You can use a Form Wizard or you can create forms from scratch in Design view. In addition, of course, you can use a combination of the two methods where you begin creating your form with a wizard and then use Design view to fine-tune the appearance of the form. See Chapter 2 for more information about creating queries.

When compared with creating a query, creating a form in Access is somewhat complicated. The reason for this added complication is that for a form you have additional considerations that you don't have with queries. These important points make form design a bit more complex than query design:

- A form might be used by someone who isn't familiar with the database, so you need to provide visual clues regarding the purpose of the form and the layout of the fields.

- Forms are often used for data input, so you may need to go to greater lengths to adjust the order in which the fields appear on the form. Making sure that field order matches the data source makes data entry move faster and reduces errors. It's certainly preferred to making users jump around the form to enter data in an inconvenient order.

- Field names that are convenient for use in a table often look strange in a form. You might need to edit the field labels to make them more understandable for the humans who will be using the form. For example, Low Estimate is probably better than LowEst.

- People are creatures of habit. Because most users are accustomed to seeing certain layouts, such as name, address, and city stacked vertically, you may throw users off if you use an unfamiliar layout, such as name, address, and city spread horizontally across the form (or stacked vertically, but out of order, such as city, address, name).

These few points aren't the only ones to consider, but they do highlight some of the reasons why creating forms takes a bit of conscious effort if you want to do it right.

Forms can be based on tables or on queries (or both). This is also true of queries and reports, of course. The examples in this chapter use forms that are based on tables, but that's simply to focus on the task at hand without the additional complication of first creating an appropriate query.

Meeting (And avoiding) the AutoForm Wizards

The Access Form Wizard is similar to the Access Query Wizard. You begin using the wizard by selecting the tables or queries that you want to use as the basis for your new form or query and then you choose which fields you want to include. In the New Form dialog box that appears (see Figure 3-1), you have several options for form layout and appearance. These additional options are divided categorically and referred to as *AutoForm* Wizards.

The AutoForm Wizards enable you to make some simple choices regarding how the basic form is built, although you'll probably still want to use Design view to touch up the form in most cases.

Figure 3-1:
The New Form dialog box offers several choices, including some AutoForm Wizards.

New Form

This wizard automatically creates your form, based on the fields you select.

Design View
Form Wizard
AutoForm: Columnar
AutoForm: Tabular
AutoForm: Datasheet
AutoForm: PivotTable
AutoForm: PivotChart
Chart Wizard
PivotTable Wizard

Choose the table or query where the object's data comes from:

OK   Cancel

The AutoForm Wizards automatically create forms by using all the fields from a single table. To use an AutoForm Wizard you simply choose the type of form you want, select the table or query to use as the basis for the form, and click OK. As Figure 3-2 shows, the resulting form isn't going to win any awards for appearance (notice that many of the labels are cut off), but this is certainly the easiest method for creating a quick-and-dirty form.

Figure 3-2:
This form was created with the AutoForm: Columnar Wizard.

ItemsTable

ItemID	11090	OwnerII		Descrip		Reserve	
State	x	DateRe	4/28/2004			NeedsC	
County		LowEst					
District/		HighEst					
LotSize		Auction					
Title							
TypeID						LotNum	
Descrip						NeedsF	

Record: 1 of 11536

For all their benefits, AutoForms have their downsides, as well. In fact, because of their extreme limitations, lack of flexibility, and often poor layout, you'll probably want to avoid using the AutoForm wizards for most purposes. Their one redeeming quality is that they give you an idea of what a particular type of form looks like in the least number of clicks. Aside from that, however, they don't seem to have much else going for them.

Making friends with the Form Wizard

I would compare the standard Access Form Wizard and the AutoForm Wizard described in the previous section, but the reality is that there is no comparison. The full-fledged Form Wizard gives you a whole lot more control over the content and appearance of your forms. In the following example, I show you how to create a simple form with the standard Form Wizard.

For maximum flexibility, always start the Form Wizard by double-clicking Create Form by Using Wizard in the Forms list (which appears on the left side of the screen) instead of choosing the Form Wizard option in the New Form dialog box. The former option allows you to select multiple tables or queries as the source for your forms, but the latter option limits you to using a single table to start with. (You can add more tables and queries to the form design in the first Wizard dialog box that appears, but why bother with the extra step?)

The following example uses a single table to keep the example easy to understand. Chapter 10 shows you how to build forms that use multiple tables.

Follow these steps to create a simple form with the Access Form Wizard:

1. **Open the Access database that contains the table you want to use as the source for the new form.**

2. **In the database window, click Forms in the Objects list.**

   The forms list appears.

3. **Double-click Create Form by Using Wizard (which appears near the top of the list of forms) to open the Form Wizard dialog box.**

   See Figure 3-3.

Figure 3-3: Choose the tables and fields that you want to include in your form.

4. **Select the table or query you want to use as the basis for your form from the drop-down Tables/Queries list box.**

   You must choose the table or query before you can select the fields.

5. **Select the fields in the order you want them to appear in the form, clicking the > button to move them from the Available Fields list to the Selected fields list.**

   You can also click the >> button to move all remaining fields to the Selected Fields list.

6. **Repeat Steps 4 and 5 if you want to add additional tables or queries to the form.**

7. **Click Next.**

   The form layout section of the Form Wizard dialog box, shown in Figure 3-4, appears.

   As you select different options, the selected layout option is displayed in the preview section along the left side of the dialog box.

   The preview is a generalized preview, not an exact representation of how your form will actually appear. For example, a PivotTable form looks something like a spreadsheet without any formulas or data.

Form Wizard

What layout would you like for your form?

- ⦿ Columnar
- ○ Tabular
- ○ Datasheet
- ○ Justified
- ○ PivotTable
- ○ PivotChart

Cancel   < Back   Next >   Finish

Figure 3-4:
Select the layout for your form.

8. **Choose the layout you want to use for your form and click Next.**

   The style section of the Form Wizard dialog box appears, as shown in Figure 3-5.

   Once again, the preview shows a generalized view that changes as you select different options.

9. **Choose the style option that you want to use for your form and click Next.**

   The final section of the Form Wizard dialog box appears, as shown in Figure 3-6.

10. **Enter a descriptive name for your form.**

   It's a good idea to use a name that is easy to remember and is related to the purpose of the form. For example, I used `New ItemsTable Items` as the name for the form to indicate that the form is to be used to add new items to the table named ItemsTable.

11. **Choose the default method for opening the form and click Finish.**

The default option is the Open Form to View or Enter Information option. Your saved form looks a little something like the one shown in Figure 3-7.

Figure 3-7:
The completed form is now ready to use.

Your form may look significantly different than the one shown in Figure 3-7, of course. You may, however, want to compare the form shown in Figure 3-7 with the one shown in Figure 3-2 to see how a small amount of extra effort on your part can pay back big dividends in creating a form that is easier to use than one created by the AutoForm Wizard.

You might want to experiment with the Form Wizard by creating several variations on the same form by using different layout and style options. The layout options can have quite an impact on how useful your form is for different purposes.

Knowing what the wizard can't do

The Access Form Wizard is easy to use, but it doesn't offer all the options you might find useful. Here are a few of the things you simply can't do with the Form Wizard:

✔ The Form Wizard always adds labels to every field on the form; there's no option to leave off the labels you don't want or need.

✔ Speaking of labels, the Form Wizard always uses the field names from the tables or queries as labels. There's no option to change the staid `Last_Name` to `Put Yer Name Here` (or whatever else suits your fancy).

   ✔ Although the Form Wizard gives you limited control over the form
     layout, it doesn't allow you to have absolute control. The `Address` field
     may *not* sit directly under the `Name` field, even though that's how you
     envisioned it in your mind's eye.

   ✔ If you want to create a hot pink form with fluorescent green labels, don't
     look to the Form Wizard. Come to think of it, don't look to me for help
     with that one, either!

Even though the Form Wizard won't handle these tasks on its own, Access
does give you the opportunity to open the form in Design view after the
wizard finishes its work.

Building Forms the Hard Way: Using Design View

Creating your first Access form from scratch in Design view can seem a bit
daunting. When you select this option you're faced with a blank grid, a floating toolbox full of strange looking icons, and no clue about what to do next.
Figure 3-8 shows you what I mean.

Figure 3-8:
Starting a
new form in
Design view
presents
you with a
whole
bunch of
unfamiliar
tools.

Introducing Design view tools

Before you begin using the Form Design view, have a quick look at the various icons that you'll encounter. Take a look at that floating toolbox shown in Figure 3-9.

Here's a brief description of the tools:

- ✓ **Select objects:** Click this button to use the mouse pointer to select objects that you've added to a form.

- ✓ **Control wizards:** Click this button to enable wizards that help you add certain types of objects such as combo boxes and command buttons to your forms. Both combo boxes and command buttons are explained elsewhere in this list.

- ✓ **Label:** Click this button to add a simple text label anywhere on your form.

- ✓ **Text box:** Click this button to add a text box to the form. Unlike a label, a text box can be set to change the information it displays when the form is used. Text boxes actually have two parts — a label and the box where a user can enter information.

- ✓ **Option group:** Click this button to create a set of related option buttons (such as Taxable and Tax Exempt). The buttons function as a group and you can only select one option at a time. For example, you can choose Taxable or Tax Exempt for an order, but not both.

- ✓ **Toggle button:** Click this button to add a button that has two states — up for off and down for on. For example, up for Taxable and down for Non-Taxable.

- ✓ **Option button:** Click this button to add option buttons that work like a toggle button or a check box. Generally, you use option buttons in an option group to restrict a user from selecting more than one item in a group.

- ✓ **Check box:** Click this button to add an item that can be selected or deselected.

- ✓ **Combo box:** Click this button to add a box in which the user can select from a list of options or enter a new value. For example, you might have a list of books by your favorite author as items to suggest, but also allow the user to enter the name of a book that isn't on the list.

- ✓ **List box:** Click this button to create a list box from which a user can select a set of preexisting values. A list box looks something like a combo box, but doesn't allow the user to enter new values.

- ✓ **Command button:** Click this button to add a button that executes a macro or a VBA *(Visual Basic for Applications)* procedure.

Option button

Label

Select objects

Checkbox

Text box

Control wizards

Figure 3-9:
The floating
toolbox
provides
these useful
tools.

Option group
Combo box
Toggle button
List box
Bound object frame
Line
Unbound object frame
Subform/Subreport

More controls

Tab control

Image

Rectangle

Page break

Command button

- ✔ **Image:** Click this button to add a digital image (such as a company logo) to the form.

- ✔ **Unbound object frame:** Click this button to add objects such as text or images that don't change when moving between records.

- ✔ **Bound object frame:** Click this button to add objects that change when the information in the database changes — such as images that are stored in fields in the table.

- ✔ **Page break:** Click this button to create multipage forms when you have too many objects to display on a single page.

- ✔ **Tab control:** Click this button to create a form with two or more tabs that group related objects.

- ✔ **Subform/Subreport:** Click this button to add a subform so that the user can see records from a related table — such as the individual line items on an order.

- ✔ **Line:** Click this button to add lines to the form to differentiate between different groups of objects on the form.

✔ **Rectangle:** Click this button to draw a rectangle on the form so that users can see how objects are related.

✔ **More controls:** This displays a listing of additional controls you have installed on your computer — such as calendar controls that enable a user to select a date from an on-screen calendar.

Okay, so you're probably scratching your head and wondering if you really have to know how to use all these tools before you can start creating your own forms in design view. The short-and-sweet answer is no. Chapter 9 gives you a lot more information on using controls on your forms.

Starting a form in Design view

Before you begin your first form in Design view, you have to understand the two different ways to open the Form Design view. When you look at the Forms list in the database window, the option at the top is always Create Form in Design View. Double-clicking this item does open the Form Design view, but using this method presents you with a blank form that is not connected to any of your tables or queries. When you're starting out designing forms you may prefer to open Design view by using a method that actually connects your form to a table or query. To use this second, easier method, follow these steps:

1. **Open the Access database to which you want to add a new form.**

2. **Select Forms in the Objects list.**

   A list of forms appears.

3. **Click the New button to display the New Form dialog box.**

4. **Make certain that the top item, Design View, is selected.**

5. **Select the table or query you want to use as the source for the form from the drop-down list box in the lower section of the dialog box.**

6. **Click the OK button to open the new form in Design view with the field list displayed (see Figure 3-10).**

If the toolbox or the field list is in your way, you can drag them elsewhere on your screen to get them out of the way. If you drag the toolbox to the top, bottom, or either side of the Access window, you can *dock* the toolbox along the edge where you dragged it. Docking the toolbox reduces your work area slightly, but it also ensures that the toolbox doesn't obscure part of your workspace the way it can when the toolbox is floating. You can't dock the field list, but unless your screen resolution is set quite small or your form is very large, you'll probably be able to find an out-of-the-way place for it.

Figure 3-10:
The field list
includes all
the fields
from the
source table
or query.

Field list

Associating a table to your form in Design view

As I mention earlier, if you double-click the Create Form in Design View option in the Forms list, you start out with a blank form that isn't connected to any table or query. In order for your new form to be of much use you need to make that connection yourself; otherwise, you won't be able to add any fields to the forms.

To manually connect a form with a table or a query, follow these steps:

1. **Right-click on the form's title bar when the form is displayed in Design view to display the pop-up menu that appears in Figure 3-11.**

Figure 3-11:
Right-click
on the
form's title
bar to
display this
context
menu.

	Form View
	Datasheet View
	PivotTable View
	PivotChart View
	Build **E**vent...
	Ta**b** Order...
	Page Header/Footer
	Form **H**eader/Footer
	Properties

2. **Select the Properties option.**

   The Form Properties dialog box for the form appears. Alternatively, you can just click the Properties button on the toolbar to display this dialog box.

3. **Click the Data tab or the All tab.**

   Either option enables you to choose a table or query to associate with the form.

4. **Click the down-arrow to the right of the Record Source box to display the list of tables and queries.**

5. **Select the table or query that you want to use as the source for the form, as shown in Figure 3-12.**

Figure 3-12:
Choose the
record
source for
the form
from the
Form
Properties
dialog box.

Form
Form
Format	Data	Event	Other	All

Record Source . . . . ItemsTable
Filter . . . . ItemsTable
Order By . . . . ItemsTable Query
Allow Filters . . . . ItemsTable Query Samp
Allow Edits . . . . ItemsTable Query1
Allow Deletions . . . . ItemsTable Select Quer
Allow Additions . . . . LowEstSplit
Data Entry . . . . LowEstSplitImport
Recordset Type . . . . OwnerContactInfo
Record Locks . . . . Dynaset
Fetch Defaults . . . . No Locks
Yes

6. **Click the Close button.**

   The Form Properties dialog box closes, but the Field list remains visible.

Although forms typically aren't very useful unless they're connected to a table or query, you can use forms that aren't connected to a table or query to display command buttons that run macros or VBA procedures. Chapter 17 provides additional information on these options.

If the field list seems to be missing in action, click the Field List button on the Access Form Design toolbar. Figure 3-13 identifies the items on the Form Design toolbar in case you need a bit of review. The Field List button has an icon that looks something like a tablet with several horizontal lines. Alternatively, choose View➪Field List.

Figure 3-13:
The Access
Form Design
tools.

Print Preview — *AutoFormat*
File Search — *Format Painter* — *Field List* — *Properties*
View — *Copy* — *Redo* — *New Object*
Save — *Cut* — *Undo* — *Toolbox* — *Build* — *Help*
Print — *Paste* — *Insert Hyperlink* — *Code*
Database Window

Adding fields to the form

After your form is connected to a table or a query, you can add fields from the table or query to the form. This is the place where you get to let your inner artist come out (but it's also where you'll probably find that laying out forms so that they look good is a bit harder than you thought).

Access provides two options to help you lay out your forms. These options appear on different menus, but you'll want to select both of them. First, make certain that the grid is visible (select View⇨Grid and make sure the option is checked). Then make certain that the Snap to Grid option is checked (select Format⇨Snap to Grid). To add a field to your form, follow these steps:

1. **Select the field in the field list and drag and drop the field into place on the form (see Figure 3-14).**

   Keep your fields some distance from the left edge of the form to leave room for the field labels. If you drop a field too close to the left edge, the label will be all scrunched together and probably unreadable.

2. **If you get too close to the edge, delete the field from the form and try again instead of trying to fix the label.**

   Trust me; I know from experience that this is the easier option.

   Don't get too hung up on trying to precisely align the fields as you're adding them to the form. See "Aligning objects on a form," later in this chapter, for more information about making Access straighten things up a bit for you.

3. **To preview how your form will look when it's in use, click the View button at the left side of the Access Form Design toolbar or choose View⇨Form View.**

Figure 3-14:
Add fields to
the form by
dragging
and
dropping
them onto
the form.

4. **To close the preview and return to Design view, click the button again (it is in the same place but with a different icon) or choose View⇨Design View.**

5. **Click the Save button or choose File⇨Save to save your work.**

   The first time you save a new form you'll be asked to name the form (use a descriptive name). You can also press Ctrl+S to save the form.

Modifying Forms You've Created

You'll probably find that your first efforts at creating forms in Design view leave a bit to be desired. It can be somewhat difficult to get the fields to line up evenly even if you have the grid displayed and the snap to grid option active. In the following sections, you see how to make your forms look like they were designed by a pro.

If you've been previewing your work as described in the previous section, "Adding fields to the form," don't forget to switch back to Design view to make any further modifications.

Figure 3-15 shows a sample form that could definitely use some improvement. The fields don't line up with each other, the sizes of the fields are inconsistent, the vertical spacing varies considerably, and the form is much larger than it really needs to be. Despite all these problems, the form is still usable, but I don't think I'd want anyone to know that I created it.

You can do a number of things to improve a form like the one shown in Figure 3-15. You won't need to do all of them to every form you create, but you eventually will need to know how to use all the various options that are available.

Access provides several commands to help you improve the appearance of your forms. Each of the commands is conveniently located in the Format menu shown in Figure 3-16. In the following sections we look at each of these commands in turn.

Figure 3-16:
The Format menu provides you with the options you need to improve the appearance of your forms.

Aligning objects on a form

The Format⇨Align submenu (see Figure 3-17) enables you to precisely align selected objects to each other or to the grid. No matter how sloppy you might have been when dropping fields onto your form, the alignment commands can make quite a difference.

Even though you may think you're aligning objects, Access really aligns labels. In other words, adjusting alignment alone may not perfect an unflattering form.

Figure 3-17: The Format⇨ Align submenu helps you to make objects line up with each other.

Before you use any of the alignment commands, be sure to select the objects that you want to align. You can drag the selection box around the objects to select them, or you can hold down the Shift key while you click each object that you want to select. If you continue to hold down Shift and click a selected object, you'll deselect the object. If you have the rulers visible, you can also click in a ruler to select all objects in a path going straight out from the ruler.

Things can get a bit tricky when you're working on cleaning up a poor form layout. For example, Figure 3-18 shows the result of selecting the four fields on the left side of the form and then choosing Format⇨Align⇨Left. All the field labels lined up quite nicely, but the boxes for the data entry certainly didn't.

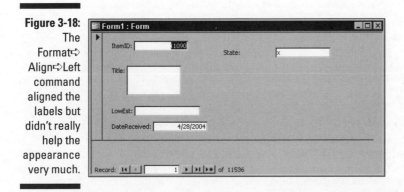

Figure 3-18: The Format⇨ Align⇨Left command aligned the labels but didn't really help the appearance very much.

One solution to the poor alignment of the data entry boxes might be to Shift+Click each of those boxes and then align the boxes independently of the field labels. In this case, though, the real answer is to adjust the size of the fields and of the data entry boxes first, and then worry about alignment after the sizes are consistent. (See the following section, "Setting consistent sizes."

Setting consistent sizes

The Format⇨Size submenu in Figure 3-19, helps you set consistent sizes for a group of selected objects. As mentioned in the previous section, "Aligning objects on a form," it's often best to set the sizes of the field objects before you attempt to align them — even though the Align menu appears before the Size menu.

Figure 3-19:
The
Format⇨
Size
submenu
helps you
make
objects a
consistent
size.

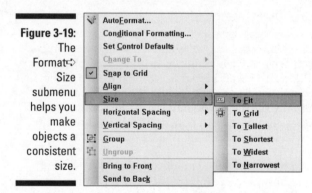

In the example form (refer to Figure 3-18), the different widths for the data entry boxes give the form a pretty inconsistent look. No amount of alignment can disguise the fact that the boxes are different sizes.

To repair this type of inconsistency in your own forms, choose Format⇨Size⇨To Widest. Voilà! Each of the boxes is now the same width.

You also have the option of making the boxes the same height, but you may want to resist that urge. One field (`Title`, for example) may need additional room for a user to type. (At least that's the case in Figure 3-18.)

After adjusting the size of the boxes, you can align the right side of the data entry boxes and align the two top fields along their top edge. Figure 3-20 shows the results.

Using the Align and Size commands together

The Align and Size commands really go together, which means that you may have to go back and forth a few times between the commands before you get the results you really want. Be patient and you'll soon develop a workflow that gives you the results you want with the least amount of effort. And then you'll be ready for even more complicated layout issues, like fixing spacing issues. See "Spacing horizontally and vertically," elsewhere in this chapter.

Figure 3-20:
A combination of consistent sizing and alignment greatly improves this form.

Spacing horizontally and vertically

One of the most difficult appearance aspects to master when you're creating forms is the horizontal and vertical spacing of the fields. That's where the Format➪Horizontal Spacing and Format➪Vertical Spacing submenus can really help. Both of these have three options: Make Equal, Increase, and Decrease.

Generally speaking, the best technique when dealing with spacing is to start out with all the fields equally spaced both vertically and horizontally before you do anything else. Choose the Make Equal command to get everything evened out. Then use the Increase or Decrease command to adjust the amount of space between individual fields. Ah. So much more efficient, yes?

Figure 3-21 shows the results of using the Format➪Vertical Spacing➪Make Equal command and then the Format➪Vertical Spacing➪Decrease command on my example form. Compare this to Figure 3-19 and you can tell that the fields in the left side of the form now use less vertical space and they're evenly distributed.

Figure 3-21:
Adjusting
the spacing
of the fields
gives the
form a
consistent
and
professional
look.

Shrinking a big form down to size

After several improvements to your form, I am sure that it will look better (just as the form in Figure 3-21 looks a lot better than the one in 3-15). But there may still be some — ahem — *room* for improvement.

Currently the form takes up more room on the screen than necessary, but you can easily fix this ailment by shrinking the form to a size that just accommodates the fields that appear on the form. Doing so is a two-step process because there are two different things that control the size of the finished form.

To begin shrinking your form's size, switch to Design view and drag the lower-right corner of the gray box (inside the Form window) that appears behind the fields, as shown in Figure 3-22. You want to make this area as small as possible without cutting off any part of any of the fields on the form.

Figure 3-22:
Resize
the gray
box inside
the Form
window
to just fit
the fields
on the form.

After you resize the gray box, drag the lower-right corner of the Form window up and to the left until you've reduced the size as much as you can without cutting off the fields (the Form window is the entire window where the form appears and has the title bar that says Form 1: Form in Figure 3-22). You'll have to switch between Form view and Design view several times to check your results. You know when you've shrunk the form too much if Access adds scroll bars to the form.

Figure 3-23 shows the final result of shrinking the form. In this case I managed to shrink the form from 283 x 532 pixels to 218 x 483 pixels — a savings of almost one-third in total screen area used by the form.

Figure 3-23:
My final
form is
much tighter
and takes
up less
room on the
screen.

You could, of course, save even more space by placing all the fields in a single column in the form or even by making two shorter columns of fields. Even so, the finished form certainly looks a lot better than the form I started out with.

I have one more neat trick that you may want to know about. If you switch the form into Form view, you can choose Window⇨Size to Fit Form to shrink the Form window to the smallest possible size to display the fields. Unfortunately, doing so often cuts off some of the record navigation tools, so you may not like the results.

Chapter 4

Building Basic Reports

*R*eports are the real icing on the cake when it comes to getting useful information from a database. They provide information in a format that almost anyone can understand, and because most reports are designed for printing, reports also give your data an element of portability. Using Access reports, you can present a membership summary at your organization's board meeting or you can show your banker that your business really is making money.

Building reports is certainly a more complex project than creating either queries or forms (see Chapters 2 and 3). Reports typically include page numbers, the dates and times the report was printed, record grouping, and summaries, all of which make creating a report a task that requires a bit more planning. In this chapter, I show you how to build basic reports so that you have a good foundation on which to build in the upcoming chapters.

Getting to Know the Types of Access Reports

You probably don't need me to tell you that there are many different uses for Access reports. Fortunately, all these different purposes can be fulfilled by a relatively small number of report types. As a result, you really only need to master a few types of reports in order to create virtually any report that Access can produce.

Even though there really are only a few different basic types of reports you can create in Access, that doesn't mean that they all look the same. Indeed, you can create a huge number of variations by using very minor changes. The important point to remember is that your reports should fulfill your needs; feel free to customize them.

Introducing simple reports

The simplest type of Access report is basically just a list that shows information as it appears in a table. Figure 4-1 shows an example of this type of simple report.

Figure 4-1:
A simple Access report shows a list of items in a table.

In this case, the report shows three of the fields that are contained within a table instead of displaying the entire set of fields. That's actually one of the advantages even a simple report has over just printing a copy of the table.

If you print a copy of a table, all the fields print in the order that they appear in the datasheet view. If you have several fields and a lot of data, the printout is likely to be very hard to follow because there are often too many fields to fit the width of a page. When you're building a report, however, you can usually create a layout that allows your data to print in a more readable format. And, of course, you can leave out the irrelevant fields. In Figure 4-1, for example, the report shows only the information that is needed for a specific purpose (taking inventory, perhaps).

Using reports that group data

Reports that group related records are still relatively simple — just a small step up from the very simple report shown in Figure 4-1. By grouping the records as shown in Figure 4-2, the report enables users to find related items. In this case the report groups the records, using the values in the State field to make viewing items by state much easier.

Figure 4-2:
This report groups the items according to the values in the State field.

	4056 Prescott, AZ Town Images.
	16891 Sterling Smelting Co.
Arizona Territory	
	16834 Lumber Camp Original Photograph, c. 1900.
	16851 Cabinet Photo, 2nd Street, Phoenix, Arizona, 1899-1900.
	17171 Santa Ana Mining Stock Certificate.
	16844 Two Photographs, Prescott, A.T. 1894.
	16840 Pimo Indian Cook Phat Cabinet Photo.
Arizona/Nevada	
	16759 Sheldon Family Albums Pages, 1902-1907.
Arizona/New Mexico	
	350 Banner MC Annual Report.
Arkansas	
	17140 New York Zinc & Lead Co.

Items Table-Simple Grouping

Page: 12

In addition to grouping records by using the entire value in each record in a specific field, you can use the grouping options to group records by using the first one to five characters in the field. This option is especially handy if your database contains typos that you haven't quite gotten around to correcting yet. Weed out the misspelled words into one report and make your changes. For example, suppose you know that someone misspelled California a number of times when entering data. If you group the report on State but only match the first two characters, you can probably find the results you want.

Using reports to summarize information

Sometimes you may need a report that summarizes the information in your database. For example, Figure 4-3 shows a report that lists the total, average, minimum, and maximum values of items in an auction, with records broken down by state.

Summary reports can include detailed records or they can simply show the summaries — the choice is yours and completely depends on your needs.

Figure 4-3:
This report provides a summary of the items in the database.

Auction Summary by State

Min	$50.00
Max	$50.00
Alaska.	
Summary for 'State' = Alaska. (8 detail records)	
Sum	$570.00
Avg	$71.25
Min	$20.00
Max	$150.00
Arizona.	
Summary for 'State' = Arizona. (42 detail records)	
Sum	$2,040.00
Avg	$48.57
Min	$20.00
Max	$150.00
Arkansas.	

Page: 1

Creating Reports by Using a Wizard

You ought to get to know the Access report wizards before you spend a lot of time and effort trying to create reports in Design view. For reports this is probably even truer than it is for forms and queries, if for no better reason than to have some good examples you can look at when you decide to give Design view a try.

Access is loaded with wizards to help you with various tasks. In fact, depending on the choices you made while installing Access, you can find something like 35 to about 55 wizards if you look hard enough. It's almost enough to make you start looking for someone named Merlin!

In the following sections, I show you how to make use of just one more wizard, the Report Wizard. This particular wizard is probably the handiest of all the wizards for most Access users.

Using the Report Wizard

The Access Report Wizard works very much like the Query and Form wizards we looked at in the previous two chapters. The Report Wizard does take you through a few extra steps that aren't necessary in those other wizards, but as long as you take your time and consider each of the options, you'll find this wizard is also quite easy to master.

Follow these steps to create a report with the Report Wizard:

1. **Open the Access database where you want to create the new report.**

2. **Select the Reports option in the Objects list to display the list of reports.**

3. **Double-click Create Report by Using Wizard near the top of the Reports list.**

   Alternatively, you can click the New button and choose Report Wizard from the New Report dialog box — both methods display the Report Wizard dialog box, as shown in Figure 4-4.

Figure 4-4:
Choose the table or query and then the fields for your report.

4. **Select the table or query that you want to use as the source of the report data from the drop-down Tables/Queries list.**

5. **Choose the fields you want in the Available Fields list, and then click the > button to move those fields to the Selected Fields list.**

   You can choose all the fields by clicking the >> button and you can remove fields by using the < and << buttons.

6. **Click the Next button to display the Grouping Levels section of the Report Wizard dialog box.**

   See Figure 4-5.

7. **If you want to group the records, choose the field (or fields) and click the > button.**

   You can't group records based on certain types of fields such as memo fields or OLE object fields.

Figure 4-5:
Choose a
field to use
to group the
records in
the report.

If you select a field to use for grouping, you can click the Grouping Options button and choose to group the records by exact match or by the first one to five characters in the field.

8. **Click Next to display the sorting options, as shown in Figure 4-6.**

   You can use these options to make sure that the report is sorted for improved readability.

Figure 4-6:
Select the
sorting
options you
prefer.

9. **To add group summarizations to the report, click the Summary Options button to display the Summary Options dialog box, as shown in Figure 4-7.**

10. **Select any summarizations you want to add to the report.**

    In my example, I selected the Sum option to show the total LowEst value by state. Only fields containing numeric values can be summarized.

Summary Options

What summary values would you like calculated?

Field	Sum	Avg	Min	Max
LowEst	☐	☐	☐	☐

OK

Cancel

─ Show ─
◉ Detail and Summary
○ Summary Only

☐ Calculate percent of total for sums

Figure 4-7:
Add group summarizations by using these options.

11. **Select the Detail and Summary option to display all the records and a summary, or select Summary Only to hide the record display.**

12. **(Optional) Select the Calculate Percent of Total for Sums check box if you want the percentage value shown for each group.**

13. **Click OK.**

    The Summary Options dialog box closes.

14. **Click Next to display the report layout options, as shown in Figure 4-8.**

Report Wizard

How would you like to lay out your report?

| XXXXXXXX |
| XXXX XXXX XXXX XXXX XXXX |
| XXXXX |
| XXXX |
| XXXXX XXXXX XXXXX |
| XXXXX XXXXX XXXXX |
| XXXX |
| XXXXX XXXXX XXXXX |
| XXXXX XXXXX XXXXX |
| XXXX |
| XXXXX XXXXX XXXXX |
| XXXXX XXXXX XXXXX |
| XXXXX XXXXX XXXXX |

─ Layout ─
◉ Stepped
○ Block
○ Outline 1
○ Outline 2
○ Align Left 1
○ Align Left 2

─ Orientation ─
◉ Portrait
○ Landscape

☑ Adjust the field width so all fields fit on a page.

Cancel | < Back | Next > | Finish

Figure 4-8:
Choose the layout options for your report.

15. **Select the report layout that you prefer.**

    As you choose different options, the selected option is previewed in the left side of the dialog box.

    Choosing Landscape orientation makes fitting reports that contain a number of fields onto a single page much easier.

16. **Click Next to display the report style options.**

    See Figure 4-9.

Figure 4-9:
Choose a
style for
your report.

17. **Choose the style you want to use for your report.**

18. **Click Next to display the final Report Wizard section, as shown in Figure 4-10.**

Figure 4-10:
Enter a
descriptive
name for
your report
so that it will
be easy to
identify.

19. **Enter a name for your report.**

    This is both the name that you want to identify the report in the Reports list and also the title that will appear at the top of the report, so you probably won't want to use the default name (the name of the table or query on which the report is based).

To include an ampersand (&) in the title (like `Nuts & Bolts`), use two of them (&&). A single ampersand will be converted to an underline.

20. Click the Finish button to build the report and then view it.

When your new report appears on-screen, you can use the navigation buttons at the bottom of the report to view each of the pages in your masterpiece. You can also use the arrow keys and the Page Up and Page Down keys to navigate.

Understanding what the wizard doesn't know

The Report Wizard does a pretty good job at creating reports, but like all the Access wizards, this wizard is more of a generalist than a detail freak. As a result, you'll almost certainly find that you want to tweak your reports after the wizard is finished. Here are some of the things the Report Wizard really doesn't know about:

- **Formatting variations:** The wizard applies the same bland formatting to every field even if you would like to make certain fields stand out by using a different font, type size, or formatting (such as bold or italics).

- **Adding divisions:** The wizard doesn't add record separators, so sometimes people find discerning where one record ends and another begins a little difficult.

- **Adding external data:** The wizard doesn't know how to use data from external tables.

- **Conserving space:** The wizard has no clue about how much money you spend on paper, so it's perfectly happy to create reports that have excessive margins, wasted space for fields that could be condensed, and group summarizations that take up several rows when one would do just fine.

If you would like to do any of these things, you have to create reports on your own in Design view (or modify ones you created with the Report Wizard). See "Designing Reports from Scratch."

Designing Reports from Scratch

Even though the Report Wizard does a pretty good job of creating a basic report, I have no doubt that eventually you'll end up using Design view to create or at least fine-tune most of the reports that you create in Access. Reports are simply too important and visible for you to accept something that's just okay — especially if the report is something you're going to be showing to other people. Sure, building a report in Design view is a bit of work, but the results can be worth the extra effort.

Take a brief look at the following section that tells you about some basic building blocks of Access reports. It's vital to understand the report bands if you want to successfully build an Access report.

Understanding the report bands

Access uses separate sections called *bands* to control the layout and grouping in reports. These report bands are always nested in a specific order that's similar to an outline in many ways. In some cases, a particular band might be empty — for example, you might not care to use the report footer if you don't have anything that you want to appear at the end of the report. It doesn't matter if you use the Report Wizard or create the report from scratch — the report bands appear in both cases.

The bands that might appear in a report (see Figure 4-11) include:

- **Report Header:** The header appears once at the beginning of a report and often includes things like a report title and the date the report was produced.

- **Page Header:** As you might guess, the header appears at the top of each page of the report. You might use this for column headings, page numbers, or the date.

- **Group Header:** When you group records in a report, the group header is used to show where each group begins. Typically, this band includes the value of the field that is used for grouping. If you have multiple grouping levels, each level has its own group header.

- **Detail:** The innermost nested band is always the detail band that is used to show the details of each record.

- **Group Footer:** Each group header can have a corresponding group footer. This footer is typically used to add separators or summaries (such as group totals).

- **Page Footer:** This footer is used to specify information that you want to appear at the bottom of each report page, such as page numbers or dates. Even though the group bands and details bands are nested within the page bands, groups and details may take up several pages. Page footers help readers know where they are so that they don't lose their place.

- **Report Footer:** This appears at the end of a report. Often, the report footer band is left blank.

The report header, report footer, page header, and page footer are optional report elements. You can add blank copies of these elements by selecting View⇨Page Header/Footer or View⇨Report Header/Footer. Both options are toggles, so if you want to view a page header, you also see the page footer. Likewise, if you hide the report footer, the report header goes away, as well. Page headers and footers are selected by default in new reports.

If you don't want one of the four elements to appear, move the mouse pointer to the bottom of the element's band and click-and-drag the band up until the element is hidden (the title bar for the element remains visible). So, if you want a report header but not a report footer, you choose View⇨Report Header/Footer to display both the report header and the report footer, and then drag the bottom edge of the report footer up until it disappears (you can always drag it down again if you change your mind and want to use a report footer).

You can resize any report band by dragging the bottom edge of the band up or down, or by dragging the right edge left or right.

Understanding the different report bands is important because you use those bands to create reports that group and summarize the records the way you want. Knowing what each type of band does is vital to building reports that function the way you intend them to. And the report bands also help users keep track of their place in a long report.

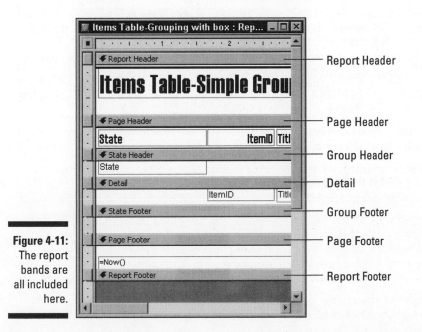

Figure 4-11:
The report bands are all included here.

Setting up the report page

You begin creating a report in Design view by double-clicking Create Report in Design View in the Reports list in the Objects list. When you select this option, Access displays a blank report, as shown in Figure 4-12.

As Figure 4-12 shows, the field list initially is empty because Access can only populate the list after you select a table or a query to use as the source for the report. The toolbox on the right side of the screen contains the same set of tools used for creating forms in Design view (see Chapter 3).

However, there are buttons on the default Access toolbar that you really should become familiar with. You are definitely going to need them when you create reports in Design view:

- ✔ **Sorting and Grouping:** Click this button to display the Sorting and Grouping dialog box so that you can sort your report or group the records. You can also display this dialog box by choosing View⇨Sorting and Grouping, but the toolbar button seems just a little easier to remember and to use.

- ✔ **Properties:** Click this button to display the Properties dialog box for a selected object so that you can control properties. For example, you can modify the table or query that is the source of data for the report by using the Properties dialog box. You can also display the Properties dialog box by choosing View⇨Properties, by right-clicking an object and choosing Properties, or by pressing Alt+Enter.

The basic report that appears when you first start a new report in Design view is completely empty. You need to select a data source (a table or a query) before you can add any fields, set up any sorting, or apply any grouping. You can, however, add a report header or footer and you can add things like page numbers or dates to the page header or footer. These objects don't depend on data from a table or query. See the previous section, "Understanding the report bands," for more information about these elements.

Adding page numbers

If you want page numbers on your report, you always add them to either the page header or the page footer because these report elements show up on every page of the report.

Toolbox   Sorting and Grouping

Field List   Properties

Figure 4-12:
Report
Design view
provides a
number of
tools you
use to
create your
reports.

To add page numbers, follow these steps:

1. **With your report open in Design view, choose Insert⇨Page Numbers.**

   The Page Numbers dialog box, shown in Figure 4-13, appears.

Figure 4-13:
Use the
Page
Numbers
dialog box
to quickly
add page
numbering
to your
report.

2. **Choose the page number format you prefer from the Format section of the dialog box.**

   The first option simply shows the page number, while the second option displays the page number and the total number of pages.

3. **Choose whether you want the page numbering to appear in the page header or the page footer in the Position section of the dialog box.**

4. **Select the alignment you prefer from the drop-down Alignment list box.**

5. **If you want to show the page number on the first page of the report, make certain that the Show Number on First Page option is selected.**

6. **Click OK to apply your selections to the report design and close the Page Numbers dialog box.**

Adding dates and times

You may want to add date and time markers to your report. These markers give readers of your report a sense of the newness of the data, which may be important if you are dealing with a database that is constantly being updated.

The date and time is updated whenever a report is previewed or printed, making it easier to make sure that you're looking at the most recent copy of a report.

To add the date or time to your report, follow these steps:

1. **With your report open in Design view, choose Insert⇨Date and Time.**

   The Date and Time dialog box, shown in Figure 4-14, appears.

Figure 4-14: Use the Date and Time dialog box to add the printing date and time to your report.

Date and Time

☑ Include Date
- ● Monday, April 04, 2005
- ○ 04-Apr-05
- ○ 4/4/2005

☑ Include Time
- ● 9:26:07 AM
- ○ 9:26 AM
- ○ 9:26

Sample:
Monday, April 04, 2005
9:26:07 AM

OK
Cancel

2. **To add the date, make certain that the Include Date check box is selected, and then choose the date format you prefer.**

3. **To add the time, make certain that the Include Time check box is selected and then choose the time format you prefer.**

4. **Click OK to apply your selections and to close the Date and Time dialog box.**

You no doubt noticed that the Date and Time dialog box did not give you the option of choosing a location in the document for the date or the time to appear. That's because when you use this dialog box, Access always places the date and time fields in the report header if it is displayed. If the report header is not displayed, Access places these fields in the Detail band. Fortunately, you can drag and drop these fields wherever you want them to appear in the report layout. For example, you might want to place the date and time fields in the page header or footer. No problem.

Adding titles and other objects

You'll probably want to add a report title and some other objects (such as a company logo or contact information) to your reports. Adding these types of objects is a bit more art than science because you're free to let your imagination take over in the area of content, placement, and even format.

Generally speaking, you'll likely find that the toolbox provides the tools you need to add titles or graphics to a report. You can also use the Insert⇨Picture or Insert⇨Object commands to add a graphic, but the Image tool is there for this purpose and is convenient.

To add a title to your report, follow these steps:

1. **Select the Label tool in the toolbox and then drag out a box in your report design where you want the title to appear**

    The report header is typically where a title appears. You can also just click where you want the label to begin, but dragging out the box for the label gives you more control over the size of the box.

2. **Enter the text you want for the title, click outside the label box, and then click the label box again to select it.**

3. **Use the options on the Formatting toolbar to modify the appearance by choosing a font, a size, and any other formatting you prefer.**

To add an image such as a logo, drag out a box in your report design with the Image tool. After you've drawn the box, Access automatically displays the Insert Picture dialog box so that you can choose a graphic image file to place in the box. Select the image and click OK to add it to the report.

Choosing your tables

Reports need to be associated with a table or a query in order to include any data. You could, of course, create a blank report with just a title, page numbers, and dates, but without any real data your report would have little value beyond serving as lining for the bottom of a bird cage.

The table or query that provides the data for an Access report is called the *record source*. You choose the record source for a report, using the Properties dialog box for the report. To open this dialog box, click the report's Title bar (in Design view) to select the report, and then click the Properties button. Alternatively, you can right-click the report title bar and choose Properties from the pop-up menu. In either case, the Properties dialog box appears, as shown in Figure 4-15.

If the Data tab isn't already selected, click this tab to bring it to the front.

Click to create a new query.

Click to select an existing table or query.

Figure 4-15:
Specify the
table or
query by
using the
Record
Source list
box.

Report	
Report	▼
Format	Data	Event	Other	All
Record Source		▼ ...
Filter	
Filter On	No
Order By	
Order By On	No

You can select an existing table or query by clicking the down arrow on the right side of the Record Source list box and choosing from the list. Alternatively, you can click the button with the three dots to build a new query from scratch. After you select a table or query, you can add the fields to your report.

Although the Data tab of the Properties dialog box includes both a Filter and Order By (sort) option, using these options can be a little confusing and error prone because you have to enter the filtering and sorting parameters manually. To avoid the possibility of typing errors, it's usually a better idea to select an existing query or create a new query as the record source instead of trying to create a filter or sort order in the Properties dialog box.

TIP

A little information about the Properties dialog box

No doubt, you've come across the Properties dialog box in your forays into the world of Access databases. When you create forms and reports, this box is indispensable. The Properties dialog box offers tabs to help you change aspects of just about every part of your forms and reports:

✔ **Format:** As you might guess (and as you've already seen in this chapter), this tab enables you to change the format of a form or report.

✔ **Data:** This tab helps you pick the records and information that you want to put into the form or report. Use this tab to exclude irrelevant data and sort relevant data.

✔ **Event:** Here you can add VBA code to control what happens when an *event* such as moving off a record, clicking a control, or changing a value occurs.

✔ **Other:** This tab is sort of the dumping ground for things that the Access programmers couldn't find a better place for like Fast Laser Printing, Record Locks, and custom help file links.

✔ **All:** If you can't find a property, look on the All tab. Sure, you'll have to scroll through every property that applies to the selected object, but if it exists, the property will be listed here.

Selecting the fields

As soon as you've selected a record source, you can begin adding fields to your report because the field list automatically includes all the available fields. Adding the fields can be a bit frustrating — especially if you're trying to be neat about it.

You typically add fields to the detail band in a report, although you can also add a field to a group band to show how the records are grouped. For example, you can add the State field to the group header if you want to group records by state. That way your report lists the name of the state above each group of related records.

You add fields to the report design by dragging and dropping fields from the field list onto the report layout. When you're dragging and dropping, remember that the mouse pointer indicates the position of the field and that the field label is farther to the left. If you intend to leave the labels in front of each field, be sure to leave enough room for those labels. I show you another alternative for the labels in the next section.

Figure 4-16 shows an example (in Design view) of a report that includes all the report bands, uses grouping on the State field, and has a number of fields added to the report design. This report is a good starting point, but it still needs some work to make it into something you'd want to show to someone.

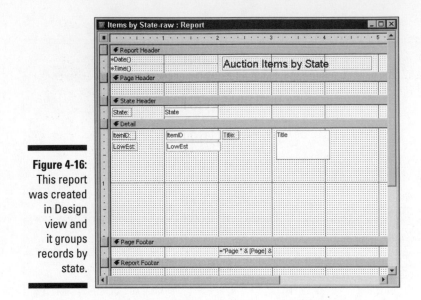

Figure 4-16:
This report was created in Design view and it groups records by state.

Modifying Report Layouts

The basic report design shown in Figure 4-16 illustrates an important point about creating your own reports — you'll probably want to do a bunch of cleanup work before you call the design finished. A few simple modifications can really improve the final result.

Deciding what needs to be done

Before just barging in and trying to fix a report's layout, it's a good idea to consider just what needs to be done. Here's a checklist of common layout issues that you'll want to evaluate and fix:

✔ **Problem: You want to change the location of date and time fields:** By default, Access puts the date and time fields along the left edge of the report header. They probably should be moved to another location. Reserve the report header for the most important details — the page footer might be a good place for the date and time information.

Solution: Drag and drop the date and time fields wherever you want them to go.

✔ **Problem: You want to change the location and position of the title of the report:** Access is pretty sloppy about where things go. Refer to Figure 4-16 and you see that the report title is offset to the right side of the report header. Centering the title improves the overall appearance.

✓ **Solution:** You can drag and drop the title or you can click the Center button on the Standard toolbar.

✓ **Problem: You want to make the layout efficient:** An occupational hazard of dragging and dropping fields into a report is that the fields *look* as though they have been dragged and dropped into the report. You need to fix this if you want the report to look like anything other than a draft. In Figure 4-16, the detail band has both field labels and the field boxes laid out in a fairly inefficient layout. The field labels could be moved to the page header and the field boxes could be tightened up underneath the labels. In addition, the bottom of the detail band should be moved up so less space is wasted between records.

Solution: Align and resize the field boxes with the Format⇨Align and Format⇨Size submenus. These tools work the same with forms that they do with reports. See Chapter 3 for more details.

You can resize a report band by dragging its bottom edge. However, moving the field labels can be a bit trickier. I discuss this topic in "Moving and formatting those pesky labels," later in the chapter.

✓ **Problem: You want to hide unused bands:** In Figure 4-16, the report footer is empty (which is fine — don't feel compelled to use every field available to you) but because the white grid in it is showing, the report footer will still take up room in the final report.

Solution: Drag the bottom of the report footer all the way up to eliminate this problem.

✓ **Problem: You want to add visual cues to help users navigate the report:** Unless you add them, your report layout gives few visual clues about where records and groups begin and end. Adding some simple horizontal divider lines can make a complicated report much easier to understand by visually delineating the records and groups.

✓ **Solution:** Drawing lines is simple, using the Line tool in the toolbox.

Moving and formatting those pesky labels

The fields that you add to a report consist of two parts. The label identifies the field and the box that follows the label displays the values. That seems pretty simple and straightforward, but there's just one little problem with this arrangement — it's a bit difficult to move the label without also moving the data box. Go ahead and try it and you'll see what I mean. When you try to select and drag the label, the whole field moves. It's almost like the two are joined at the hip!

Actually, there is a simple trick for moving the label separately from the data box, but you'd probably have little success discovering the trick on your own, and even if you did, you'd find that it doesn't work quite the way you might expect.

When you click a field to select it, you select both the label and the data box. But if you carefully move the mouse pointer to the upper-left corner of the label, the pointer changes into a hand with the index finger pointing upwards (see Figure 4-17). This is your chance! As long as the mouse pointer looks like that, you can drag and drop the label without moving the data box.

Mouse pointer with upward-pointing index finger

Figure 4-17: Look for this mouse pointer if you want to move the field label but keep the data box where it is.

As promising as this trick seems to be, there's a catch to it (isn't there always?). The catch is that you can't use it to move the field label into a different report band than the data box. As a result, this trick doesn't help you move field labels into the page header in order to save space by having a single field label above each column on a page. Likewise, you can't save a little space (and make the report easier to read) by moving labels to the group header.

So, how can you move the field labels to a different report band? The answer is that you have to separate the labels from the data boxes by using cut-and-paste techniques. There simply isn't any drag-and-drop method for moving the labels to one report band while leaving the data boxes in another.

Here's how to move those pesky labels:

1. **Click the label to select it.**

2. **Choose Edit⇨Cut, click the Cut button, or press Ctrl+X to move the label to the clipboard.**

   The data box won't move when you cut the label.

3. **Click the band where you want to place the label.**

4. **Choose Edit⇨Paste, click the Paste button, or press Ctrl+V to paste the label into the band.**

5. **Repeat Steps 1 through 4 for each of the labels you want to move.**

6. **Use the Format⇨Align commands to line up each of the label and data box pairs.**

TIP

You may need to do some moving and resizing of the data boxes in the detail band before aligning the labels with the data boxes. Remember that you can select two or more objects by holding down Shift as you click each object.

To make the text in each field align with the left side of the field labels, first select the data boxes. Then right-click the selection and choose Properties from the pop-up menu to display the Properties dialog box. Click the Format tab and select Left from the drop-down Text Align list box, as shown in Figure 4-18. Click the Close button to close the dialog box. Of course, you may prefer different alignment options for numeric or currency fields, but that's just a matter of choosing what you want.

Figure 4-18:
Make the data align with the labels by setting the text alignment for the field.

Pulling the layout together to save paper

After you move your labels and otherwise clean up the mess you started with (as described in the previous sections), be sure to drag the bottom of each report band up to prevent your printer from spitting out a bunch of blank paper when you print your report. When you drag the bottom of a band up, Access won't allow you to shrink the band to less than the height necessary to show whatever fields are in the band. Even if you drag the bottom of the band up higher than the bottom of a field, the band won't shrink that far because the bottom of the lowest field in a band limits the amount you can shrink the band.

Figure 4-19 shows the completed report in Design view. You may want to compare the completed design with the preliminary design shown in Figure 4-16 to see how the report was changed. Of course, this isn't the way the report will look when it's printed.

Figure 4-19:
The completed report design is much cleaner than the original.

Figure 4-20 shows how the completed report looks when it's in its printable version. To preview the report, click the View button. The finished report is compact but it clearly displays the data in an understandable format. What more could you ask for?

Figure 4-20:
The completed report also looks good in Print Preview mode.

Adding Data from External Linked Tables

Creating your reports within the same Access database that holds the records you need for the report is not always possible — or even desirable. Perhaps you need to use data from an Access database that is maintained by Mr. Smith in Accounting, who doesn't want you messing around with his creation (Mr. Smith doesn't get out much). Or maybe you're dealing with a situation where you don't want to add anything to the primary database file because you've split the database into *front end* and *back end* applications — basically a database where the tables are in one file and all the forms, reports, and queries are in another file. Or perhaps you simply want to know how to add data from external linked tables to your report so that you'll have another fancy Access trick up your sleeve. Regardless of the reason, you *can* base Access reports on tables that exist in another Access database.

Choosing a method for accessing external data

To use data from an *external* table you must first establish a connection between your current database and the database file that holds the table you want to use. There are two ways you can create this connection:

✔ **You can *import* the table from the other database file into your current database file.** This method places a *static* copy of the table into your database file. That is, after you import the table, there's no remaining connection between that imported copy of the table and the external database file. If Mr. Smith in Accounting makes changes to the information in his database after you import the table, those changes won't be reflected in the imported table. Likewise, if you make a change to the table after you import it, Mr. Smith's database won't be affected. Obviously, this option has some merits. Mr. Smith can sleep well, knowing that you haven't turned his database into a disaster. On the downside, if Mr. Smith's changes to the table are important to your report, you don't have access to them.

✔ **You can *link* to the table in the external database file.** The link ensures that you're always working with current data, but it also requires that the external database file remains available whenever you need to access the information. Another issue that's near and dear to Mr. Smith's heart is that you can screw up his tables. Of course, in the interest of maintaining peace in the office, you may not want to point out to Mr. Smith that his changes to the tables can monkey with your report. Rather, just be careful.

If you know that the external database file will always be available, you probably want to link to the external table instead of importing the table. That way you can be sure that whenever you run your report it is accurate and up-to-date. If, on the other hand, the external database file might not always be available (or it might be moved and break the link) and you can live with a snapshot of the data as it existed when you imported it, importing the table may be your best choice. Only you can choose the best option for your situation.

Importing or linking external data

After you decide which method you want to use to connect to external data to your report, you can create that connection. You need access to the external database file, but you don't have to open that file.

The process is pretty much the same whether you decide to import the data or link to it. To create a connection to an external table in a different Access database file so that you can use the data in a new report, follow these steps:

1. **Open the database file where you want to create your report.**

2. **Choose File⇨Get External Data⇨Import to import the table or File⇨Get External Data⇨Link Tables to create a link to the table.**

   In my example, I chose File⇨Get External Data⇨Link Tables. Doing so displays the Import or the Link dialog box (shown in Figure 4-21). The two dialog boxes are essentially the same except for their title.

Figure 4-21: Locate and select the external database file.

3. **Select the external database file that contains the table you want to import or link to.**

   If you need to navigate to another server or folder in the network, you can do that, just as you would when looking for any file in Microsoft Office.

4. **Click Link (or Import) to display the dialog box showing the list of tables.**

   Figure 4-22 shows a list of tables. Once again, the two dialog boxes are quite similar. If you're importing, not linking, the dialog box shows tabs for all database objects — not just the tables.

Figure 4-22:
Choose the
tables you
want to
import or
link.

Link Tables

Tables

CURRENTA
CURRENTB
FORFREDSTOP3
GeneralInfo
IntInvoicing(Aug13)
LIVEWINBID
LotNumberbyOwner
Low_High
MANAGER
OWNERS
Paste Errors
TOP THREE BIDS

OK
Cancel
Select All
Deselect All

5. Select the tables you want to use and click OK.

You can select multiple tables by holding down Shift or Ctrl as you click
each table. You can select all the tables by clicking the Select All button.

After you click OK, the dialog box closes and the connection is created.
Figure 4-23 shows the Tables list with two linked tables, CURRENTA and
LIVEWINBID, and one imported table, CURRENTB. You can tell that
CURRENTB is imported because there is no arrow next to it. The arrow
indicates an active link between the table and your report.

Figure 4-23:
Two tables
are linked
and one
was
imported.

UsingExternal : Database (Access 2002 - 2003 ...

Open Design New

Objects

Tables
Queries
Forms
Reports
Pages
Macros
Modules

Groups

Create table in Design view
Create table by using wizard
Create table by entering data
CURRENTA
CURRENTB
LIVEWINBID

After you import or link the external tables, you can use them exactly as you
would any table you created within the current database. Being able to use
external tables in your Access reports gives you many additional possibilities
for creating reports (as well as forms and queries) that you may not have
considered before. There's really no difference between internal and external
tables. Whether you import the table or create a link to it, the table acts the
same way.

Part II
Creating Effective Queries

The 5th Wave   By Rich Tennant

"Let me run a quick Select query for
you in the Life_Preferences table
before I tell you where you're headed."

In this part . . .

Queries enable you to choose which information is included in your forms and reports. You don't have to include everything in a form or report when applying a little focus can make you so much more efficient. This part shows you how to create very effective queries that improve your forms and reports. You also get an introduction to the language that is at the heart of all Access queries, SQL — *Structured Query Language* — so that you can soup up your queries for even better results.

Chapter 5

Creating Multi-Table Queries

· ·

· ·

In Part I, I get you up to speed on the basics of queries, forms, and reports. In Part II, you get to tackle some really meaty topics. In this chapter you see how to effectively use multiple tables in a query so that you can get even more useful information from your Access databases. Multi-table queries enable you to use information from two or more tables as if you had a single table containing a combination of the data from those multiple tables.

Using information from two or more tables requires that there be a *relationship* between the tables so that Access can determine how to combine the data. Table relationships are fundamental and extremely important for making your Access databases powerful and efficient. This chapter shows you how to create these relationships, as well.

Understanding Multi-Table Queries

Queries act almost as surrogates for tables. That is, you can use a query in place of a table in nearly any place where you would ordinarily use a table. For example, you can just as easily use a query as the basis for a report as you can use a table for that purpose. You can't, of course, use a query as a place to store data — that's a job that can only be handled by a table. But if what you need is a data source, a query can easily serve the bill.

A query must ultimately have a table as the source of its data, but one query can build on the results from another query as long as the lowest level of the chain is a table.

A query typically extracts a group of information from one or more tables by using criteria you specify. That's why queries are so useful. Instead of showing every record in a report or in a form, you can choose to include a *subset* of the records in order to bring some focus to the report or form. You can also choose to include only the fields you want.

Understanding the benefits of multiple tables

You may be asking yourself why you'd ever want to use multiple tables in a single query. Simply stated, using multiple tables in your queries gives you more flexibility, just as using multiple tables in a database gives you many benefits. The following list gives you a few of the many good reasons to use multiple tables to hold your data:

- ✔ **Efficient data storage:** Multiple tables can actually be a more efficient means of storing related data because they enable you to enter certain information once and then reuse that information in the future without reentering it. For example, if you have a contact database, you can enter basic information about a company, such as the address, when you add your first contact at that company. After that, you can then simply refer to the same information when you enter additional contacts from the same company.

- ✔ **Easy updating:** Multiple tables are also far more convenient when you need to update information because you can make a single change and have it apply to all related records; you don't have to go in and change every single one of the records. A good example of this efficiency is when telephone area codes change and you can update the records for everyone in the old area code in a single step.

- ✔ **Easy data access:** Using multiple tables makes setting up lookup lists in forms much easier so that you can give users limited choices in specific fields and prevent keying errors. This also makes it easier for users to find the data they need.

- ✔ **Keeping remote relationships intact:** Many databases contain information that is only remotely related. Multiple tables provide a means of keeping that information together so that it's easier to exploit the few, distant relationships.

These are all great reasons to use multiple tables in a database, of course, but how do they relate to using multiple tables in a query? Using multiple tables in a query enables you to perform the following tasks:

✔ **To bring information together in one place:** Multiple tables are efficient for storing related information, but sometimes you simply need to bring that information together in one place — such as in a report. A multiple-table query often provides the best way to bring that information together.

✔ **To update information in a table based on its links to another table:** You guessed it — a multiple-table query provides the solution for this, too.

✔ **To create a table that combines specific fields and records from several tables:** A multiple-table query is really the only way to go. For example, you might want to provide your customers with a year-end summary of the business they've done over the year, and this could require you to pull information from your orders table in addition to your items list table.

You can probably think of a number of other examples of how using multiple tables in a query can help you accomplish your specific goals. Just as Access databases have thousands of functions, there are countless ways to use the information they contain.

Establishing relationships between multiple tables

Storing various pieces of information in different tables is easy. The hard part is linking the information that's in one table to the information in another table so that you can create *relationships* between the tables. When information in two tables is related through linking, you can find records in each of the tables that are somehow connected. For example, Figure 5-1 shows two related tables in an auction database. The two tables share a common piece of information that makes finding related records in the two tables much easier.

If you study Figure 5-1, you notice that there are no common fields between the two tables. That's because table relationships can be created between fields with different names as long as the two fields contain the same type of information. The USERBIDID and BIDID fields in this example are both used to identify the bidder.

Figure 5-1 demonstrates one of the important points about using data from multiple, linked tables — that you can combine information in useful ways very easily. Suppose, for example, that you have a table named CURRENTA, which holds information about an auction's bidders, and that you have a table named LIVEWINDBID, which contains information about the items that are sold in an auction. When you combine the two, you can create a list of the items that were won by each of the bidders. In this case a single bidder might be the winner of a number of items, so the number in the BIDID field could show up multiple times in the LIVEWINBID table. That's why the line indicating the relationship between the tables has a 1 on the CURRENTA table side and an infinity symbol on the LIVEWINBID table side — a single record in the LIVEWINBID table can match any number of records in the CURRENTA table. This is called a *one-to-many* relationship between the tables.

Figure 5-1:
These two
tables are
related
because
they share a
common
value.

See the section, "Understanding Relationships in Queries," later in this chapter, for more information on creating relationships if they don't already exist in your database.

Adding Multiple Tables to Queries

In Chapter 2, I show you how to use both a Query Wizard and the Query Design view to create simple queries with a single table as the source of the data. Now I give you the lowdown on building queries that include fields from more than one table. (Using fields from another query works exactly the same way except that you choose a query instead of a table as the record source.)

Selecting multiple tables upfront

The method you use to select the tables for your query depends on the option you select to begin the query. Here's a brief review of the two methods:

✔ **Query Wizard:** If you decide to use the Query Wizard, you choose the first table from the drop-down Tables/Queries list box in the first section of the simple Query Wizard dialog box and then add the fields you want to use from that table to the query. Then you select the next table that you want to use and add its fields to the query. You continue this process until you've added all the tables and their fields to the query.

✔ **Design view:** If you create your query in Design view, you select the tables for the query by using the Show Table dialog box. You can add more than one table at a time by selecting all the tables you want to use before you click the Add button (see Figure 5-2). Use Ctrl+click to add each table you click to the selection or Shift+click to add a contiguous range of tables to the selection. Click Close to close the Show Table dialog box after you've added the tables to the query.

Figure 5-2:
Select all
the tables
you want to
add to the
query and
click Add.

You can use whichever method you prefer to add the tables to the query. Adding the tables in Design view means that you still need to add the fields you want to the query (see Figure 5-3); on the other hand, you may prefer doing the Design view method because you can more easily control the order in which the fields appear in the query.

Table links

Figure 5-3:
When you
add the
tables to the
query in
Design
view, none
of the fields
are auto-
matically
added to the
design grid.

Notice that in Figure 5-3 the links between the tables in the query automatically appear when you add those tables to the query design. In this case, the selected tables are the same ones shown in Figure 5-1, so the tables are linked the same way as they were in the earlier figure.

Sometimes you may see the link but won't be able to see the fields that are related because not enough space is allocated to display all the fields in a table. You can display the linked fields by scrolling the field list with the scroll bar along the right side of the list of fields, or you can drag the edges of the list to expand the list so more fields are visible.

If you add multiple tables to a query and no links appear in Design view, you have to create the links before you can run the query. Access won't allow you to save your work or run the query if the links don't exist before you begin creating the query. One way to add the links is to drag the field name from one table to the other, making sure, of course, that you drop the field onto the field that it is supposed to link to in the second table.

Each table in a query must be linked to at least one other table in the query. It's not necessary for every table to be linked directly to every other table, though. In fact, if you have three or more tables in a query and every table is linked to every other table directly, your database design is probably pretty messed up! (I show you a tool in Chapter 20 that may help you deal with this type of problem.)

Adding the tables you forgot about to your query

Inevitably as you start to create more complex multiple-table queries, you'll discover that you need to add a bit more information, but that the information you need is stored in a table that you forgot to add to your query. This isn't quite the disaster that it might seem because it's pretty easy to add tables to a query that you've already started working on.

If the new table that you want to add already has an established table relationship with at least one of the tables in your query, you simply need to open the Show Table dialog box and add the new table. Follow these steps:

1. **Choose Query⇨Show Table or click the Show Table button on the toolbar.**

   The Show Table dialog box appears.

2. **Add the new table by selecting it and clicking Add.**

If the new table you want to add doesn't have an established table relation-ship with one of the existing tables in the query (or if you're not sure whether it does), things are a bit trickier. You need to establish that relationship (as discussed later in this chapter in the section "Understanding Relationships in Queries") before adding the new table.

How can you tell whether the new table is related to one of the existing tables in the query? Probably the most straightforward way is to first save your query design by choosing File⇨Save, by clicking the Save button, or by press-ing Ctrl+S. By saving your query design first you avoid the dreaded possibil-ity of losing the query if something goes wrong and you can't save it later. After you save the query design, add the new table to the query and look for a link to an existing table. If the link is there, you're home free. If there's no link, right-click on the new table and choose Remove Table from the pop-up menu. Then create the link before trying to add the table again.

Choosing the fields to use

You have several methods you can use to add fields from the query tables to the design grid. They include the following:

- ✔ You can drag and drop fields from the tables at the top of the Query editor onto the columns in the lower section of the Query editor window.

- ✔ You can double-click fields in the tables at the top of the Query editor window.

- ✔ You can click in the Field row of the design grid to display a list of the available fields, and then choose a field from the list.

- ✔ You can use the asterisk (*) at the top of either the field list in each table or in the Field row of the design grid to add all the fields from the speci-fied table to the grid.

Adding the fields to the grid is the easy part. Choosing the fields that should be included and the order in which they appear is just a touch more compli-cated. There are no hard-and-fast rules about which fields you should include or their order in the design grid, but the following guidelines may help you decide what will work best in your queries:

- ✔ **List the most important fields first.** That is, if you intend to do any grouping, add the grouping fields first in the order that you plan to use them to group the records — with the least selective grouping (such as State) coming before more selective grouping (such as City).

- ✔ **Follow grouped fields with nongrouping fields that you want to use for sorting the records.** Once again, place the most important sorting fields to the left of fields that aren't so important.

- ✔ **Finally, include fields that you want to use to select which records you want included in the results.** You don't have to include these criteria fields in the results if you don't want them there. You can deselect the Show check box for any fields you don't want included in the results.

- ✔ **Be sure to include every field that you want to show in the results.** The results can be a simple datasheet view, a form, or a report.

- ✔ **Exclude any fields that aren't important to your results.** The idea here is to keep the results just a bit cleaner and easier to use. For example, you might not need to include fields like automatically generated indexes that Access uses to create unique records. Typically, these types of values aren't very useful in a report.

You can delete fields by clicking the column header to select the field in the query design and pressing the Delete button on your keyboard.

You can use and adapt these guidelines to best suit your needs. If you're more comfortable throwing in every available field just to make sure they're all there, feel free to include them all. Just be aware that it's really easy to add an extra field later if you've left one out of your original query design.

Making Access use the correct table

The second row of the query design grid shows the table that is the source for the field in that column. If all of your query designs in the past have been single table queries, you might not have given the table entry much thought. But when you begin creating multiple-table queries, the table entry can be very important.

Commonly, you may have fields with the same name in different tables. For example, you might use State as a field name in several different tables in a single database. Generally these duplicated field names aren't a problem, but consider the following scenario where the problem is very real.

Imagine for a moment that you have two tables in your database that use State as a field name. The first table lists the names and addresses of your customers. The second table lists the items that were won by bidders in a recent auction. Now, suppose that you're required to file a report with the tax department showing all the items sold to buyers in your state. If your query uses the State field from your customer list, there's no problem. But suppose you accidentally used the State field from the items table and that table showed the state where the item originated instead of the state where the buyers live. Clearly, in the second case, your report isn't going to satisfy the tax collector. (And when have you known a tax collector who had a sense of humor?)

Access allows you to choose a table and field name that don't match. That is, if you have already selected a field and then change the source table by making a different selection in the Table cell, the field name remains the same even if no field by that name exists in the new table. If you change the source table, be sure that the field exists because otherwise the query results will be meaningless.

Linking to External Databases in Your Queries

Chapter 4 briefly touches on the idea of using information from external databases in your reports. Here I expand on that idea and consider some additional ways that you can use external data with your queries.

Understanding the types of external data you can use

If you read Chapter 4, you already know that you can use data that exists in another Access database. But Access isn't the only application that produces databases. Fortunately, Access can work with information from many different types of databases without a whole lot of fuss and bother.

Access uses *drivers* — small helper applications — to import or link to external data. You won't usually notice when Access is using a driver because quite a few of them are built into Access. Depending on the version of Access you're using, different drivers may be built in. For example, Access 2003 has built-in drivers that provide the ability to import or link to the following types of files:

- Access databases and projects
- dBASE databases
- Excel spreadsheets
- Fixed-width and delimited text files
- HTML and XML files
- Lotus 1-2-3 spreadsheets
- Microsoft Exchange databases
- Microsoft Outlook databases
- Paradox databases
- Windows SharePoint Services

Importing versus linking external data

The File➪Get External Data submenu offers two options. You can choose to *import* data or to *link* to the data. Access is perfectly content to use the information either way, but you should be aware of the important differences between the two options. If you import data, the copy of the data that you import only exists within your Access database. Any changes that are made to the external data after you import the information won't be included in your version of the table. If you want to maintain an active link so that you're always working with current information, you must choose to link to the external data instead of importing it.

In addition, Access can use *ODBC* (Open Database Connectivity) drivers to connect to quite a few other types of database files such as SQL Server, FoxPro, and Oracle. Some of these ODBC drivers are installed automatically when you install Access, but Access can also use ODBC drivers that are supplied by other manufacturers.

Every driver provides a different level of support for features that are native to other file types. In some cases, you may not be able to use every type of data that a foreign file can contain. This problem is usually the result of ancient ODBC drivers that came with an old database application and can sometimes be corrected by searching the manufacturer's Web site for newer drivers that you can install.

Even after you successfully import or link to external data, keep in mind that some types of information make no sense in an Access database. For example, if you link to an Excel worksheet that is laid out as a database but which contains formulas in the database range, those formulas mean nothing in Access. You can create the link, but you'll probably see a cryptic message that says something like `Method 'Columns' of object 'IImexGrid' failed`. If you see a message like this, be sure to have a look at the linked (or imported) data to see whether it makes sense before you try to use the information in Access (the message in this example is simply a strange way of telling you that Access couldn't import everything from the Excel worksheet).

Linking to tables in another foreign database format

It's just a fact of life that different people like to do things different ways. That's one reason why, from time to time, you may need to use data that was created in a format other than Access. In order to use that information, though, you need to bring it into Access. To link to data in another database format, follow these steps:

1. **Open the Access database where you want to use the external data.**

2. **Choose File⇨Get External Data⇨Link Tables.**

   The Link dialog box appears (see Figure 5-4).

Figure 5-4:
Use the Link
dialog box
to link to
external
data.

3. **Select the type of file you want to use from the drop-down Files of type list box at the bottom of the dialog box.**

4. **After you select the type of file, select the file you want to link to in the file list.**

5. **Click the Link button to continue.**

6. **If you are prompted to select an index file, select the file and click Select. If there is no index file, click Cancel to bypass this step.**

   A message box appears, telling you that the file was successfully linked (see Figure 5-5).

7. **Click OK.**

Figure 5-5:
Access
informs you
that the
link was
successfully
created.

8. **Click Close to close the Link dialog box.**

    The linked table will appear in the Tables list with an arrow in front of the table name to indicate that it is a linked table. If you linked to a non-Access table, the table's icon shows the type of the file.

Depending on the type of file you're linking to, you may encounter different steps and prompts during the linking process. For example, if you link to an Excel worksheet, you're asked to indicate whether the top row of the data includes the field labels.

Knowing what you can and can't do with a linked external database

After you've successfully created a link to an external database table or spreadsheet database range, you can use that linked table just about the same way you would use an ordinary Access table that is contained within your database file. There are some things you *can't* do to a linked table, however. As Figure 5-6 shows, if you attempt to open a linked table in Design view, Access informs you that you can't modify some of the properties in a linked table. In truth, in most cases you can't modify any of the properties in linked tables — except for the name of the table.

Figure 5-6:
You cannot
modify most
of the
properties
in linked
tables.

Microsoft Office Access

! Table 'AddressLink' is a linked table with some properties that can't be modified.

Do you want to open it anyway?

    Yes   No

See Chapter 6 for information on how to use a query to create a new table. Creating a new table is an easy way to get around the fact that you typically can't modify the properties of a linked table.

Understanding Relationships in Queries

In order to use multiple tables in a query, the tables have to be related. In the following sections, I give you a closer glimpse at those relationships; you can see how to create the relationships necessary for adding extra tables to a query.

Getting to know how tables are related

When you add related tables to a query, Access shows you that the tables are related by drawing lines between the tables in the Query editor. You must make sure that the table relationships are established before you begin creating your queries. If you begin creating a query and attempt to use tables that aren't already related, you have to create the table relationships, and then continue building your query.

Except in unusual circumstances, all the tables in a typical Access database are generally related in some way. The relationships may be distant and travel through several intermediate tables, but tables that are unrelated to any other tables usually signify that either the relationships have not yet been established, or that the unrelated table may not actually belong in the database.

Although you can view table relationships in the Query editor, Access provides a better option for working with table relationships. The Relationships window, shown in Figure 5-7, not only displays any existing relationships, but it also enables you to create and edit relationships.

In Figure 5-7, two relationships are displayed. The TypeID field is shared by both the TypeTable and ItemsTable tables, and those fields were used to create one relationship. The ItemsTable and OWNERS tables are similarly related, using a common field.

Figure 5-7:
The Relation-
ships
window
enables you
to view,
create, or
edit table
relation-
ships.

Access includes the symbols showing the type of relationship between the tables if you choose to enforce *referential integrity* for a link. Referential integrity is a method of ensuring that your related data is protected and is covered in the section "Setting up table relationships" later in this chapter.

You can create relationships between fields in two different tables as long as those fields contain related information and are of the same type (you can link an `AutoNumber` field to a `Number` field if the `Number` field has its `Field Size` property set to `Long Integer` or `Replication ID`). It's not necessary for the fields to have the same name, although using the same name for the field in the two tables does give you a good clue when you're creating the links. You can't, however, create links to memo or OLE Object fields.

Making sure that you choose the right relationships

You need to choose the right relationships. No, I'm not talking about family matters or dating here. Tables can be related to each other in several different ways:

- ✔ **One-to-many** relationships have a single value in one table that is matched up with more than one value in the other table. This is the most common type of relationship. For example, in the typical relationship between a customer table and an orders table, each customer is usually assigned a unique ID in the customer table. That ID can appear in the orders table many times — once for each order placed by the customer.

- ✔ **One-to-one** relationships have unique values that can appear only once in each table. This type of relationship is far less common because one-to-one relationships aren't very useful in most instances.

- ✔ **Many-to-many** relationships are actually just two one-to-many relationships with an intermediary table that is used to create the link.

Don't worry too much if the types of table relationships seem a little confusing right now. Usually, Access automatically creates the correct type of relationship, which is usually a one-to-many relationship. In Chapter 15, you can find out how to make Access use a different type of relationship if necessary.

Setting up table relationships

The relationships between the tables in your database are what make your database into a *relational* database and therefore far more efficient and useful than a *flat-file* database like one you might create in an Excel worksheet. Although this book isn't intended to cover basic database design issues such as creating table relationships, you should know the process in case you somehow missed that step in designing your databases.

If you need more information, check out *Access 2003 For Dummies* by John Kaufeld (Wiley).

Setting up table relationships does require some initial planning. When you're creating the tables for your database, you need to think about how those tables will be related. This means that you have to include fields that are common to two or more tables and that contain information that is shared between the tables. Say you have a `Customer ID` field and a `Catalog Number` field; these are but two examples of the types of fields that are likely to occur in multiple tables — you use the same customer ID in both a customer table and in an orders table. Likewise, you use a catalog number in both an inventory table and an order detail table. To add table relationships in your database, follow these steps:

1. **Open the Access database in which you want to create the table relationships.**

2. **Choose Tools⇨Relationships to display the Relationships window, as shown in Figure 5-8.**

Figure 5-8: Open the Relationships window to create new table relationships.

3. **Click the field in the first table that you will use to link to the second table, hold down the left mouse button, and drag the pointer onto the related field in the second table.**

   You may need to first scroll the field display in the two tables to make the two fields visible.

4. **Release the mouse button.**

   The Edit Relationships dialog box appears, as shown in Figure 5-9.

Figure 5-9:
Use the Edit
Relation-
ships dialog
box to
specify the
parameters
for the
relationship.

```
Edit Relationships                              ? X
 Table/Query:        Related Table/Query:
 ItemOwners    ▼    WinningBids    ▼         Create
 DBOWNERID    ▼    OWNERID         ▲         Cancel
                                   ▼
                                            Join Type..

 ☐ Enforce Referential Integrity             Create New..
 ☐ Cascade Update Related Fields
 ☐ Cascade Delete Related Records

 Relationship Type:   One-To-Many
```

5. **Select the Enforce Referential Integrity check box if you want Access to make sure that certain rules are applied when you make changes to the records in the tables.**

   Referential integrity insures that you cannot delete or otherwise change data under specific circumstances. For example, you can't delete a customer's record in your customer table if there are still active order records under the customer's ID.

6. **If you chose to enforce referential integrity, choose the Cascade Update Related Fields check box if you want Access to automatically update the related tables when the primary table is modified.**

   For example, if you assign new customer ID numbers in the customer table, you want the orders table to reflect those new ID numbers, right?

7. **If you chose to enforce referential integrity, choose the Cascade Delete Related Fields check box if you want Access to automatically delete the associated records in the related tables when the primary table is modified by deleting a record.**

   For example, if you remove a customer from the customer table, you should also delete any remaining records for that customer in the orders table.

8. **Click the Join Type button.**

   The Join Properties dialog box appears, as shown in Figure 5-10.

   What Access calls a *join* is what I would call a relationship. A join simply brings records from various tables together.

9. **Choose the type of join that's most appropriate for your database from the three choices.**

   In most cases the first choice is the correct one because you want to match the records between the two joined tables. The other two choices create what is called an *outer join,* where records from either the left or the right table are included even if the other table does not have matching records.

Figure 5-10:
Use the Join
Properties
dialog box
to specify
which
records
to use.

Join Properties   ? X

- ⦿ 1: Only include rows where the joined fields from both tables are equal.
- ○ 2: Include ALL records from 'ItemOwners' and only those records from 'WinningBids' where the joined fields are equal.
- ○ 3: Include ALL records from 'WinningBids' and only those records from 'ItemOwners' where the joined fields are equal.

    [OK]   [Cancel]

10. **Click OK to close the Join Properties dialog box.**

11. **Click Create to create the link (or *join*) between the two tables.**

12. **Repeat Steps 3 through 11 for each of the table pairs where you want to create a relationship.**

After you finish creating the table relationships, those relationships appear in the Relationships window. You can drag the tables and resize them as necessary to make the links between the tables easier to visualize.

While viewing the relationships in the Relationships window, you can see a copy of the relationships by using the File➪Print Relationships command. This command displays an on-screen report showing the relationships, and clicking the Print button gives you a printed the report. You might need to move the tables to fit one printed page.

Chapter 6

Modifying Data with Queries

· ·

· ·

You can do a lot more with queries than simply selecting data to show in a datasheet view, form, or report. You can also use queries to actually change the information that's contained in your database. This capability opens up whole new worlds of tasks that you can accomplish with Access because you can easily make either mass changes or very selective ones simply by creating the proper query.

In this chapter, you see what you can do with a data-modifying query. The topics include creating new tables by using a query, updating existing information by using a query, removing specific data with a query, and adding new records with a query. Armed with these techniques, you'll become more efficient in manipulating your Access databases so that you can get more done in less time and maybe even find time to do some things that are a bit more fun with the spare time that you'll gain.

Understanding What You Can Modify with a Query

Queries are very powerful tools. They give you the ability to automate a broad range of actions in your Access databases without requiring you to master some strange-looking and difficult-to-understand computer programming language, such as SQL *(Structured Query Language)*.

Knowing what you can modify

One of the most frustrating things about using queries to modify your databases is simply getting a handle on just what you can do with a query. Oh sure, you already know that you can use a query to select specific records and specific fields, but what else can you do with a query? Just what kinds of modifications are possible by using queries?

Here are some of the things you can modify by using a query:

- ✓ **Modify field values in a table:** You can change the prices of items you want to put on sale, change the name of a customer's company if another company buys it out, update telephone area codes for customers who live in a specific city, or modify the descriptions of a series of products based on some new requirement from your attorney that says you have to warn customers that the kites you sell aren't intended for flying in winds above 2 miles per hour.

- ✓ **Remove specific records from a table:** With this type of query you can remove all of your old flames from your address list when you become engaged, get rid of all of your cousin Larry's vegetable-flavored ice cream varieties (you knew they were a dumb idea in the first place, didn't you?), or delete any one-of-a-kind products from your inventory table after they're sold.

- ✓ **Add new records to an existing table:** You can quickly add a new series of products that you've just begun selling, add the latest members to your club's local membership list by using the list e-mailed to you from the national office, or add shipping and handling charges for each customer based on the amount of stuff they bought at your most recent auction.

- ✓ **Create a new table, using a specified group of records from a single table or records that you generate from several tables:** You can create a table to send to your bookkeeper that lists the customers who purchased items so that the bills can be prepared, you can create a table for your newsletter editor that lists the members' birthdays for the upcoming month, or you can create a table of customers who bought your canned lizard meat spread so that you can send them a mailing announcing your new line of pickled banana products (are you sure it was cousin Larry who thought up that line of ice cream?).

I'm the first to admit that this list barely scratches the surface, but it does give you at least a few ideas about how queries can do so much more than simply select a set of records.

Knowing what you can't modify

As powerful as queries are, they can't do everything. It's important that you get a feel for the limitations of queries. Here are some things that you can't modify with a query:

- **You can't use a query to modify the basic structure of an existing table.** For example, you can't use a query to change the data type or size of a field in a table.

- **You can't directly change the values used in** `AutoNumber` **fields.** However, you can use an *append query* to add enough records to change the next value used indirectly.

- **You can't use a query to change the names of objects in your database.** You can work around this limitation by using a *make-table query* to create a new table, but this solution doesn't really help if you have already created queries, forms, or reports based on the existing table.

Append and make-table queries are different kinds of *action* queries. Action queries are designed for the specific purpose of modifying data in a table. If you want to make changes to data by using queries, you'll become familiar with these queries. Lucky for you, I discuss action queries in the following section, "Being Called to Action: Data-Modifying Queries."

- **You can't change the sort order of a table so that an *OLE Object* field is used as the sort key.** Even if you use a make-table query, you're stuck because OLE Object fields simply can't be used for sorting.

- **You can't create a whole new database file with a query.** Queries can only exist within an existing database.

These limitations aren't so bad when you get right down to it. After all, a query is really intended to manipulate data, as opposed to modifying the basic building blocks of your database. You can easily make those types of changes yourself and use queries for what they do best.

Being Called to Action: Data-Modifying Queries

When you begin creating a new query, Access automatically sets the query type as a select query. But if you want to modify data in a table, a select query just won't cut it. In Access, queries that modify data are called *action* queries. If you want to create an action query you must select the query type when the query is open in Design view.

Action queries include the following types:

- *Append* queries add new records to an existing table. Those new records can come from a single table or they can be built up from records in two or more tables. The only fields append queries deal with are the ones that are already in the existing table, so if you create an append query that includes fields that aren't already in the target table, Access simply discards those extra fields when the records are appended.

- *Delete* queries remove records from a table. Any records that match the specified criteria are completely deleted even if you only specify some of the existing fields in the query.

    If you only want to remove certain field values from a table without deleting the complete records, use an update query instead of a delete query.

- *Make-table* queries create a new table that includes all the fields specified in the query.

    Make-table queries always delete any existing table that has the same name as the specified target table, so you need to use some caution to make certain you don't accidentally overwrite a table that you really need.

- *Update* queries modify values in an existing table. Only the fields specified in the query are changed, so any fields that you don't specify are left untouched. When you want to delete only some fields (but not all the records), this is your action query of choice.

SQL-specific queries can also modify data. Although many people consider SQL queries to be a separate type of Access query, in reality, all Access queries are SQL queries. SQL — *Structured Query Language* — is discussed in Chapter 7.

I often find that I need to create a couple of different types of queries and then run those queries in the proper sequence in order to accomplish a particular goal. For example, to create a table that contains the billing information for an auction, you might first create a make-table query that builds a new table containing information about the prices of the items that were sold at the auction. Then you would create an append query to add the buyer's premium and one that adds shipping and handling charges to that new table. This combination of different query types enables you to produce results that wouldn't be possible with a single query.

Making sure you don't do any damage

Because all action queries modify your data in some way, you need to be a little careful so that you don't make changes to your database that you later regret having made. That's one of the primary reasons that all new queries start out as select queries. You can always safely run a select query without worrying about changes to your tables because select queries simply don't make any changes. After you've verified that your select query returns the results you want, you still have to be sure that you choose the proper type of action query and that you specify the correct tables to modify, but at least you know that your query is using the right records.

You must keep the differences between the types of action queries in mind as you create your own action queries. A simple mistake such as choosing to create a make-table query when you actually should have used an append query or an update query can have some pretty extreme consequences — especially if you ignore the warnings that Access provides when you try to run one of these queries! If you're not sure what you're doing, it's okay to experiment. Just back up the work you don't want to lose.

If Access isn't warning you about changes to the records when you run an action query, choose Tools⇨Options to display the Options dialog box. Then click the Edit/Find tab and select the Action Queries check box in the Confirm section. For that matter, you should probably make sure that all the options in the Confirm section are selected. Click OK to close the dialog box and apply the changes.

Creating New Tables with Queries

Okay, you may find this a little strange, but I happen to think that make-table queries are actually kind of fun to create and use. After all, can you think of another way that you can so quickly create a new table and fill it with selected data from a couple of different tables? It almost seems magical the way a make-table query allows you to be both creative and extremely productive at the same time.

Why you would want to create new tables

There are often several different ways to accomplish the same goal. That's certainly true in Access. For example, if you consider the example of selecting and gathering data for a report from a set of tables, one method to meet your objectives would be to create a complex select query and then base your report on that query. If you need to summarize the data in the report and perform calculations based on various subtotals, your report design could become quite intricate and difficult to troubleshoot or even to verify.

As an alternative to that option, you may want to consider using a make-table query to first bring together the basic data for your report. After you set up the new table, you can continue to use the same complex report design or you can use another query to perform the calculations, and then base your report on the already summarized data. This second method offers a couple of advantages because it means that you have an actual table where you can examine and verify your data, your report is easier to design, and you don't need to deal with so many troubleshooting issues. In addition, having the data in a new table makes exporting that data to another application such as Excel, Word, or even QuickBooks a snap.

Creating your first table with a make-table query

A make-table query enables you to create a new table by using records from one or more existing tables. For example, you can convert an existing select query into a make-table query that creates a table that shows the winning bidder for each item in an auction.

To create a make-table query, follow these steps:

1. **Create the select query that you want to use as the basis for your make-table query.**

   Figure 6-1 shows an example query. Be sure that you save the query before continuing.

2. **Test your query by choosing Query⇨Run or by clicking the Run button.**

   You want to make sure that your query returns the expected results before you convert the query into a make-table query. Figure 6-2 shows a sample query that returned the expected results.

3. **Choose View⇨Design View or click the View button to return to Design view.**

   If your query didn't return the results you expected, correct the errors and test it again. When you're satisfied with the results, continue to Step 4.

Figure 6-1:
Begin by
creating
your select
query.

Basis for make-table query example : Select Query

CurrentAuc...
*
BKEY
FirstName
LastName
BIDID

WinningBids
*
ID
AuctionNumbe
LOTNUMBER
BIDID

Field:	AuctionNumber	LastName	LOTNUMBER	BIDAMOUNT
Table:	WinningBids	CurrentAuction	WinningBids	WinningBids
Sort:				
Show:	☑	☑	☑	☑
Criteria:	40			
or:				

Figure 6-2:
Run your
select query
to make
certain that
it actually
produces
the results
you
intended.

Basis for make-table query example : Select Query

AuctionNumber	LastName	LOTNUMBER	BIDAMOUNT
40	Webster	180	$60.00
40	holabird	181	$20.00
40	O'Neill	182	$50.00
40	Brown-1	183	$25.00
40	Petersen	184	$15.00
40	Dawson	185	$50.00
40	kille	186	$45.00
40	Dougan	187	$60.00
40	Blythe	188	$200.00
40	Sale	189	$0.00
40	Duppa-Mille	190	$150.00
40	Sundstrand	191	$110.00
40	Livingston	192	$25.00
40	Sale	193	$0.00

Record: 1 of 661

4. **Choose Query⇨Make-Table Query or click the down arrow at the right side of the Query Type button and choose Make-Table Query.**

   The Make Table dialog box appears, as shown in Figure 6-3.

5. **Enter a name for your new table in the Table Name text box.**

   Be careful not to use the name of an existing table unless you really do want to completely replace the existing table with the new table.

6. **If you want to create the new table in a different Access database file, select the Another Database option button and then specify the name of the database file in the File Name text box.**

   You can click the Browse button if you prefer to browse for the file and avoid the possibility of typing the filename incorrectly.

Figure 6-3:
Enter the
name for the
new table
that you
want to
create.

7. **Click the OK button.**

   The Make Table dialog box closes and you return to Design view. The only visual clues to show that your query is now a make-table query (and not a select query) are the description in the Design view title bar and the icon that is displayed on the Query Type icon on the toolbar.

8. **Save the query before continuing.**

   Choose File⇨Save, press Ctrl+S, or click the Save button on the toolbar.

9. **Choose Query⇨Run or click the Run button to run your query.**

   A warning message similar to the one in Figure 6-4 appears. The warning message indicates the number of records that will be added to your new table. You can't undo the action you're about to agree to, so be careful (refer to Step 8).

Figure 6-4:
This
warning
tells you
what will
happen next
and gives
you a
chance
to change
your mind.

10. **Click Yes to continue and create your new table.**

If, instead of displaying a message similar to the one shown in Figure 6-4, Access displays a message telling you that an existing table will be deleted before you run the query, be sure that the correct table name is shown before you click the Yes button. Otherwise, you could destroy an existing table that you actually want to keep.

Updating Data by Using Queries

There's no doubt that creating new tables by using a query (as described in the previous section) is both useful and interesting, but you may have even more call for updating existing data with a query. With update queries, you can make changes throughout a database quickly and efficiently.

Imagine for a moment how bored you would be to search through a table containing several thousand records to find and manually change a specific value. For example, suppose you have a database that contains, among other things, a customer list of several thousand people and businesses. You've just found out that the telephone area code for a city where a hundred or so of your customers live has just been changed from 702 to 775. Sure, you can spend a whole bunch of time looking for all the affected customers and then manually changing their area code, but an update query can do the job in moments (and you wouldn't have to wonder whether you missed anyone when you nodded off somewhere at about the 83rd on-screen page of the Datasheet view).

You might be tempted to use the Edit⇨Replace command to change the value 702 to 775 in the table and, indeed, that option would work if you wanted to change *all* occurrences of the values to something else. But in the case where you want to change only certain instances of that specific value based on the contents of another field, Edit⇨Replace won't do the job because you'd still have to manually verify each change. (What if several people paid $702 for an item?) For this more complex situation you really need to use an update query to make the changes easily and efficiently.

Creating an update query example

You can use an update query to modify a series of records. In the following steps, I use the example mentioned in the previous section where the telephone area code needs to be changed for a group of clients. It's always a good idea to have more than one criterion to cross-check your queries. For example, if you want to change a current area code, you should also make sure that the city and state match. Each of these items is important to check before making any changes because if any of them don't match you don't want to make any changes.

To create an update query, follow these steps:

1. **Create the select query that you want to use as the basis for your update query.**

   Figure 6-5 shows an example query in which the state must be NV, and the city must be Reno, and the phone area code must be 702. (In this case the `Phone` field just contains the area code, not the whole telephone number.)

Figure 6-5:
Create your select query that selects the records you want to update.

2. **Test your query by choosing Query⇨Run or by clicking the Run button.**

   Figure 6-6 shows the results of running the query.

Figure 6-6:
Verify the query results before you update the records.

3. **Choose View⇨Design View or click the View button to return to Design view.**

4. **Choose Query⇨Update Query or choose Update Query by clicking the Query Type button and making your choice from the pop-up menu.**

5. **In the Update To row of the Phone field, enter the new value you want to apply to the selected set of records.**

   In this case, you would enter **"775"** as the new value (Access automatically adds quotation marks when you enter values in a text field, but you can add them yourself, too).

   Figure 6-7 shows how the query looks after being changed to an update query and having the update value added.

Figure 6-7: The update query is now ready to run.

6. **Choose Query⇨Run or click the Run button to run your query.**

   Access displays a message similar to the one shown in Figure 6-8 to tell you how many records will be updated. This number should be the same as the number of records that the select query selected. If it's not, click No in Step 7 and review your actions.

Figure 6-8: Access tells you how many records will be updated.

7. **Click Yes to continue and update the records.**

   Figure 6-9 shows the result of running the update query and then creates a new select query to show all the records where the state is NV.

If Figure 6-9 has you a little confused, that's okay. I specifically set up this example so that it would produce results that you might not expect. It's very important that you take an analytical eye to every change you make to your database; otherwise, you'll have real problems down the road. Read the following section, "Understanding the update query results," for information about interpreting your results.

Figure 6-9:
This is a sampling of the records after the update query was run.

STATE	CITY	PHONE
NV	Carson City	702
NV	Las Vegas	702
NV	Carson City	702
NV	Virginia City	702
NV	Fallon	702
NV	Fallon	702
NV	Reno	775
NV	Virginia City	702
NV	Reno	775
NV	Laughlin	702
NV	Fernley	702
NV	Reno	775
NV	Reno	

Query1 : Select Query

Record: 1 of 94

Understanding the update query results

If you refer to Figure 6-9, you might be scratching your head. That's a good thing. In my example, the area code for any cities other than Reno remained as 702 and *most* of the Reno records were changed to 775. But why is there a record for Reno without an entry in the Phone field? Why wasn't that record updated to show 775?

The answer is simple. The select query I set up had three criteria. To be selected (and therefore updated), each record had to match all the criteria. One of the criterions was that the existing value in the Phone field had to be 702. In this case, the last record that is visible in Figure 6-9 didn't meet that criterion because there was no value in the Phone field for that record.

The original value may have been a different area code — not an uncommon occurrence in some large cities where several area codes are used — and you wouldn't want to change that value incorrectly. Or for some other reason (pilot error?), the field might have been empty. The update query actually does work exactly as it's supposed to because the nonmatching record was left untouched.

Deleting Data with Queries

Any action query has the potential for being destructive, but delete queries are the ones that seem the scariest. After all, with just a couple of clicks a delete query can permanently wipe out years of data entry work. If the potential damage a delete query can do doesn't scare you into backing up your database files, you may be one of those people who keep rattlesnakes as house pets.

Delete queries remove all trace of the selected records from your database. Because of this simple fact, it's even more important to first create your query as a select query and test it to see what results it returns before you change the query type to a delete query. Did I mention that you should be careful?

As an alternative to permanently deleting records by using a delete query, you may want to consider adding an `active` field to your table and marking the records you were thinking of deleting as `inactive`. That way, you can retain those records for possible future use, but exclude them from any reports by only including active records.

Creating a delete query is virtually an identical process to that of creating an update query. Here's how to proceed:

1. **Create a select query, as shown in Figure 6-10.**

   In this case, I specified that the state must be NV and the phone area code field is empty (Access refers to this as a *null* value).

2. **Test your query by choosing Query⇨Run or by clicking the Run button.**

   When you change the query type, all the selected records are slated for deletion, so make sure the results are correct before moving on.

3. **Choose View⇨Design View or click the View button to return to Design view.**

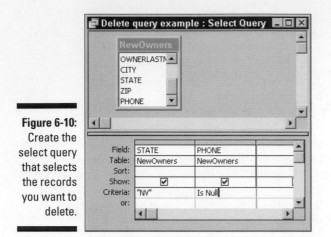

Figure 6-10:
Create the
select query
that selects
the records
you want to
delete.

4. **Choose Query⇨Delete Query or choose Delete Query, using the Query Type button.**

   Doing so changes the query design slightly, as you can see in Figure 6-11.

Figure 6-11:
The delete
query is
ready to
delete
records
from your
database.

5. **Choose Query⇨Run or click the Run button to display a warning message similar to the one shown in Figure 6-12.**

   If something doesn't seem right, you should click No and go back over your work.

6. **Click Yes to continue and delete the records.**

Figure 6-12:
This message gives you your last chance to save the records before they're gone for good.

Access won't allow you to delete records from a table if doing so would violate referential integrity rules. For example, if you have a customers table and an orders table that are linked with referential integrity enforced, you can't delete customers who still have open orders. See Chapter 5 for more information on referential integrity.

Adding New Data with Queries

Compared with delete queries, append queries seem almost tame. Instead of permanently removing records from your database, an append query adds new records to a table. Any existing records remain untouched and you can sleep a little easier.

Even though append queries seem benign, you should still exercise a bit of caution with append queries just as you should with any other action query. After all, you're still modifying the data, and that can have its consequences — if you aren't careful, an append query can add a whole bunch of bogus information to your database in the blink of an eye. The old saying *garbage in, garbage out* certainly applies here!

Using an append query

If you've been following along in this chapter, by now you've had some practice creating action queries from a select query. The process is pretty much the same no matter which type of action query you want to create. First you create your select query and make certain that it is actually producing the set of records that you expect. After you're sure that the select query is functioning, you change the query into an action query, supply any additional parameters, and run the query to perform the action. You can read more about parameters in Chapter 15.

Creating an append query generally follows the same path as any of those other types of action queries. However, you have some additional options that may make an append query even more useful to you.

The purpose of an append query is to add new records to a table. That's nothing new, of course, but stop for a moment and think about the implications of that statement. Notice that I didn't say where the new records were coming from. It's not necessary for the source of the new records to be a table in your current database file. This simple fact opens up a whole bunch of possibilities:

- ✔ You can use a table in another Access database on your PC as the source of the new records.
- ✔ If you are on a network, you can use an append query to add records to your database from a database file on your server or on another PC.
- ✔ If several people are using copies of the same database file on their laptop PCs, you can use an append query to consolidate the information from each of them when they stop into the office.
- ✔ You can import or link to files from other applications such as Excel, so the source of the new records doesn't even have to be an Access database.

You can also use something called *database replication* to synchronize different copies of a database, but the process can be pretty complex to set up and administer. Database replication is a topic that's beyond the scope of this book, but if you're really inclined to give it a try you'll find some sketchy information on it in the Access help files.

The following steps show you how to use an append query to add records to a table. In my example, I'm using for the basis of these records some data in an Excel worksheet that need to be added to an existing Access database table. Here are the steps you need to follow:

1. **Choose File⇨Get External Data⇨Link Tables to open the Link dialog box.**

   You can also use the File⇨Get External Data⇨Import command if you don't want to create a live link to the data. In this case you use the link option, but you need to consider how you want to add records on an ongoing basis before making a choice. The import option might be a better choice if you intend to continue adding new records to the external file rather than starting with a clean set of records the next time you run the append query.

2. **In the Files of type drop-down list box, choose Microsoft Excel (or the appropriate file type if your data is in another format).**

3. **Select the file, as shown in Figure 6-13.**

   In my example, I selected an Excel worksheet file.

Figure 6-13:
Choose the external file you want to use as your data source.

4. **Click the Link button to display the Link Spreadsheet Wizard dialog box, as shown in Figure 6-14.**

Figure 6-14:
Select the worksheet or range that is the source of your data.

5. **Select the worksheet or the range that you want to use in Access.**

   The sample data area shows how the selected worksheet or range appears.

6. **Click Next to continue.**

7. **Select or deselect the First Row Contains Column Headings check box as appropriate for your data.**

   It's much easier to use data from an Excel worksheet that has column headings that match the field names in your Access table than to use data from a worksheet with different names or none at all.

8. **Click Next to continue.**

9. **Specify a name for your linked table and click Finish.**

10. **When Access displays the message saying that the link is completed, click OK.**

11. **Create your new select query by using the linked table as the data source.**

    You can choose the asterisk at the top of the list to add all the fields to the table.

12. **Choose Query⇨Append Query to display the Append dialog box, as shown in Figure 6-15.**

Figure 6-15:
Specify the
table to
which you
want to add
the new
records.

Append	? X
Append To	OK
Table <u>N</u>ame: [▼]	Cancel
⦿ <u>C</u>urrent Database	
○ <u>A</u>nother Database:	
<u>F</u>ile Name: [ ]	
	Browse...

13. **Click the down arrow at the right side of the Table Name list box and then choose the table where you want to append the new records.**

14. **Click OK to continue.**

15. **Choose Query⇨Run or click the Run button.**

    A message similar to the one shown in Figure 6-16 appears, telling you how many new records will be added to the table.

Figure 6-16:
Access
is ready
to append
your new
records.

> **Microsoft Office Access** ✕
>
> ⚠ **You are about to append 661 row(s).**
>
> Once you click Yes, you can't use the Undo command to reverse the changes.
> Are you sure you want to append the selected rows?
>
> [Yes]   [No]

16. **Click Yes to add the new records to your table.**

As this example demonstrated, you can easily add records from sources other than tables that already exist in your database to your tables. This capability really expands your options — especially when you realize the possibilities it opens up for you.

Combining make-table and append queries

I've found that neither a make-table query nor an append query can always fill the bill, but sometimes a combination of the two is exactly what I need. In the auction database I regularly need to generate a table that the bookkeeper can import into QuickBooks. Here's a quick-and-dirty description of how it works.

1. **Create a table, using a make-table query.**

   This query generates the initial table with, say, the winning bids. Of course, your make-table query could generate a table with final sales, lowest temperatures, or any other data.

2. **Use an append query to add additional records.**

   In my example, of course, these additional records are for shipping and handling and the buyer's premium.

You could create a table with one extremely complex query, but if a couple of simple (and easy to troubleshoot) queries can do the job, why not go for the easier solution?

Action queries certainly give you a much higher level of automation and control than the simpler select queries that I discuss in the beginning chapters of this book. As long as you respect the power of action queries, as well as their capability to really mess up your database if you're not careful, you can find many uses for action queries in the future.

Chapter 7

Expanding Queries with SQL

- -

- -

*Y*ou've been using Access for a while, and if you've been reading the book from the beginning, you probably have a pretty good handle on the various types of Access queries — with one big exception, that is. I haven't really talked much about *SQL* queries. Well, now it's time to acknowledge the elephant over in the corner. This chapter sheds some light on what SQL is and how it affects your Access databases.

If you're completely happy writing queries with a Query Wizard or in Design view, you can just skip this chapter and avoid being exposed to another programming language. But if you want to supercharge your queries, or you want find out something about Access that you can use to impress your computer geek friends when they start spouting off a bunch of incomprehensible jargon, this is the chapter for you. After all, how cool will it be to drop something like, "Oh, I use a SQL union query to merge results in my Access database all the time"? Well, okay, maybe it's not all that cool, but it might impress your boss. And don't you want to discover just a bit more?

Getting the Scoop on SQL

SQL is an acronym for Structured Query Language, and it's a computer programming language that is used in most modern database applications.

Yes, that's right! SQL is actually a pretty common language that is used to create queries in most of the popular general database applications on the market today. For example, IBM DB2, Microsoft SQL Server, MySQL, Oracle, and Sybase are all SQL databases. Although it's not as obvious, Access fits right into that crowd, too. (Don't worry if you've never heard of those other types of databases, you can stick with Access and forget about them without really missing anything.)

Understanding the "S" in SQL

The S in SQL stands for *structured*. What that means is that SQL commands always follow a defined *syntax*. This syntax is pretty basic:

```
COMMAND object OPTIONS;
```

SQL statements include a command; they specify the object, such as a database, a table, or a field on which to execute the command; and they specify any options that are needed to alter how the command functions. Also, SQL statements always end with a semicolon (;) to tell the SQL application that the end of the command has been reached and it's time to execute the command. For example, the following snippet demonstrates a SQL select query that shows records for customers from Nevada:

```
SELECT CustomerName FROM Customers WHERE State = "Nevada"
```

So, there's your SQL lesson, now let's move on. Okay, just kidding, but that's really SQL in a nutshell. To use SQL effectively you have to know a bit more — such as some of the commands you can use.

By convention, SQL documentation always shows all the SQL commands and options in uppercase. In fact, some SQL database applications may not understand commands that aren't in uppercase; fortunately, Access isn't one of them. You can use any capitalization (or lack thereof) that you want and Access will still understand. However, if you think you may eventually advance to using SQL with other database programs, get into the habit of using the correct capitalization. In all the commands you see in this chapter (and throughout the book), I follow the correct SQL conventions.

To put the idea of a structured language into a bit clearer focus, consider the difference between human languages and computer programming languages. Humans are typically quite adaptable and can usually understand statements that don't follow normal sentence structure. Computer programs, on the other hand, are easily confused and need to have commands structured in a very precise way so that the program can understand what to do. To further understand what I mean, consider something my father told me about that happened when he was young and working in a local butcher shop. An elderly immigrant came in and said, "Give you to me a chicken." Although that wasn't the normal syntax he was used to hearing, my father clearly understood what was being requested. Imagine what a hard time a computer would have trying to figure out a statement that was so different from what it expected. The lady would probably still be waiting for her chicken!

Putting SQL in its place (at the heart of all Access queries)

Maybe you're surprised to discover that every Access query is actually a SQL query. No matter what method you use to create a query in Access, that query is converted to SQL and stored in your Access database as SQL. For example, Figure 7-1 shows a simple append query in Design view.

Figure 7-1: This simple append query is actually stored as a SQL query.

The query shown in Figure 7-1 looks like this in SQL:

```
INSERT INTO LIVEWINBID
SELECT [Auction 67].*
FROM [Auction 67];
```

Here's a quick look at what this all means:

```
INSERT INTO LIVEWINBID
```

says to insert records into the LIVEWINBID table.

```
SELECT [Auction 67].*
```

tells Access to select all the fields in the table named Auction 67 (the asterisk is a *wildcard* for all the fields in a table).

```
FROM [Auction 67];
```

tells Access to get the records from the table named Auction 67.

Okay, so I agree that this isn't quite normal human language, but you probably didn't have any real trouble understanding the gist of it even before the explanation.

Understanding How SQL Can Help

By now you're probably wondering what the big deal is and why you should even care about SQL. After all, can't you simply go on using the Query Wizard or creating your queries in Design view?

Actually, you can just ignore SQL — if you're willing to give up some of the power that's packed into Access, that is. However, there are some powerful reasons for expanding your knowledge of SQL. Put simply, SQL can help you improve your forms and reports in ways you might not imagine right now. For example, you might discover that using a SQL *data-definition query* enables you to change the type of existing data so that it can be more accurately displayed in a report.

Going beyond the automated query functions

Even though the Query Wizard and Design view enable you to do an awful lot, you simply can't create some types of queries without resorting to SQL. These are what Access calls *SQL-specific* queries, and include the following types of queries:

- **Data-definition:** These queries allow you to create or alter objects in the database by using *Data Definition Language* (DDL) statements.

- **Pass-through:** These queries allow you to send commands directly to an ODBC database server so that you work directly with tables on the server. Usually, the Microsoft Jet database engine that Access uses processes the data.

- **Subquery:** With this type of query you use a SQL SELECT statement in a select or action query.

- **Union:** You use this type of query to combine the results of two or more select queries into a single query.

Access doesn't actually support all the SQL statements that are available in some other SQL databases, but it does allow you to use the most common and useful statements. Access 2002 and later versions support a few additional SQL statements that aren't supported in older Access versions, but only if you use the latest Access 2002 or Access 2003 file format for your database.

Creating an indexed table with SQL

SQL-specific queries can't be created with a Query Wizard or in Design view. Even though you have to do some manual work, SQL queries *do* enable you to do some things you can't do with an ordinary query.

Chapter 6 shows an example of how you can use a make-table query to create a new table in your database by using fields from one or more existing tables. When you use a make-table query in this way, the fields in the new table have the same data types as the existing fields. This limits you in creating tables because you can't specify the data type, and you also have no way to specify a *primary key* (or index) for the table.

The following SQL data-definition query demonstrates a totally different way to create a new table. Working from scratch, you can

🖛 Specify the data type for each field.

🖛 Set a specific size for two fields (in my example the fields are Lastname and Firstname, but you probably have different names for your own).

🖛 Set those two fields as required fields.

🖛 Define a field (in my example, the ContactID field) as a primary key for the table.

Here's how the SQL query looks:

```
CREATE TABLE Contacts
([ContactID] integer,
[Lastname] text (25) NOT NULL,
[Firstname] text (25) NOT NULL,
[Phone] text,
[City] text,
[State] text,
[ZIP] text,
CONSTRAINT [Index] PRIMARY KEY ([ContactID]));
```

Figure 7-2 shows how my Contacts table appears in Design view after the SQL query is run.

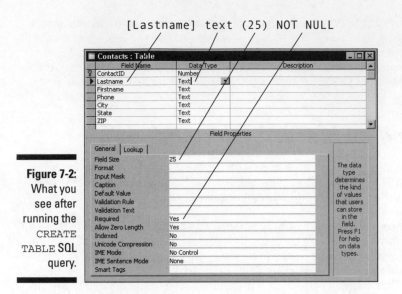

Figure 7-2:
What you
see after
running the
CREATE
TABLE SQL
query.

Modifying a table with SQL

You can use a SQL query to make modifications to the structure of an existing table. Examples of this might include

✔ Adding a key to a table

✔ Changing the data type of a field

✔ Changing the size of a field

✔ Making a field into a required field

Any of these functions might be especially handy if you use a make-table query to create a new table by using records from one or more other tables.

The following SQL query example adds a primary key to an existing table (such as one you might create with a make-table query):

```
CREATE INDEX Lot
ON [Auction40] (Lotnumber)
WITH PRIMARY;
```

In this example, the table is named Auction40 and the field on which the primary key is based is named Lotnumber. The new index is named Lot. By creating a primary key, you can use the table in a relationship where referential integrity is enforced and you can ensure that the values in the Lotnumber field are unique.

After you become comfortable with creating SQL queries, you can use the same SQL statements for the query as the RecordSource or RowSource property in a form or a report. You usually use a query or a table as the RecordSource or RowSource, but an SQL statement works just as well.

These examples barely scratch the surface of what you can do with SQL in Access, but they do show you the possibilities that await you when you move beyond an ordinary query.

Viewing the SQL You've Already Created and Didn't Know About

Every query that you create in Access is actually defined by a set of SQL statements that Access automatically generates from your query design. It simply isn't possible to create a query without generating the corresponding SQL statements — even if you didn't know they were there.

Switching to Design view

If you're still stuck on using the Query Wizard to create all of your queries, it's time to bite the bullet and switch to Design view. You have to open the Query editor (Design view) before you can have a look at the SQL statements that are behind your queries.

If you want to create a SQL query from scratch, it's unnecessary to add any tables to the query by using the Show Table dialog box — even though Access automatically shows the Show Table dialog box when you double-click the Create Query in Design View option in the Queries list.

To have a look at the SQL statements in a query you've already created, open the query in Design view, as shown in Figure 7-3. To open a query in Design view, select the query in the Queries list and click the Design button.

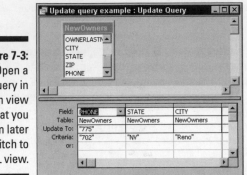

Figure 7-3:
Open a
query in
Design view
so that you
can later
switch to
SQL view.

Changing to SQL view

To see the SQL statements underlying your queries, you need to switch the Query editor from Design view into SQL view. To change to SQL view, choose View⇨SQL View or right-click the Design view window and choose SQL view from the pop-up menu.

Figure 7-4 shows the same query from Figure 7-3, but this time it is shown in SQL view.

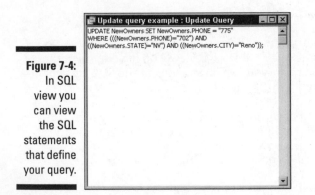

Figure 7-4:
In SQL
view you
can view
the SQL
statements
that define
your query.

Figure 7-4 illustrates an important point about SQL statements. You don't have to worry about line breaks in the code because line breaks are simply ignored when the statement is executed. On the other hand, line breaks do make it a bit easier for humans to understand the statements. Here I've added some line breaks (by pressing Enter) to break down the SQL statements into more understandable pieces:

```
UPDATE NewOwners
SET NewOwners.PHONE = "775"
WHERE (((NewOwners.PHONE)="702")
AND ((NewOwners.STATE)="NV")
AND ((NewOwners.CITY)="Reno"));
```

Even without any previous knowledge of SQL, this set of SQL statements is pretty easy to understand. It tells Access to update the NewOwners table by setting the value of the PHONE field to 775 only when three important criteria are met: The existing value in the PHONE field must be 702, the value in the STATE field must be NV, and the value in the CITY field must be Reno. You might even say that the SQL statement is easier to understand than trying to understand the same query in Design view!

Seeing the results in Datasheet view

Before you actually run your query, you can check the Datasheet view to get an idea of what the query will do. Figure 7-5 shows how the query shown in Figures 7-3 and 7-4 appears when you switch to Datasheet view.

To switch to Datasheet view, choose View⇨Datasheet View or right-click the query and select Datasheet View from the pop-up menu. You'll probably want to switch back to SQL view after you've checked the results in Datasheet view.

Figure 7-5:
In
Datasheet
view
you can
see how
records will
be affected
by your
query.

Datasheet view doesn't actually show the results of running the query. Rather, it shows the set of records that will be selected and processed when you run the query. In other words, the Datasheet view of your query shows you which records will be selected or changed by running the query, but it shows you how those records appear before any modifications occur. That makes the Datasheet view a good way to verify that your query is going to choose the correct records before you commit to any changes to those records.

Going back to Design view

Usually, you can switch back to Design view by choosing View⇨Design View or by right-clicking the query and choosing Query Design from the pop-up menu. But Figure 7-6 shows that sometimes you simply don't have this option available.

Figure 7-6:
The pop-up menu has the Query Design option disabled for this query.

Figure 7-6 illustrates all too well the fact that you can't create certain types of queries in Design view. When you create a SQL query that isn't possible to create in Design view, Access simply has no way to represent that query in Design view.

This might seem frustrating to you, but imagine how exasperating it would be if Access did switch to Design view and your SQL query was changed into something that could be shown in Design view — you'd probably have a few choice words to say to someone at about that point.

Even though you can't always switch back to Design view from SQL view, in most instances you'll be able to make the switch back and forth as often as you like. Switching between the two types of views is actually an excellent way to gain a better understanding of SQL because you can see what happens to the SQL statements when you make a change in Design view (or what happens in Design view when you make a change in SQL view).

Don't forget that you can copy and paste SQL statements to and from the SQL view in the Query editor. This makes it easy for you to keep copies of your SQL queries in a text document for documentation purposes, for example.

Getting Your Feet Wet with Simple SQL Statements

Although this book doesn't have the space for anything resembling a full course on SQL programming, I can at least get you headed in the right direction with some good tips and best practices.

Earlier in this chapter, in "Changing to SQL view," I show you how to switch from Design view to SQL view so that you can examine the SQL statements that Access automatically generates whenever you create a query. Although you can use SQL statements as either `RecordSource` or `RowSource` properties in a form or report, the more common use for SQL statements is to enter them in the SQL view of the Query editor.

When you start playing with the powerful tools, Access treats you like a pro, assuming that you're a database expert. In many cases, it doesn't display the warning messages you typically see when you run a query. Just to be safe, use a copy of your database rather than the real, working copy you depend on.

You'll likely want to begin working with SQL by making small changes to existing queries so that you can switch back to Design view to see the results of your changes. That way, you can build your experience and confidence at the same time.

Before you make any modifications, though, make certain to follow some important do's and don'ts:

- ✔ **Don't put a semicolon (;) anywhere but at the end of a command.** The only place that a semicolon (;) can appear in a statement is at the very end of the statement. The semicolon tells Access that the statement is complete and ready to execute.

  If you happen to forget the semicolon, the world might end tomorrow, but Access ignores your little error and runs the query anyway.

- ✔ **Do get in the habit of using uppercase even though you don't have to.** SQL *keywords* (such as commands and options) are always shown in uppercase by programming convention, but you aren't required to follow this convention if you are only preparing SQL statements for use in Access.

  Even though using uppercase for SQL keywords isn't required, it's not a difficult convention to follow and it can help you to find problems later. Most SQL examples you'll find online or in books do follow the convention and this will make it easier for you to compare what you've entered to the examples.

TIP

✔ **Don't forget brackets.** If a table name or a field includes spaces, such as `Auction 40 Results`, enclose the name in square brackets, as in `[Auction 40 Results]`.

Actually, it's always safe to enclose names in square brackets, so using them is a good habit to develop — that way you won't forget to add the brackets when they're important.

✔ **Do specify the table name.** You can get away without specifying the table name when you specify a field name if there's only one table in the query, but it's safest to always specify the table name in square brackets just before the field name. Use a period after the closing square bracket just before the first character of the field name. For example, type `[Customers].State` to specify the `State` field in the `Customers` table.

✔ **Do use wildcards, but don't be fooled.** When you use wildcards in SQL statements in Access, you use a question mark (?) to match a single character and an asterisk (*) to match any number of characters (including none).

In *ANSI* (American National Standards Institute) SQL, the version of SQL used by some other SQL database software programs, an underscore (_) is the wildcard for a single character and a percent sign (%) is the wildcard for any number of characters. If you attempt to experiment with SQL examples you find on the Web or in other sources, be sure to look for these differences because they can cause your statements to fail (and the error message you see probably won't provide a lot of help, either).

✔ **Don't forget that you're using a nonstandard form of SQL.** Access supports some nonstandard SQL features such as the `TRANSFORM` command for creating crosstab queries, the `PARAMETERS` declaration for creating parameter queries, and a few extra built-in functions for analyzing data. You can't use these commands and functions with other SQL programs.

✔ **Don't forget that you're using a nonstandard form of SQL, Part II.** Access doesn't support all the keywords that are defined in the ANSI standards. If you attempt to copy an example from another source (say from an online resources) and you find that it doesn't work, you'll probably want to check the Microsoft Jet SQL Reference in the Help file to see if you're using unsupported keywords.

✔ **Do consult the Help files when you need to.** The actual application that processes the SQL statements you create in Access is called Microsoft Jet. As a result, you'll find Help file information that lists various language elements you can use in the Help file section called Microsoft Jet SQL Reference.

✔ **Do consult the Help files when you need to, Part II.** If I haven't stressed this point already, let me tell you that there are some important differences between the ANSI data types and those that are supported in Access. You probably won't encounter any problems unless you try to copy an example of a SQL data definition query, but if you do, check the Help file to see how to modify the query to use Access data types.

You don't have to use SQL in order to make awesome forms and reports. But as you expand your knowledge of Access, a little SQL here and there can only help you. Although some of the points I mention here may seem a bit heavy, you can certainly create SQL queries without fully understanding all of them.

Making Useful SQL Statements

SQL queries can be useful and surprisingly simple. You don't have to write a best-selling novel in SQL in order for SQL statements to be effective.

If you've created an especially useful query, use it as a template for future queries. You can quickly and easily create a variation of that query by copying, pasting, and editing the SQL statements as necessary. This technique certainly beats going through the whole process of building a new query in Design view or by using the Query Wizard.

Updating records with SQL

Updating records is one of the more common uses for queries, and it's also a good place to start if you're just starting out making SQL statements. SQL update queries are pretty easy to understand because they're simple and straightforward.

Consider the following example:

```
UPDATE [AuctionResults]
SET [AuctionResults].[AuctionNumber] = 87
WHERE [AuctionResults].[AuctionNumber] = 85;
```

This query changes the value in the AuctionNumber field of the Auction Results table from 85 to 87. Another, shorter way to create this query is:

```
UPDATE AuctionResults
SET AuctionNumber = 87
WHERE AuctionNumber = 85;
```

You can, of course, create the entire SQL statement on a single line. In addition, if you don't need to specify any criteria, you can leave off the line that begins with WHERE and simply place the semicolon at the end of the second line.

If you need to update more than one field, simply add a comma after each field and then specify the additional field updates, as in this example:

```
UPDATE AuctionResults
SET AuctionNumber = 87,
Status = "Sold",
WHERE AuctionNumber = 85;
```

Creating and filling tables using SQL

A make-table query both creates a new table and fills the new table with data from an existing table. In SQL, this type of query is known as a *select into* query because the query first selects records and then places them into the new table.

One very handy use for this type of query is to create a backup of an important table as in the following example:

```
SELECT AuctionResults.*
INTO AuctionBackup
FROM AuctionResults;
```

In my example, I've created a simple backup of the entire AuctionResults table (remember that the asterisk is a wildcard, so it includes all fields) into a new table named AuctionBackup. In a real world example you might want to add the auction number to the end of the new table's name, as in Auction Backup85 so that you can keep a running history of each sale in a new table.

To modify this query to make it into an append query rather than a make-table query, you need to use INSERT INTO, as in the following example:

```
INSERT INTO AuctionBackup
SELECT *
FROM AuctionResults;
```

This example adds all the records from the AuctionResults table into the AuctionBackup table. To be useful, you would probably want to empty the AuctionResults table between sales so that only new records would be added to the AuctionBackup table when you run the query.

If you want to add a single record into the table and specify the field values in the query, you use a slightly different syntax:

```
INSERT INTO AuctionBackup (AuctionNumber, AuctionTotal)
VALUES (87, 300);
```

Notice that both the field names and the values must be enclosed in parentheses. If you forget to add parentheses, Access displays an error message when you attempt to run the query.

Making the most of SQL's flexibility

Each of the examples in this chapter have been relatively simple to create and to understand, and using SQL view makes it very easy for you to quickly and easily modify an existing query to suit your needs. But don't be fooled. SQL is a powerful and complex language that takes practice to perfect. By understanding how these examples work, you can create new queries and change existing ones with speed and flexibility.

You may want to consider keeping a selection of your favorite SQL queries in a file for quick reuse in the future. One excellent way to do this is to create an Access table that contains two text fields. The first field could be used to hold a query type or description, and the second field could hold the text of each of your saved queries. Having a set of prebuilt query templates could make you into the real Access Query Wizard!

Summarizing values using SQL

You can also do a number of different calculations using *SQL aggregate functions*. These are built-in functions that are similar to the functions you've probably used in formulas in Excel worksheets hundreds of times. For example, the following query returns the sum of the winning bids from Auction 87:

```
SELECT Sum(WinningBid)
AS Total
FROM AuctionResults
WHERE AuctionNumber = 87;
```

In addition to Sum, you can use Avg for the average value of the field, Count to return the number of records, First or Last to return the first or last value in the selected records, Min or Max to find the minimum or maximum value, StDev or StDevP for the population or population sample standard deviation, and Var or VarP for the population or population sample variance.

Deleting records using SQL

Delete queries are the bad boys of queries because they have the potential for being so destructive. Even so, here's an example of a SQL query that deletes records from a table that match a specified criteria:

```
DELETE FROM AuctionResults
WHERE AuctionNumber = 87;
```

A Nod to VBA Programmers

As useful as SQL queries are to ordinary people who want a bit more control over their Access queries, those SQL queries become more valuable than gold when you start automating your Access applications with *VBA* (Visual Basic for Applications). VBA is the programming language that enables you to automate various operations in the Microsoft Office programs.

This book isn't the venue for a VBA tutorial, but I do want to touch on one aspect of VBA — using SQL queries as the basis for VBA programming code. When I create Access applications for my clients, I often use SQL queries in my VBA code. You can produce fully automated procedures that run much faster than manual queries when you do this. In addition, you can combine a number of operations in a single VBA procedure so that there's no chance that a user will forget to perform an important step that's necessary to successfully complete the task.

To a great extent, you can practically drop an SQL query into VBA code without changing a thing. For example, consider the following VBA statement that executes a delete query:

```
DoCmd.RunSQL "DELETE Customer.* FROM Customer"
```

Even without any background in VBA, you can probably recognize the SQL query portion of the statement:

```
DELETE Customer.* FROM Customer;
```

Although I can't give you a full VBA lesson, I can give you a set of guidelines about using SQL statements in VBA code. VBA is slightly less forgiving of creative syntax than SQL, so following some general rules is pretty important:

- ✔ To execute a SQL statement, the line of VBA code must begin with `DoCmd.RunSQL` followed by a space.

- ✔ Any double quotes within your existing SQL statement must be replaced by single quotes. You can very easily make this change using the Edit⇨Replace command in Notepad. Place all text strings within single quotes.

- ✔ Use the ampersand (&) to *concatenate* (link strings of) values within the statement. For example, the following adds the value in the `LotNumber` field from the LiveWinBid table to `Lot:` to produce a result such as `Lot:101` to be placed in the `LotNumber` field of the new table:

  ```
  'Lot:' & LiveWinBid.LotNumber AS LotNumber
  ```

- ✔ Your entire SQL statement must be enclosed within double quotes — this is the only place where double quotes should appear in the VBA statement unless you're building the SQL statement on the fly.

✔ Use the plus sign (+) to concatenate the values of VBA variables with your SQL statement and create a new SQL statement on the fly. For example, the following code creates a string by using the word Auction and the value of a VBA variable called myNumber to produce a string value based on the current value of the myNumber variable (this is the one place where you use double quotes other than at the beginning and end of the SQL statement):

```
'Auction" + myNumber +"' AS AuctionName
```

✔ The semicolon at the end of the SQL statement has to go. Just go ahead and delete it and the world will be a happier place.

Even if you've done a bunch of VBA programming, the rules about concatenating values might require some experimentation before you'll fully grasp how they work. But other than those two rules, this set of rules are really just about all you need to take your SQL queries and throw them into some VBA code and dazzle the world.

The rules regarding single and double quotes are very important and they're also frequently stated incorrectly in other texts. Using the two types of quotes improperly makes for runtime errors that can be awfully confusing to decipher.

Chapter 8

Dealing with Quarrelsome Queries

*O*ne of the most frustrating things about computers is that sometimes they just don't seem to work correctly. You think that you've done everything right, but the next thing you know some cryptic error message that seems to have been translated through about six languages pops up. Or even worse, no messages appear but the darn thing just produces really screwy results. Don't you just hate it when that happens?

A lot can go wrong with Access queries. It really doesn't take much to throw the whole process off base, and discovering the real problem is sometimes pretty difficult. In this chapter, you can see a number of things that commonly make queries act up. I also examine the ways that you can send those problems packing.

Troubleshooting Queries That Don't Quite Work

If you really want to see the cause of most problems with your Access queries, get up from your desk, walk to your bathroom, and look in the mirror. Yes, it's really true — you're the ultimate source of the issues that make your queries misbehave. Actually, you shouldn't feel too bad about your role in the problem; it's good news, because it means that you can fix most query-related problems by getting a handle on what you did wrong. Rarely do you have to worry about some bug in Access, so you can concentrate specifically on what's in your query to figure out what isn't quite right.

Understanding the clues Access gives you

Troubleshooting any type of problem requires a certain mindset if you want to find and fix the problem as quickly as possible. The first rule of trouble-shooting is to be as methodical and logical as possible. Very few problems are ever solved by simply throwing up your hands and saying, "It just doesn't work."

The methodical approach to solving problems with Access queries can be summarized like this:

1. **Read the error message and click Help.**

   If an error message appears, read it carefully and click any help links that are included in the message. You may have trouble understanding what the message means, but it's the best clue you're likely to get.

2. **Think over every change you've made or identify the parts of your query that relate to the Help information.**

   If a query was working before you changed something, you have a pretty good clue about why the error occurred. Try to remember every little change you've made, not only in your query, but also in your database file.

   If the query runs but produces unexpected results, remember that Access is only doing what you've told it to do and is not getting creative on its own.

3. **Modify the parts of the query related to the issue noted in the Help file for the error to see whether your actions make things better.**

4. **Finally, if you see nothing obvious wrong or your changes don't improve your results, you may need to just start over and create a new copy of the query from scratch.**

   Starting over and repeating what you think are the exact same actions often corrects a problem (and this solution is frequently faster than con-tinuing to agonize over a query that won't give up its secrets).

Locating the problem

Locating the specific cause of a problem you encounter when you attempt to run a query isn't always easy. After all, if you knew that something was going to be a problem you wouldn't try to put it in your query in the first place.

Each error you encounter will be a bit different, but here's a look at a typical Access query (containing deliberate errors) to see how you may go about locating the problem. In this example, I'm using an append query as it appears in SQL view (see Chapter 7 for information about using SQL to write queries):

```
INSERT INTO AuctionBackup
AuctionNumber, AuctionTotal
VALUES 87, 300;
```

You may not see anything wrong with the query, but Access sure does. When you attempt to run the query, Access displays the message shown in Figure 8-1.

Figure 8-1:
Access
encountered
an error
trying to run
the query.

To troubleshoot the problem, follow the steps in the previous section, "Understanding the clues Access gives you," to methodically identify, repair, and re-run the append query. Specifically,

1. **Click the Help button in the warning message box.**

   Figure 8-2 shows an example of the Help information you might see.

Figure 8-2:
Access tries
to explain
the error
when you
click Help.

Access usually tries to identify potential causes when it identifies the error. In my example, Access points to two possible causes. Either something is misspelled or there is a punctuation error.

2. **Armed with the information you receive, click the Close button and then click OK in the warning message box.**

   At this point, Access does its best to pinpoint the first instance of the error by highlighting the item that triggered the error message, as shown in Figure 8-3.

Figure 8-3:
Access
highlights
the item that
triggered
the error.

```
Query1 : Select Query          _ □ ×
INSERT INTO AuctionBackup
AuctionNumber, AuctionTotal
VALUES 87, 300;
```

Now you're getting somewhere. In my example, you can say for certain that the error seems to be caused by the highlighted item, the field name `AuctionNumber`.

3. Modify the parts of the query that seem to relate to the error message you received.

In this case, you can quickly rule out a spelling error in any of the keywords because `INSERT`, `INTO`, and `VALUES` all appear to be correct. This leaves you with a punctuation error as the probable cause, and `AuctionNumber` as the location of that punctuation error.

If you're baffled, choose Help⇨Access Help and look for terms in the Help file that can make things more clear.

For example, if you look up `INSERT INTO` in the Help file, you discover that the field names belong in parentheses — your punctuation error is that the field names should be surrounded by parentheses. So, armed with this information, you should modify the query like this:

```
INSERT INTO AuctionBackup
(AuctionNumber, AuctionTotal)
VALUES 87, 300;
```

Unfortunately, my example has more than one problem in it, so even with this change, if you try to run the query again, Access greets you with the same error message that you received before. But this time when you click OK, Access highlights 87 in the third row because values also have to be enclosed in parentheses. You have to change the query one more time so that it looks like this:

```
INSERT INTO AuctionBackup
(AuctionNumber, AuctionTotal)
VALUES (87, 300);
```

4. Continue the process until no error messages appear and you get the results you expect; alternatively, if you can't make the error messages go away, scrap the query and start from scratch.

After making the changes prescribed in my examples and running the query again, Access displays a message telling you that you're about to append one row to the table. That's more like it!

If there is an error that prevents Access from executing a query, Access will always try to help you find the error first by displaying an error message and then by highlighting the item that seems to be the cause. If you're working in Design view, try switching to SQL view to get more informative information about the error as shown in this example.

Using Datasheet view as a troubleshooting tool

Often, the problem with a query isn't that the query won't run but rather that it doesn't produce the results that you expect. Access is more than happy to run a query that doesn't really do anything (or that does something other than what you intend), and because the query doesn't produce any errors, you can easily miss the fact that the query results are empty or incorrect — especially if you're in a hurry.

Always check your results! Don't assume that just because you see no error message that there's no error.

One quick check for record selection errors you can make is to switch the query to Datasheet view before you run the query. Datasheet view shows you which records will be selected without actually performing any actions. Datasheet view is an excellent option for verifying that your query is correctly structured, especially if the query you want to run will delete records or update a table.

Figure 8-4 shows a select query that displays a list of city names and a count of the number of customers in each of those cities. The `State` field is used to specify which states are included in the results. The figure shows a subtle error in the query.

Figure 8-4:
This query is supposed to display a list of cities with the number of customers in each of the cities.

Field:	City	City	State
Table:	CurrentAuction	CurrentAuction	CurrentAuction
Total:	Group By	Count	Group By
Sort:	Ascending		
Show:	☑	☑	☐
Criteria:			"NF"
or:			

As Figure 8-5 shows, switching to Datasheet view displays an empty result. (Remember to choose View⇨Datasheet View or right-click on the query and choose Datasheet View from the pop-up menu to switch to Datasheet view.)

Figure 8-5: Datasheet view shows that the query isn't returning the expected results.

If you get into the habit of switching to Datasheet view just before you run your queries, you can train yourself to identify subtle errors before they muck up your forms and reports. When you see, for example, a Datasheet view like the one in Figure 8-5, your uh-oh detector is going to turn on automatically, and you'll immediately ask yourself what's wrong. Remember that typing error I mentioned? In this case, the selection criterion for the State field is mistyped as NF rather than NV. Switching back to Design view and correcting the typing error solves the problem, as Figure 8-6 shows.

The errors you're most likely to discover by using Datasheet view are record selection errors. These types of errors can be directly traced to problems with any criteria you have specified, so if you don't see the expected results in Datasheet view, examine the criteria you have entered.

Correcting thorny problems

After you locate a problem with a query, the fix is usually pretty obvious. Sometimes, though, you may have a *really* messed up query that leaves you at a loss as to the best way to fix it. For example, if you're working in Design view and you change the table that's associated with one of the fields in the design grid to a table that doesn't have the field, your query won't work until you correct the table association. The difficulty with this type of error is that you may not realize what's causing the problem.

If you encounter a really nasty situation in a query that seems to defy correction, step back for a moment and think about what's going on. If possible, delete a field or two from the query to simplify it, and then check the results in Datasheet view. When the simplified query starts producing the results you expect, add back one field at a time until you find the culprit.

TIP

Empty results in Datasheet view aren't always the result of an error, of course. It's also possible that you've specified your criteria properly, but that your database simply doesn't contain any matching records.

Figure 8-6:
After you correct the typo, the query selects the correct records.

City	CountOfCity
Carson City	9
Elko	1
Ely	2
Fallon	3
Fernley	2
Gardnerville	2
Goldfield	2
Henderson	1
Incline Village	1
Las Vegas	12
Manhattan	1
Midas	1
Minden	2
Reno	54

Using datasheet to troubleshoot : Select Query

Record: 1 of 23

Troubleshooting Sassy SQL

SQL-specific queries can present their own set of potential errors. Because you create these types of queries as text instead of by making selections in the Query editor, you really have to watch out for things like spelling and punctuation in addition to syntax errors.

Figuring out what went wrong

Because there are so many different types of errors that are possible in queries you create in SQL view, you really need to give yourself all the advantages you can. That way you can concentrate on being productive.

One very important point to remember when you're creating SQL queries is that, as I mention in Chapter 7, you should always enter any SQL keywords in all uppercase characters. Access won't protest if you don't capitalize, but it's still a good idea because the caps make spotting typing errors in keywords a bit easier in your finished query. For example, Figure 8-7 shows a SQL query with a common typing error and the error message that Access displays when you try to run the query.

In this case the word *TABLE* is misspelled as *TABEL*, and Access highlights the misspelling when you click the OK button in the message box. But even if Access didn't highlight the misspelled word, the caps help make the error jump right out at you with even a quick glance at the SQL statement.

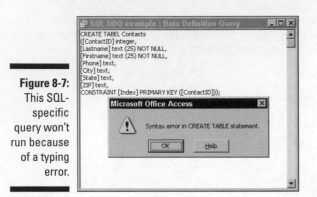

Figure 8-7:
This SQL-
specific
query won't
run because
of a typing
error.

If your SQL query runs without any errors but produces unexpected results, you must dissect the query to figure out the source of the problem. It can be quite difficult to locate a logic error because, after all, you wouldn't have created the query like that if you didn't think you had the logic all worked out. Your best bet in such a situation is probably to put on your Sherlock Holmes hat and then carefully read through the query as if it were a story. When you find the place where the story doesn't seem to make any sense, you've found the problem!

Trying Design view

Another method that you may find helpful when you're troubleshooting a SQL query is to switch to Design view. This option isn't available for SQL-specific queries that cannot be shown in Design view, of course. If the View⇨ Design View command is grayed out (Query Design on the right-click on the pop-up query menu), you won't be able to switch to Design view. But if the option is available, your query is one of the types that can be shown in Design view.

Switching to Design view is a handy way to determine whether the problem with your SQL query is a language problem or a logic problem. If you have a language problem (also called a *syntax error*) such as a keyword spelling error, missing or incorrect punctuation, or items in the wrong place in the SQL statement, Access displays an error message when you try to switch to Design view. If Access can show the query in Design view, your problem is one of incorrect logic — not incorrect use of the SQL language elements.

Things to watch out for in SQL queries

Frankly, a lot of things can go wrong with SQL queries. Here's a list of some common problems to watch out for:

✔ **Spelling errors:** Misspellings are easy to make and they can stop a query cold. Watch for not only misspelled SQL keywords, but also for table and field names that are misspelled.

✔ **Punctuation:** SQL often uses somewhat confusing punctuation and the online help examples may not seem very, well, helpful. A handy thing to remember is that you should include any punctuation shown in the examples with the exception of square brackets (but you should use square brackets around filenames and around field names if either of them includes any spaces) and ellipses (. . .).

✔ **Correct order:** The elements in a SQL statement have to appear in the correct order. If you have keywords, table names, or field names in the wrong place, it's even possible that the query will run but that it will do something (probably destructive) to the wrong table.

✔ **Correct dialect:** ANSI SQL and Access SQL are two dialects of the same language, and sometimes you need to modify examples you find on the Web or in books so that they work correctly in Access.

Simplifying your SQL to find the problem

If you create a complex SQL query that runs without producing an error message but doesn't do what you expect it to, you may want to try simplifying the query to pin down the problem. This is the place where you find the cut-and-paste options awfully handy!

Many SQL queries look extremely complicated, but when you break a typical "scary" SQL query down to its components, it's basically a select query combined with an action query. It's reasonable, therefore, to begin your trouble-shooting by first testing the select query. To test a select query, follow these steps:

1. **Copy your existing query, paste the SQL statement into a blank SQL view window, and then delete everything except the pieces that fit neatly into a select query.**

2. **Test your select query and then modify it as necessary.**

   You know you're done when the records you want to see appear when you switch to Datasheet view.

3. **When you're satisfied that the correct records are being selected, add back the fancy bits such as the ORDER BY clause for sorting or the GROUP BY clause for grouping.**

4. **When the select query is functioning properly, save it with a new name.**

Remember that you can use a query as the data source for a query instead of using a table as the data source. After you debug your select query you may want to consider using it as the source for the remainder of the action query.

Avoiding Improper Relationships

It's the relationships between the various tables in your Access databases that make it possible for you to combine the data in those tables effectively. You really can't create a useful query involving multiple tables if you haven't specified the proper relationships between those tables.

Understanding how bad relationships can mess you up

How you deal with your in-laws has nothing to do with this discussion, so you can stop making any wisecracks right now. No, what I'm talking about here are the kinds of problems you face when trying to create Access queries that produce reasonable results. If there are problems with the way the table relationships are defined in your databases, your queries will not produce good results.

Access uses *primary keys* and *unique indexes* to ensure that table relationships are properly defined. Both primary keys and unique indexes enable Access to ensure that each record in a table is unique. Some records may be similar, but each record must have at least one piece of information that ensures that no other record is an exact duplicate. Primary keys are unique indexes. A table can have only one primary key, but the same table can have more than one unique index. The primary key controls the sort order of the records.

When you create table relationships, you generally use a primary key or a unique index in at least one of the tables to define the relationship with the other table. For example, in Figure 8-8 the relationships between three tables are shown. Each of the tables is linked, using a field that is a unique index in one of the tables. In this case, the OWNERID field is a unique index in the Item Owners table, and the BIDID field is a unique index in the CurrentAuction table (you'd have to open the tables in Design view to examine the field properties to know that these fields are unique indexes).

Unfortunately, Access doesn't require you to use either primary keys or unique indexes to define table relationships. If you create a relationship between two tables by using fields that aren't defined as primary keys or unique indexes in either table, Access creates an *indeterminate* relationship, as shown in Figure 8-9.

Figure 8-8:
These three tables are linked using unique indexes.

Figure 8-9:
Indeterminate relationships result from linking fields that aren't primary keys or unique indexes in either table.

When there's an indeterminate relationship between tables, Access can't determine which records are actually related. In the case of the relationships shown in Figure 8-8, for example, you can't tell whether the winning bidder is Søren or Cole because they may both have the same BIDID. If you create a report that generates invoices for the winning bidders by using a query that included these tables, you could send an invoice to the wrong bidder.

Making sure your relationships make sense

Even though Access allows you to create relationships that are pretty meaningless, that doesn't mean that you should do so. See Chapter 5 for more information on table relationships, but here are some quick do's and don'ts to consider so that the links you create between tables produce the results you want:

- ✔ **Do use a field that is a primary key or a unique index in one of the tables to create your links.** Making sure that one of the fields is either the primary key or a unique index enables you to create a one-to-many relationship, which is generally the most useful type of table relationship.

- ✔ **Don't create relationships in which fields are primary keys or unique indexes in both tables.** This action creates a one-to-one relationship. In most cases, the tables in one-to-one relationships should be combined into a single table (the exception to this rule is when you need to allow certain users access to some of the fields without allowing them access to other fields).

- ✔ **Do define the fields that you use for links so that the fields have the same data type in both tables.** You can create links between fields with different types, but you won't be able to enforce referential integrity if you do.

Correcting relationships that don't work

The method you use to correct a problem with a relationship depends on the type of problem you need to fix. You can, for example, simply open a table in Design view and change a field's Indexed property to Yes (No Duplicates) to make the field into a unique index. This type of change doesn't require you to delete the existing relationship before you make the change.

Often, however, you may need to right-click on the relationship in the Relationships window and select Delete from the pop-up menu before you can make the necessary changes. For example, if you want to change the data type of a field that's part of a relationship, you need to delete the existing relationship before you can change the data type. After you save the modified table design you can re-create the relationship.

Junking Joins That Don't Join

A problem that you may encounter that is closely related to the table relationships are *joins* that don't produce the results that you want. Joins determine which records from the two tables are included in the results of the query.

Understanding why default joins may not work

When you create a table relationship, Access automatically creates a default type of join that may not work for you.

There are three basic types of joins you can create:

✔ **Inner joins** are the default type of join. All records from both tables that match are selected.

✔ **Left outer joins** include all the records from the first (left) table in the relationship even if there are no matching records in the second (right) table.

✔ **Right outer joins** include all the records from the second (right) table in the relationship even if there are no matching records in the first (left) table.

The terms inner and outer are sometimes left out, so a left outer join is also simply called a *left join,* for example.

You typically want your queries to only return the records where there were matching values in both tables, and for this purpose the default inner join is the perfect choice. But in some cases you want slightly different results. For example, if you have one table that lists all the items in an auction and another table that listed the bids that were received, you probably want to be able to produce a report that lists all the items — even those items for which there were no bids. If the table of items is on the left side of the join, you need to create a left outer join to produce this result. Choosing a default inner join would leave out the items that didn't receive bids.

Correcting your joins

There are two primary ways to change the type of a join. Generally, the easiest way to modify a join is to edit the relationship by using the Relationships window. You can also modify the join in a query by changing the SQL statement in SQL view.

To modify the join type by using the Relationships window, follow these steps:

1. **Choose Tools⇨Relationships.**

   Alternatively, click the Relationships button on the toolbar to open the Relationships window.

2. **Right-click on the relationship you want to modify and choose Edit Relationship from the pop-up menu.**

   The Edit Relationships dialog box appears.

3. **Click the Join Type button.**

   The Join Properties dialog box appears, as shown in Figure 8-10.

4. **Click to select the join type you want.**

   Option 1 produces an inner join, option 2 produces a left outer join, and option 3 produces a right outer join.

5. **Close the Join Properties dialog box by clicking OK.**

6. **Click OK to close the Edit Relationships dialog box.**

You can also modify your query directly in SQL view to create a different type of join. For example, a default inner join that selects only matching records from two tables may look like this:

```
SELECT ItemOwners.OWNERLASTNAME, WinningBids.LOTNUMBER
FROM ItemOwners
INNER JOIN WinningBids
ON ItemOwners.OWNERID = WinningBids.OWNERID;
```

To change this to a query that selects all the records from the left side table (ItemOwners in this example), modify the query to look like this to create a left outer join:

```
SELECT ItemOwners.OWNERLASTNAME, WinningBids.LOTNUMBER
FROM ItemOwners
LEFT JOIN WinningBids
ON ItemOwners.OWNERID = WinningBids.OWNERID;
```

Steering Around Empty Query Results

One of the more frustrating things that can happen when you're creating queries is to have the results of the query turn up empty. And with no results, your forms or reports won't be very useful, either.

Understanding some of the causes of empty query results

Sometimes a query produces empty results for a very good reason — there simply aren't any records that match the criteria you've specified. Although this can happen when you've specified just one criterion, it's far more likely to happen if you've specified a number of them.

For example, suppose you set up a select query that has three fields, `CustomerName`, `State`, and `NumberOfWinningBids`. If you specify that the value in the `NumberOfWinningBids` field must be greater than zero and no other criteria, your query will probably return quite a few results. Now imagine that you also specify that the `State` field should contain `RI`. If you don't actually have any customers in Rhode Island, the query won't return any records when you run it.

Sometimes (more often than anyone wants to admit) a query returns an empty result because you've specified criteria that don't make any sense. For example, say you mistyped the selection value for `California` as *CQ* rather than *CA*. Access will return exactly the results it should — none!

Correcting a query that doesn't return any data

It's pretty easy to correct a query that uses a single criterion and produces no results. You simply have to look at the query and correct whatever error you've made in entering the criteria (or, if there is no error, accept that returning no records is the correct result).

Correcting a query that uses multiple criteria is a bit harder because you have to locate the error before you can correct it. One method you can use is to remove the criteria one at a time until you start seeing results (use the Datasheet view for this). If you set up your query so that the most important fields are to the left of less important ones, remove the criteria starting at the right and moving left. Eventually, you'll discover what's causing the problem and then you can determine why the last criteria you removed was causing a problem.

Preventing Data Destruction

Suppose you spend several thousands of dollars on a fancy new PC with all the bells and whistles. But just before you transfer all the files you've created over a number of years from your old clunker of a PC to the new one, you suddenly realize that your house is on fire and you've only got time to grab one PC before you rush out the door. The question is which PC do you save?

If you said that you'd save the old PC and all of your data, give yourself an A. If you decided on the new PC, you either have an off-site backup of all of your data or you don't understand the value of your data. A new PC is a lot easier to replace than the years of work that could be lost on your old PC.

Beginning by backing up

If you don't keep an up-to-date copy of your really important files someplace off-site, you're asking for trouble. But you're not alone, because most people think that backups are something they'll do when they have time. Anything I say here probably isn't going to change your behavior in that regard.

Instead of trying to convince you to back up all your data, let me just suggest that you at least make a copy of your important Access databases so that they're safe from anything you do while practicing creating queries. Really, it's not going to take you any time at all to make a copy, now is it?

Access even has a command, Tools➪Database Utilities➪Back Up Database, that's designed specifically to make backing up database files much easier. Now you can't even use the "it's too complicated" argument.

Avoiding destructive query results

Whenever you create an action query, you're creating a query that has the power to modify or destroy data. Access tries to warn you before committing any changes, but we all know how easy it can be to ignore those warning messages. "Sure, I want to delete 661 records; why else would I run this query?"

One of the surest ways to avoid destructive query results is, of course, to never create an action query. Simple select queries don't make any changes to your databases, so they're always safe to create and run. In the real world, though, action queries are a fact of life.

You can give yourself one extra chance to make sure you've got things right by switching to Datasheet view to check the results before you run your query. That way, you can review the records your delete query is going to destroy.

What to do if your database seems to be kaput

If you try to open your database and Access displays an error message that indicates that the file is corrupt, you'd better hope that your backup isn't too far out of date. But if you have no backup, you're stuck with what seems like your only copy of a bad file. Not the best situation. Here are some things you can try:

Any repair attempt has the potential for causing even more problems, so be sure to make a copy of your database file before trying to fix a kaput database file.

- ✔ Choose the Tools➪Database Utilities➪Compact and Repair Database command. In some cases, this command actually repairs minor errors, but it's actually more useful for removing the junk from your database file and making the resulting file smaller.

- ✔ Databases that have been converted from one Access file format to an older Access file format with the Tools➪Database Utilities➪Convert Database commands can sometimes act a little strange in some types of list views. If tables, forms, reports, or queries seem to have disappeared after a file format conversion, try clicking the different view mode icons (Large Icons, Small Icons, List, or Details) to see whether the objects reappear.

- ✔ If the tools built into Access don't seem to be able to recover your database file, try one of the big-gun third-party software options like the AccessFIX utility discussed in Chapter 20. This tool can often correct problems just when you think all hope is lost.

Part III
Building Really Useful Forms

The 5th Wave   By Rich Tennant

I've never seen a form so dense with color and data.

Oo-look! Stare long enough at the center and a 3-D image of a bird in flight pops out.

In this part . . .

Forms put a much friendlier face onto your database by making data entry and editing much easier tasks. This part shows you how to create forms that are really useful, and it tells you how to create forms that tackle data from more than one table at a time for even more efficiency.

Chapter 9

Building Better Forms by Using Controls

C reating better, more usable forms is an art. This chapter introduces the various types of objects (known in Access-speak as *controls*) that you can add to your forms; it shows you how to make effective use of those controls.

Forms can have the most direct effect on how friendly your database application seems to users. The controls that you choose to use in your forms can make or break this impression because the right set of controls that are properly configured make for a form that is logical and easy to use. A haphazard selection of controls that are simply thrown onto a form without some forethought about how users will actually use the form can make the form an odious tool that people hate using.

Getting to Know the Controls

You build Access forms by using various controls. Even when you can use a Form Wizard or Design view to create a form, the objects that you use as building blocks for your forms are called controls. (See Chapter 3 for the basics of creating forms.)

There's nothing particularly meaningful behind the name. Programmers like to have names for the objects that they use, and it happens that they like to call the objects that appear on forms (and reports) controls. I guess that's better than calling them Ralphs (not that I have anything against the name Ralph, of course). You could probably make the argument that the name control fits because controls control what you see when you view a form, but the name itself isn't as important as understanding just what controls are. Here's a brief explanation of the types of controls:

- ✔ **Bound controls:** Each of the fields that you add to a form is what is known as a *bound* control. This simply means that this type of control is connected — bound — to some data in your database. Most of the controls that you add to your forms are bound controls.

- ✔ **Unbound controls:** The things that you add to a form that isn't connected to any data are called unbound controls. These unbound controls typically serve to make your form look fancier — such as a company logo — or to convey useful information — such as a label that explains the purpose of a bound control.

- ✔ **Calculated controls:** Objects that display data that is the result of an *expression* (or *formula* for you spreadsheet fans) are called calculated controls. You use these types of controls to show things like shipping charges, sales tax, or order totals.

You add most controls to a form in Design view by selecting the control you want in the Toolbox and then dragging out the size you want for the control on the form design, or by dragging a field onto the form from the Field List.

Common Controls You Can Use

The most common type of control that you're likely to add to a form is a labeled field box, a bound control. Figure 9-1 shows a very simple form that has the LastName field (a labeled field) added from the Field List (which is shown over the right side of the form.

A field box is also called a text box, but a text box is not always associated with a particular field. Text boxes are also used for calculated controls.

The label control and the text box control appear next to each other in the Toolbox and they appear to be quite similar. But they're not the same type of control and you should always use a label instead of a text box when you want to display static, unchanging text in a form.

Figure 9-1:
Add a field
box for the
`LastName`
field by
dragging it
from the
Field List for
the Current-
Auction
table.

List box controls

Another type of control you may find very useful is the list box. This type of control enables a user to select from a set of predefined choices (and sometimes to enter a new value). There are actually two variations of list boxes you can use on your forms:

- ✔ **Combo box:** When you use combo boxes, the list isn't displayed until you open it by clicking the down arrow at the right of the combo box. You can set up a combo box to enable users to enter new values in addition to selecting an existing value.

- ✔ **List box:** When you use an ordinary list box, the whole list of values is visible at the same time. Users can only select the values that are shown in the list — they can't add a value that's not in the list.

Figure 9-2 shows how a combo box (top) compares to a list box (bottom) when both are added to a form design. Both controls show the word Unbound because neither of them has been associated with a field yet.

Figure 9-2:
A combo
box and a
list box
were added
to this form.

A third variation of the list box control that you're probably familiar with is the *drop-down list*. Drop-down lists are only used on *data access pages* — Web pages that ask users to input information. Drop-down list boxes look a lot like a combo boxes, but they don't allow users to add new values to the list.

Option button controls

Option buttons used to be called radio buttons because they acted like the station selection buttons on old-time car radios — when you pushed in one button to select a station, all the other buttons popped out. But because radios no longer have buttons like that, what had been a useful and descriptive name for a particular type of form control became less intuitive, and, alas, anachronistic for many users. The name *option button* won out. My nostalgic lapse has helped define the key element that makes an option button an option button: When you choose one option, you elect not to choose any of the other options.

Option buttons usually present users with a fixed set of mutually exclusive choices. If they choose vanilla, they can't have chocolate or banana. Option buttons serve a similar purpose to list boxes (but not to combo boxes, from which users can enter a new value). Option buttons can be used individually to offer users a simple yes or no choice, but this is seldom a good idea because users don't expect it and can become confused.

Check box controls

Check boxes give users two choices — true or false. Although forms seldom show the choice as true or false, that's really what a check box does. When a user selects a check box, the value is set to true. When the check box is deselected, the value is false. This type of choice is called *Boolean*, and it's associated with the Access Yes/No data type.

Adding Controls to Your Forms

The controls may look interesting sitting in the Toolbox, but they don't serve any purpose in your database until you add them to a form. In Chapter 3, I show you how to create simple forms, but this section gives you a gander at how you can use some of the more advanced controls to create even more useful forms.

Earlier in this chapter in the section "Getting to Know the Controls," I show you that controls can be bound to a field, unbound (not associated with a field), or be associated with a calculated value. In most cases you can use bound controls so that the control actually selects or modifies values in the database. Bound controls require a record source — an associated table or query that stores the data.

If you drag a field from the Field List onto a form, you create a bound control. If, on the other hand, you simply select a control and click the form design without dragging a field from the Field List, you create an unbound text box control. You can change an unbound control into a bound control by following these steps:

1. **Right-click on the control and choose Properties from the pop-up menu.**

   The Properties dialog box appears.

2. **Click the Data tab.**

3. **Select the field you want to bind to the control from the Control Source list box.**

   Figure 9-3 shows an example of binding a list box control to a database field.

Figure 9-3:
Selecting
a control
source
changes an
unbound
control into
a bound
control.

You can use the drop-down list box at the top of the Properties dialog box to select a different object if you want to view or modify the properties of another object.

Adding list boxes to your forms

List boxes (and their combo box variants) enable users to select a value from a list. The source of that list can be a table, a query, or a fixed list of values that you load into the control when you create the control. The selected value is stored in the table that is associated with the form.

The table that's associated with the form is *not* the source of the list of values that are displayed in the list box. This terminology can be a bit confusing until you realize that each field in a record can only hold a single value. So, in order for the list box to return a single value, the list box has to get its values from a source other than the table where the selected value will be stored.

So how do you choose the type of source that will best serve your needs? Here are some guidelines that can help:

  - ✔ **If the list of values is relatively short and won't be changing, you can use a value list that you enter into the control or a database table.** A list entered directly into the control is easy to create, but so is a small table. Database users are less likely to modify a list that is typed directly into the control, if for no better reason than that they don't know where the list resides.

  - ✔ **If the list of values can change over time, you can use a table or a query as the source of the list.** In most cases it's easiest to simply use a table as the source.

  - ✔ **If the list of available values must be conditional based on some other value, you must use a query as the source of the values.** For example, say you have a set of shipping options, but you want to restrict the methods depending on what the product is. (Who wants to send a piano FedEx Next Business Day?)

You can add a list box to a form with a wizard or you can use Design view and build the list box yourself. The following steps show you how to add a list box to a form without using a wizard. In my example, the list box uses an existing table as the source of the values for the list box.

To add a list box to a form, follow these steps:

  1. **Open the Access database where you want to create the new form.**

  2. **In the Objects list, click Forms.**

     A list of forms appears.

3. **Double-click the Create Form in Design View option.**

   A new, blank form opens.

4. **Right-click on the title bar of the new form and choose Properties from the pop-up menu to display the Properties dialog box for the form.**

   You can also click the Properties button on the toolbar to display this dialog box.

5. **Click the Data tab and choose the table to associate with the form from the drop-down Record Source list box.**

   In this example I selected a table called ItemsTable, which stores information about items that are consigned for auctions.

   You can leave the Properties dialog box open but move it if it is in your way.

6. **In the Toolbox, click the List box icon to select it, but don't drag a list box onto the form design just yet.**

   Selecting the List box icon before dragging the associated field onto the form tells Access to create a list box when you later drag the field onto the form. Make certain that the Control Wizards icon is not selected so that you can complete these steps without using the wizard.

7. **Drag the field that you want to appear as a list box onto the form.**

   In this example I selected the `TypeID` field.

8. **With the list box you added to the form still selected, choose the table that holds the values you want to appear in the list box from the Row Source drop-down list on the Data tab of the Properties dialog box.**

   In this example I selected the table named TypeTable, as shown in Figure 9-4.

9. **Choose View⇨Form View or click the View button on the toolbar to see how your form and the new list box appear.**

   Figure 9-5 shows the form I created in this example.

10. **Return to Design view and save your work.**

Although the list box displays the proper values, Figure 9-5 does demonstrate one area where the default setup for a list box leaves a little bit of room for improvement. When a list box displays values from a table, the values are shown in the order that they appear in the table. Often, this means that the values aren't sorted intuitively, which can make locating a specific value difficult — especially if the list of choices is quite long.

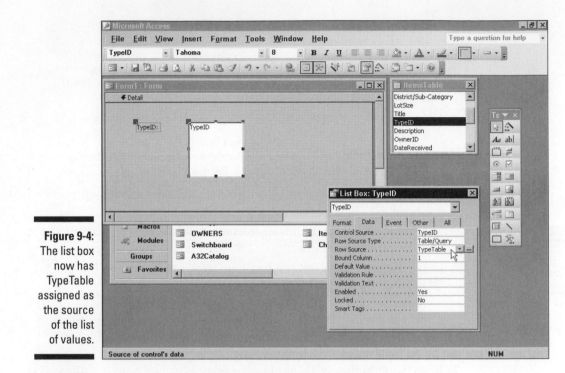

Figure 9-4:
The list box
now has
TypeTable
assigned as
the source
of the list
of values.

Chapter 17 shows you how to improve your forms by making sure that values
that are shown in list boxes are sorted for easier selection.

Figure 9-5:
The list box
displays the
list of values
from the
table that is
the row
source.

The form used in this example also demonstrates something about form
design that you may not have given too much consideration in the past. In
this case, the form allows users to select a value for one of the fields in the
associated table, but it doesn't give users enough information to enable them

to make an intelligent choice. To be of much use, the form needs to display additional fields so that users can tell which record they're modifying. The record counter at the bottom of the form simply doesn't do the job!

Adding option groups

Option buttons also enable a user to select one item from a list of choices, but unlike a list box, option buttons always use a fixed set of choices that all appear together on the form. Option buttons enable users to determine which of the choices is currently selected.

Creating an *option group* (the structure that ties the option buttons together so that users' choices are properly recorded) can be a bit complicated, but Access provides a very handy wizard, the Option Group Wizard, that simplifies the task considerably. This wizard not only helps you create the various option buttons, but it also helps you create the option group. Option buttons are pretty useless without an option group.

To add an option group and option buttons to a form, follow these steps:

1. **Open the form you want to use in Design view.**

2. **Make sure that the form has a table associated with the form's Record Source property.**

3. **Click the Control Wizards icon in the Toolbox to select it.**

   Toggle to select the wizard.

4. **Click the Option Group icon in the toolbox.**

5. **Click inside the form design where you want the option group to appear.**

   The Option Group Wizard dialog box appears, as shown in Figure 9-6.

Figure 9-6:
The Option Group Wizard helps you create option buttons and an option group.

Option Group Wizard

An option group contains a set of option buttons, check boxes, or toggle buttons. You can choose only one option.

What label do you want for each option?

Label Names:

Cancel   < Back   Next >   Finish

6. **Enter the labels that you want to appear next to each of the option buttons in the rows under the Label Names heading.**

   In this example, I'm using Taxable and Tax Exempt as the two option button labels.

   Press the Tab key to move from one label to the next.

7. **Click Next to continue.**

8. **Choose either to make one of the option buttons selected by default or to not have a default selection and then click Next.**

9. **Enter the values you want to save in the database for each choice.**

   You can enter numeric values, accept the default numeric values, or you can enter Boolean values such as True/False, Yes/No (you can only use the Boolean values if you only have two option buttons in the group). If you enter Boolean values, Access changes the values to -1 for true and 0 for false.

10. **Click Next to continue.**

11. **Choose the option for storing the value. You can save the value in a *variable* for later use or store it in a field in the table.**

12. **Click Next to continue.**

13. **Select the appearance options you prefer, as shown in Figure 9-7, and then click Next.**

Figure 9-7:
Use these
options to
determine
how your
option
buttons will
appear.

14. **Enter the label that you want the option group box to display in the form.**

15. **Click the Finish button to complete the task.**

   Figure 9-8 shows how the pair of option buttons from this example appears in Form view.

Buttons, toggles, check boxes, and other options

Option buttons, toggle buttons, and check boxes do complicate your life as a database designer somewhat because of the way these controls store information in your database. This complication comes about because various controls don't store the values you see on the form. Instead, they store numerical values that you need to interpret before you can use those values effectively. In the option button example in the nearby section, "Adding option groups," you need to set up your reports so that the value you associate with the Taxable button causes the report to calculate and add sales tax. A little complex, yes. But this added complexity is offset to an extent by the fact that you have complete control over the values that users can enter into your database. With only taxable and tax exempt choices available, you can be certain that users can't add something meaningless like, "Read my lips; no new taxes," to the field.

Figure 9-8:
The completed option group and option buttons as they appear in the form.

If you will only have two options that a user can select, you might want to consider using a toggle button control instead of option buttons. A toggle button typically takes up less space on a form than what is required for option groups.

Using check boxes on forms

Check boxes are very familiar elements you can use on forms. They, like the closely related toggle button, have two possible states. When a check box is selected (or a toggle button is depressed), they return a value of Yes, True, or -1, which are equivalent values as far as Access is concerned. The deselected value is No, False, or 0.

Although the Option Group Wizard (see "Adding option groups," earlier in this chapter) gives you the options of creating option groups containing check boxes or toggle buttons, these two types of controls are not usually used as mutually exclusive members of an option group. To avoid confusing users it's probably best to use controls in ways that are familiar to users — otherwise you greatly increase the possibility of errors.

It's usually best to associate check boxes or toggle buttons with a field whose Access data type is Yes/No because then you won't have to do any conversions to use the value returned by the control. You can also use these types of controls as unbound controls if you use their value in a VBA procedure or in an Access macro. I don't address these subjects in this book because I don't have the space to do them justice. The *Access 2003 All-In-One Desk Reference For Dummies,* by Alan Simpson, et al. (Wiley) covers all these topics, as well.

Adding a check box or a toggle button to a form as a bound control is very easy. First you select the control in the Toolbox, and then you drag the field from the field list onto the form. Figure 9-9 shows how these two controls appear after they have been added to a form design.

Figure 9-9:
A check box (upper) and a toggle button (lower) appear in this form design.

Adding labels to toggle buttons

If you refer to Figure 9-9, you see important differences between a check box control and a toggle button control. Even though both were added to the form as bound controls, Access added a label for the check box control but not for the toggle button control. Unlabeled buttons are an accident waiting to happen, so you may want to add some indicator that tells the user the purpose of the button. There are three options for you to consider:

✔ **Use the label control:** You can use the label control to add a label on the form. This may be the best choice if you need to use a lot of text to explain the purpose of the button.

✔ **Add a caption:** You can add a caption to the button by using the Caption text box on the Format tab of the button's Properties dialog box (see Figure 9-10). Captions have to fit onto the face of the button, so this option is best if you can create a one- or two-word description.

✔ **Use a picture:** If you have an image that clearly indicates the button's purpose, you can use that image by selecting it — using the Picture text box on the Format tab of the button's Properties dialog box. Access has a selection of images you can use or you can browse for another image. Unless the image you choose is very easy to understand, though, you probably want to use a label, too.

Figure 9-10:
You can use the Format tab of the button's Properties dialog box to specify a caption or a picture for the face of a toggle button.

Toggle Button: NeedsPhoto	
NeedsPhoto	
Format	Data	Event	Other	All
Caption	
Picture	(none)
Picture Type	Embedded
Visible	Yes
Display When	Always
Left	0.7083"
Top	0.8333"
Width	0.5"
Height	0.5"
Fore Color	-2147483630
Font Name	Tahoma
Font Size	8
Font Weight	Normal
Font Italic	No
Font Underline	No
Reading Order	Context

Incorporating ActiveX Controls

There's something fun about finding cool stuff that's hidden on your PC and playing around with what you've found. Okay, so I admit that this isn't on par with finding out that you've just won the grand prize in some contest you forgot about months ago, but if you're a curious person who likes to tinker, trying out some of the extras that are stashed away on your hard drive is something you won't want to miss.

You might be wondering just how all these extra controls happened to end up on your hard drive. Was this some plot to hide a bunch of strange stuff on your PC so that you'd eventually run out of space? Who did this, anyway?

Actually, the answer is a lot simpler and less intriguing than you might think. The programs you install on your PC are made up from a whole series of small components, including a bunch of pieces that are called *ActiveX* controls. When you install programs, those ActiveX controls are *registered* on your system to make them accessible to the programs. And it turns out that any program that can use ActiveX controls can also access all those registered controls — not just the program that installed the ActiveX control. Access just happens to be one of the programs that can use ActiveX controls, so you've got a whole bunch of new toys to play with!

Before you get too excited, though, I do have to bring you down just a notch. Sure, you can add almost any ActiveX control that's registered on your system to an Access form, but that doesn't necessarily mean that you can do anything useful with it. Some ActiveX controls are pretty cool and some can do useful things, but the only way to know for certain is to give them a try.

Because the ActiveX controls that are available on your system depend completely on what programs you have installed, it's impossible for me to predict which ActiveX controls you find. Your set of ActiveX controls will certainly be very different from the set that are on my test system.

Okay, I've teased you enough. Try adding an ActiveX control to an Access form. I know that you've always wanted an Access database that has a form that plays music (humor me), so that's the example I use — a copy of the Windows Media Player ActiveX control. Of course, you may find something much more appropriate and business-y to add.

Here's how to amaze your friends by adding an ActiveX control to a form:

1. **Open a new form in Design view.**

2. **Choose Insert⊳ActiveX Control.**

   The Insert ActiveX Control dialog box, shown in Figure 9-11, appears. You can also click the More Controls button on the Toolbox to display a list of ActiveX controls that are registered on your system.

3. **Scroll down the list until you the ActiveX control that suits your purpose (or fancy).**

   I chose the Windows Media Player ActiveX control, not just because I love cool music, but also because this control should be available on any Windows PC (antitrust laws be darned).

4. **Click OK to add the control to the form.**

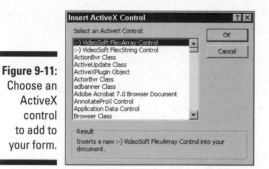

Figure 9-11:
Choose an
ActiveX
control
to add to
your form.

5. **Choose View➪Form View or click the View button to change the form to Form view.**

   Figure 9-12 shows the Windows Media Player ActiveX control in an Access form while it's playing an Internet radio station stream. Groovy.

Figure 9-12:
Access
provides a
bit of enter-
tainment by
way of an
ActiveX
control.

In order to make the Windows Media Player ActiveX control play something like an Internet radio station, you need to set the URL property on the Other tab of the control's Properties dialog box. You can find the proper URL for your favorite Internet radio station by opening the station's stream in Windows Media Player (not the ActiveX control) and choosing File➪Properties to display the Properties dialog box. Copy the URL shown in Location and paste it into the URL property of the ActiveX control.

Modifying the Characteristics of Controls

You can modify the characteristics of any control that you add to a form. Whether you're adding a button, a list box, or the Windows Media Player ActiveX control, you have access to many different properties that you can set and tweak to your heart's content.

An example of setting default values

Often, setting up a form so that certain values are automatically entered in specific fields can be quite handy. For example, Figure 9-13 shows a simple form that is used to check in items as they're received. In most cases, items are checked in immediately, so the DateReceived field value will almost always be the current date. Why not make the form a bit easier to use by automatically entering the current date in this field? That's what I thought, too.

Figure 9-13:
Make this simple form even better by setting a default value for the Date Received field.

Here's how to set up a date field so that the current date is automatically entered (but can be overwritten if necessary):

1. **Create your basic form with a** Date **field on the form.**

2. **Right-click on the** Date **field and choose Properties from the pop-up menu.**

   The Properties dialog box for the Date field appears.

3. **Click the Data tab, and then click the Default Value text box.**

4. **Click the Build button (the button with three periods) to the right of the text box.**

   The Expression Builder dialog box appears. It contains three columns, or list boxes.

5. **In the first list box (the one on the left), click the Common Expressions option.**

   This option appears toward the bottom of the list.

6. **In the second list box (the one in the middle), click the Current Date option.**

   Again, this option is toward the bottom of the list.

7. **Click the Paste button.**

   The term `Date()` appears in the text box at the top of the Expression Builder dialog box. See Figure 9-14.

Figure 9-14:
The
Expression
Builder
dialog box
helps you
create
expressions
for setting
default
values.

Expression Builder

Date()

OK
Cancel
Undo
Help

+ - / * & = > < <> And Or Not Like ( )   Paste

ItemsTable1 | Page Number | Date()
Tables | Total Pages
Queries | Page N of M
Forms | Current Date
Reports | Current Date/Time
Functions | Current User
Constants
Operators
Common Expressions

8. **Click OK to close the Expression Builder dialog box.**

9. **Switch to Form view to see the results. The date field shows the current date.**

You can type expressions directly into the Default Value text box without bothering with the Expression Builder dialog box. In this case, you simply enter **=Date( )** to indicate that you want today's date to be the default value.

Blocking access to certain controls

In some cases, you may want to prevent users from changing the values that are entered in certain fields. For example, you may not want users to be able to change the value for a date field if you set a default of the current date as the date the record was created. Access makes blocking users from making changes to values in specific fields pretty darn easy.

To block access to a field, first open the Properties dialog box for the field. Figure 9-15 shows the Properties dialog box for the date field used in the last exercise.

Figure 9-15:
Use this
Properties
dialog box
to block
users from
changing
values.

```
Text Box: DateReceived                      ✕
DateReceived                          ▼
Format  Data │ Event │ Other │ All
Control Source . . . . . . . . .   DateReceived
Input Mask . . . . . . . . . . . .
Default Value . . . . . . . . . .  =Date()
Validation Rule . . . . . . . . .
Validation Text . . . . . . . . .
Enabled . . . . . . . . . . . . .  Yes          ▼
Locked . . . . . . . . . . . . . .  No
Filter Lookup . . . . . . . . . .  Database Default
Smart Tags . . . . . . . . . . .
```

To prevent a user from entering values in a field, you have two options:

- You can set the `Enabled` property to No to prevent the user from moving the cursor into the field. When this property is set to No, the field still appears on the form, but it is grayed out. Users expect this type of behavior, so this is the recommended option.

- You can set the `Locked` property to Yes to allow users to move the cursor into the field, but to prevent them from making any changes. Using this option can cause confusion, so I recommend avoiding it.

Improving controls by using tab order

When you add controls to a form, Access sets up the *tab order* so that users can press Tab to move to the next control or Shift+Tab to move to the previous control. But if you move controls around on a form, the tab order can get a bit out of whack. Fortunately, there's an easy way to correct this problem.

Figure 9-16 shows the Other tab of the Properties dialog box for a control. You use the `Tab Index` property on this tab to specify the tab order for your form. When a user presses the Tab key, the cursor moves to the next highest Tab Index and Shift+Tab moves the cursor to the next lowest Tab Index.

You can also use the Tab Order dialog box (Choose View➪Tab Order) to change the tab order for the controls.

Figure 9-16:
Use the
Tab Index
property to
control the
tab order of
the controls
on a form.

Text Box: DateReceived	☒
DateReceived	▼

Format	Data	Event	Other	All

Name	DateReceived
IME Hold	No
IME Mode	No Control
IME Sentence Mode	None
Status Bar Text	
Enter Key Behavior	Default
Allow AutoCorrect	Yes
Vertical	No
Auto Tab	No
Tab Stop	Yes
Tab Index	2
Shortcut Menu Bar	
ControlTip Text	
Help Context Id	0
Tag	

Using Multiple Tables in Forms

Multiple, related tables help you organize the information in Access databases efficiently. But to use that information effectively, you must often access data from more than one table at a time. You may, for example, want to see all the items that you have for sale (easy enough), but what if you want to see that information split into groups according to which of your clients owns the items? That's where using multiple tables in the same form comes in handy. With multiple tables feeding data to a form, you can easily access related groups of items.

This chapter shows you how to create and use forms that incorporate data from more than one table. It explores the sometimes confusing line between forms and subforms, and it shows you how to use different types of subform views to most effectively present the information. In addition, this chapter discusses the unique navigation challenges that are presented by multiple-table forms.

Using multiple tables in a form enables you to deal with your database in a more logical and intuitive manner in many cases. Tasks like navigating between records are slightly more complicated in multiple-table forms, but proper form design can help reduce any possible confusion.

Understanding Forms and Subforms

The form examples that have been discussed so far in this book have all been pretty much ordinary forms. That is, the forms have been ones that enabled users to view and edit records from a single table. In the following sections, I turn your attention to forms that are made up of a main form and a *subform*.

You need to be very clear about one point that can easily lead to confusion. Forms and subforms are most definitely *not* the same thing as the list boxes I discuss in Chapter 9. List boxes enable a user to make a selection from a list of values and store the selected value in the current table. The list of values can come from values that are stored in another table or from a set of values that are stored in the list box control itself. Subforms, on the other hand, enable you to use a form and a subform to store and edit values in two related tables at the same time.

Understanding the needs subforms fill

If you recall the discussions of table relationships from Chapters 5 and 8, you know that the most useful type of relationship is the *one-to-many* relationship. In this type of relationship there is one record in the main table that can be related to multiple records in the detail table. If you want to create a form that shows the related information you need a main form that shows the *one* side of the relationship and a subform that shows the *many* side of the relationship.

Say you have a form that showed the various foods that are available from an online store. In the main form you can select the category of food, such as cheeses, meats, or beverages, and in the subform you can select the specific foods in one category such as bleu cheese, Swiss cheese, or cheddar cheese. In a nutshell, subforms greatly increase your ability to logically organize information in your forms.

Getting to know the subform place

As the name implies, subforms are usually displayed inside a main form. Subforms can be displayed by using any of the standard Form views, and the view you select for the subform does not have to be the same as the view you use for the main form. In most cases, though, the subform is shown in the standard Form view or in Datasheet view.

Figure 10-1 shows a typical arrangement for a form and a subform. In this case, the subform has a very different background color than the main form to make the subform a little easier to identify in the figure.

Subforms can also be displayed as a separate form window that pops up when the main form is opened. Unfortunately, this *Linked Form* view is somewhat confusing for users so you may want to avoid using this option.

Main form

Subform

Figure 10-1:
The subform
inside the
main form is
shown in
standard
Form view.

Subform navigation bar

Main form navigation bar

It's important to understand the connection between a main form and a sub-form. Because the two forms typically show the records from two tables in a one-to-many relationship, you navigate through the records in the two forms in a different manner than you do in a single table form. Think of the main form acting as a query that feeds the subform. The record you select in the main form determines which records you can view in the subform. When you move to a different record in the main form, a different set of records is displayed in the subform.

You can also nest more than one subform within a main form; you can nest subforms as deep as seven levels by placing subforms within subforms. Frankly, even though this is possible, you need to do some awfully heavy-duty planning to keep the whole mess understandable — much less to find room for the gigantic main form you'd need to hold such deep nesting. Just because you *can* do something doesn't mean that you *should*.

Adding Fields from Multiple Tables to Your Forms

If you're interested in finding out the mechanics of adding fields from more than one table to your forms, you've come to the right section. Using fields from more than one table adds some additional complications compared to using fields from a single table (or from a query).

Verifying relationships and adding fields

To build a form with a subform, you need to begin by making sure that the tables you want to use as the record sources have the proper one-to-many relationship established. You can choose the Tools⇨Relationships to display the Relationships window so that you can verify and establish relationships before you begin building the form.

If you aren't sure whether a relationship is a one-to-many relationship, right-click on the relationship line in the Relationships window and choose Edit Relationship to display the Edit Relationships dialog box. The dialog box identifies the type of the relationship.

After you're sure that the tables have the proper one-to-many relationships, you can add any of the fields from those tables to the form. You add the fields from the *one* (or *master*) table to the main form and the fields from the *many* table to the subform. It's far easier to use the Form Wizard to add the fields because the wizard automatically adds the fields to the proper places on the forms.

Linking forms to external databases

Chapter 4 discusses using external database tables in reports and Chapter 5 follows up with a discussion of using external database tables in queries. You can link an external table to the current database to ensure that you're using the most recent data or you can simply import the external table so that you lose the currency of the data but gain independence from the external database file. You can also create a multiple-table form that accesses data in an external database table, either by linking or importing the data.

Your decision to link to the database or import database information will depend on your specific project. However, I generally recommend that you link to the database if you can. When you're working with a form, you probably have the expectation that you're working with live data; that is, if you make a change to some data by using a form, you almost certainly expect that the information in the database will be updated to match the changes that you've made. This will only happen if the external table is linked rather than imported.

With the exception of making certain that your external table is linked rather than imported, using an external database table in a form is no different than using a local table, regardless of whether you're using multiple-table forms or single-table forms.

Because Access understands how to *synchronize* the main form and the sub-form based on the table relationships, you don't have to include the fields that are used to create the table links unless you want those fields to appear on the forms. Even so, it's important to include the fields that will help users understand which set of records they're dealing with when they use the form. For example, if you're creating a form that shows order details in a subform, make sure that the main form displays the information that enables the users to identify whose order is being shown.

Adding subforms with the Form Wizard

You can use several methods to create forms with subforms. The most straightforward method is to use the Form Wizard and add the related tables and fields by using the wizard. It's also possible to create your main form and subform separately and then add the subform to the form.

To create a form with a subform by using the Form Wizard, follow these steps:

1. **Open the Forms list under Objects.**

2. **Double-click the Create Form by Using Wizard option.**

    The Form Wizard dialog box appears.

3. **Select one of the tables whose fields you want to include from the drop-down Tables/Queries list box.**

    Which of the tables you add first doesn't make much difference; you can specify the *master table* shortly (in Step 7).

4. **Add the fields from that table to the Selected Fields list.**

5. **Repeat Steps 3 and 4 to add the next table and its fields to the Selected Fields list.**

6. **Click Next to continue.**

7. **Select the master table as the table by which you want to view the data, as shown in Figure 10-2.**

    You can only select the Form with Subform(s) option if you've selected the correct master table — otherwise your only option is to show all the data on a single form.

Figure 10-2:
Choose the
master table
as the way
you want to
view your
data.

8. **Make sure the Form with Subform(s) option is selected and click Next to continue.**

   If you select the Linked Forms option, your subform will be created as a separate form that isn't embedded in the main form. Many users find the results of choosing this option to be confusing, so I don't recommend choosing it.

9. **Choose the layout option for your subform and click Next.**

   For now, the default Datasheet view is okay — I show you how to modify the subform view in an upcoming section, "Choosing the Best Subform View."

10. **Select the appearance you prefer and click Next to continue.**

11. **Specify the titles you want for your form and subform and then click Finish to view the finished form.**

    Figure 10-3 shows an example of how your form and subform might appear.

Figure 10-3:
A completed
form with
the subform
displayed in
Datasheet
view.

Adding a subform after the fact

If you don't want to create the form and subform at the same time, you can still add the form you want to use as a subform to the main form later. To do so, follow these steps:

1. **Open the main form in Design view.**

2. **Make certain that the Control Wizards icon is selected in the Toolbox and drag the subform from the Forms list onto the main form.**

3. **Clean things up.**

   You probably need to do a bunch of cleanup work in order to produce acceptable results, depending on how carefully you planned before you added the subform to the main form.

Choosing the Best Subform View

If you've ever tried to enter or edit data by using the Access Datasheet view, you're probably wondering why it is the default view selection for subforms. It is hard to imagine a more difficult subform view to use, and yet, that's what Access really wants to give you.

Fortunately, you can change the subform view into something that's far more user friendly than the Datasheet view. The setting for doing so is just a bit difficult to find, though, because it's not really where you might expect to find it.

Making the switch from Datasheet view to another subform view

You can change the subform to a different view in one of two ways:

- ✔ The best method is to open the subform in Design view without having the main form open. When the subform is open in Design view, right-click on the subform and choose Properties from the pop-up menu to display the Properties dialog box for the subform.

- ✔ The second-best method is to click the Properties button on the toolbar to display the Properties dialog box for the subform. In the Properties dialog box, click the Format tab and then choose the view you want to use for the subform from the drop-down Default View list box, as shown in Figure 10-4.

Figure 10-4:
Choose the
view
settings for
the subform
on the
Format tab.

Figure 10-4 also hints at the reason why opening the subform in Design view and setting its properties by using its Properties dialog box is the preferable method for setting the view for the subform. Although the drop-down list box partially covers the four options immediately below the list box, the labels for these properties are still visible. The four important options are Allow Form View, Allow Datasheet View, Allow PivotTable View, and Allow PivotChart View. You can set each of these options to either Yes or No so that you can lock out views that you don't want users to select. This is a great little feature because it enables you to reduce the possibility that a user will mess up the subform by selecting an inappropriate or confusing view.

Access also offers an option for displaying a subform in its own window. ChooseView⇨Subform in New Window to enable this option. But use this display option sparingly (if at all) because displaying a subform in its own window may prevent users from seeing a clear relationship between the main form and the subform.

Figure 10-5 demonstrates the other option for changing the Subform view. This option is available when the form and subform are open for entering or editing data — not when they're open in Design view. To use this option you right-click the subform to display the pop-up menu. Then you choose the view you want for the subform from the Subform submenu.

Users can also modify the subform view. As an Access application designer, you can probably imagine the panicked calls you might get from your users when all of a sudden "the form looks completely different and I didn't do anything." Right. And I've got some swamp land and a bridge to sell you, too! So if you're worried that users may get confused and you want to head off panicked phone calls before they occur, lock the subform to the view you want by setting the Allow properties for those other views to No.

Figure 10-5:
When the
form and
subform are
open for
editing data,
you can
change the
view by
using the
pop-up
menu.

Introducing your subform view options

Even though the pop-up menu for the subform typically shows four options, you actually have five different view options available for subforms. That's because there are two different Form views (but you can only choose between the two by using the Default View list box of the subform's Properties dialog box).

The view options for a subform include the following:

- ✔ **Single Form:** This is the standard view for ordinary forms and it is arguably the best choice for subforms in a large percentage of situations.

- ✔ **Continuous Forms:** This is a strange combination of Form view and Datasheet view that displays multiple copies of the subform in a scrolling window on the main form.

- ✔ **Datasheet:** This is the standard Datasheet view and the one that appears by default. It's also somewhat difficult to use because all the fields are displayed in a single row so the user has to do considerable horizontal scrolling if more than just a few small fields are included on the subform.

✔ **PivotTable:** This view shows the data summarized in a *PivotTable*, which is typically used for data analysis rather than data entry or editing.

✔ **PivotChart:** This view is similar to the PivotTable view, except that the data is charted rather than summarized in a table.

The PivotTable and PivotChart views really aren't very useful for most of the purposes for which you'd use a form, so I don't discuss them further. Figure 10-6 shows you how the Continuous Forms view looks.

Figure 10-6: The subform here is displayed in Continuous Forms view.

As Figure 10-6 shows, the Continuous Forms view of the subform displays as many copies of the subform as necessary to show all the matching records from the many table based on the selection in the main form. In addition, one extra, blank copy of the subform is added to the bottom of the set of subforms so that you can add additional records to the database. Users can view the individual copies of the subform by using the subform's navigator bar or by using the scroll bar along the right side of the subform's section of the main form.

The Continuous Forms view is the same as the Tabular view option offered by the Form Wizard.

Choosing the best subform view can be a real challenge. You need to balance usability with efficiency, and you also need to consider the amount of space your form and subform combination will require in order to show all the required information.

Adding Multiple Subforms

You can create forms with two or more subforms or even make forms with subforms that have their own subforms. The key to creating these complex types of forms is making sure that each level of form has a one-to-many relationship with its subform through the underlying tables.

The most common example of this type of arrangement is probably that of an order tracking system. In this type of system, you have a Customers table that has a one-to-many relationship with an Orders table. The Orders table then has a one-to-many relationship with a Line Item table.

You add multiple subforms to a form with the same techniques you use to create a form with a single subform. That is, you add the first table and its fields to the design, and then you add the next table and its fields, and then the third table, and so on. If you have the proper table relationships set up, the Form Wizard creates the multiple subforms, as shown in Figure 10-7.

Main form

Figure 10-7:
This form
has an
Orders
subform and
an Order
Details
subform.

Order details subform

In Figure 10-7, I modified the appearance and layout of the subforms just a bit to make them stand out a little better. You can tell that there are two subforms because there are three record navigator bars — each form or subform has its own record navigator because each shows the records from different tables. (See "Navigating Records in Multi-Table Forms" for more information about this topic.)

Navigating Records in Multi-Table Forms

Whenever you have a form that draws records from more than one table, you need a method of navigating the records in each of those tables. To make this navigation possible, Access adds a *record navigator bar* to the bottom of each form and to the bottom of each subform.

Choosing the right navigator bar

Figure 10-8 shows a form with a subform and the two record navigator bars. It also identifies the purpose of the navigation buttons.

Figure 10-8:
The main form and the subform have separate navigator bars.

CurrentAuction

FirstName: Jeff

State: CO

WinningBids

LOTNUMBER: 254

TITLE: Gold Lode Mining Co

Record: 1 of 3

Record: 12 of 683

First record

Previous record

Record number   Last record

Next record

Main form navigator

Insert new record

Subform navigator

Users can sometimes get confused about which navigator bar they need to use — especially if you've been a little careless with your form design and forced users to scroll the form or the subform in order to see the navigator bars.

In Figure 10-8, the main form's navigator bar indicates that record 12 out of 683 records in the main table is visible in the form. In this case record 12 is for the customer named Jeff. The subform's navigator bar shows that record 1 of 3 is visible — the record for lot number 254.

You can also move through the records by using the Page Up and Page Down keys in addition to using the buttons on the navigator bar. The insertion point must be in the section of the form — that is, the main form or the subform — that you want to navigate.

Finding records with filters

One method of finding records in a multiple-table form isn't very efficient. Scrolling through the records by using the main form or even the subform navigator bar gets old awfully fast. You could create a query, of course, but when you've already got the form, why start from scratch?

Figure 10-9 shows another way to locate records, using an existing form — with *filters*. Simply right-click on a field on the main form and enter a value. For example, I clicked the FirstName field on the main form in Figure 10-9 and entered Fred as the value for the filter. Now The form produces all the records in which the FirstName field contains Fred.

A filter functions pretty much like a query except that filters are temporary and can easily be used with existing forms.

	Filter By Selection
	Filter Excluding Selection
	Filter For: Fred
	Remove Filter/Sort
	Cut
	Copy
	Paste
	Sort Ascending
	Sort Descending
	Insert Object...
	Hyperlink
	Properties

Figure 10-9: Use a filter to help you find records.

Figure 10-10 shows the results of applying a filter to the main form. Just as with the navigator bars, you need to apply the filter to the correct section of the form or subform to obtain the results you want.

Figure 10-10: The filter limits the main form to six records.

CurrentAuction

FirstName: Fred
State: NV
WinningBids:
LOTNUMBER: 127
TITLE: Thomas Flyer Original Photo Postcard, 1908

Record: 1 of 30
Record: 1 of 6 (Filtered)

Chapter 11

Fixing Form Faults

Forms are the primary windows into your Access databases, so problems with your forms can cause a whole range of difficulties. Controlling how users can interact with your forms and presenting the data in a clear and understandable fashion can save you a whole lot of trouble.

You work hard to create Access forms that do the job, so the last thing you want is to have problems with those forms. No one wants problems, of course, but sometimes it's hard to avoid them. You are only human, after all.

This chapter discusses several types of problems that you may encounter with forms, and proposes solutions that may work for you. For example, this chapter shows you methods that you can use to help prevent users from entering invalid data. In addition, you see how to present data by using formats that reduce the possibility of error and confusion.

Preventing Invalid Data with Input Masks

No doubt, you put a lot of time and effort into creating your Access databases. But all that time and effort can be wasted if someone is careless about entering data. Queries and reports end up being meaningless if they're loaded with invalid data.

You actually have several methods at your disposal for controlling what data a user can place in your database. Your first line of defense comes when you design the table. When you define how the tables, and the fields they contain, function, you can also define both the type of data that can be entered into each field, and you can create a validation rule for the fields in the table.

If that's not enough, another method of validating the data that the user enters it is to create validation rules for the fields on a form. This method offers one important advantage over setting validation rules in your tables: On a form, you can set validation rules for any control that accepts input even if that control is *unbound* (not tied to) a field in a table. In addition, you can specify a message to display if users attempt to enter an invalid value.

Setting up an input mask with the wizard

An *input mask* helps to prevent users from inputting invalid data by automatically converting the appearance of the data into the proper format so that the user can easily tell whether there's a problem. For example, you can use an input mask in a phone number field to let users know when they've typed an incorrect number of characters.

To set up an input mask for a field on a form, follow these steps:

1. **Open the form in Design view.**
2. **Right-click on the field you want to modify.**
3. **Choose Properties from the pop-up menu.**

   The Properties dialog box for the selected field appears.

4. **Click the Data tab.**

   See Figure 11-1.

Figure 11-1:
Use the
Input Mask
property of
the Data tab
to create an
input mask.

Text Box: PHONE#

PHONE#

| Format | Data | Event | Other | All |

Control Source . . . . WORK#
Input Mask . . . .
Default Value . . . .
Validation Rule . . . .
Validation Text . . . .
Enabled . . . . Yes
Locked . . . . No
Filter Lookup . . . . Database Default
Smart Tags . . . .

5. **Click the Build button to the right of the Input Mask text box.**

   The Input Mask Wizard dialog box, shown in Figure 11-2, appears.

6. **Select a mask and click Next to continue.**

   Some of your options include Phone Number, Social Security number, Password, and so on.

7. **Make modifications to the input mask if necessary.**

   One useful modification is that you can choose placeholder characters to indicate to users the number of characters that they should type.

8. **Click Next to continue.**

9. **Answer any additional questions on the remaining screens of the Input Mask Wizard dialog box and click the Finish button when you're finished.**

   Different input masks require different information, of course. For example, with a phone number mask you can specify whether you want placeholders to indicate the correct number of characters and whether you want the value formatted to look like a phone number.

Making an input mask from scratch

You can also create your own input mask from scratch (or modify an existing input mask) by using the characters shown in Table 11-1. Sometimes, starting from scratch is the only way to create exactly the input mask you want given the limited choices that are available in the Input Mask Wizard dialog box.

Table 11-1	Input Mask Characters
Character	*Purpose*
0	A number 0 to 9 is required, and no other characters are allowed.
9	An optional number from 0 to 9.
#	A number, a space, plus sign, or minus sign is optional.
L	An uppercase letter from A to Z is required.
?	A letter from A to Z is optional.
A	Any letter A to Z or any number 0 to 9 is required.
a	Any letter A to Z or a number 0 to 9 is optional.
&	Any character or a space is required.
C	Any character or a space is optional.
. , : ; - /	Decimal placeholder and thousand, date, and time separators (based on the current settings in the Regional Settings area of the Control Panel).
<	Converts all characters to lowercase.
>	Converts all characters to uppercase.
!	Displays the input mask from right to left, rather than from left to right.
\	Displays the character that follows as itself (so you can show input mask characters).

To create an input mask from scratch or to modify one, follow these steps:

1. **Open the form in Design view.**

2. **Open the Properties dialog box for the field you want to modify.**

3. **On the Data tab, enter the input mask by using the characters shown in Table 11-1.**

   For example, enter **00000\-0000** to create an input mask for a nine-digit U.S. postal code. This input mask displays an entry like 895216315 as 89521-6315.

Limiting a User to Specific Values with Validation Rules

Although an input mask (which I describe in the previous sections) provides the user with some visual feedback, it's really difficult to create a good enough input mask to prevent a user from entering inappropriate values. For that, you need to create a *validation rule*.

If you've used Excel or another spreadsheet program, you'll probably find the task of creating a validation rule pretty familiar. Validation rules are created by using *expressions* that look very much like the formulas in a spreadsheet. Validation rules are actually somewhat more flexible than spreadsheet formulas, but the idea behind them is similar.

Setting up your own validation rules

In an auction database, validation rules come in handy all the time. For example, you can create a validation rule that specifies that bids in an auction must be at least $100. The validation rule could also specify a maximum amount, of course, but I will keep the example simple.

To create a validation rule, follow these steps:

1. **Open the form that you want to create a validation rule for in Design view.**

2. **Open the Properties dialog box for the field that you want to validate.**

   In this case, I choose the BIDAMOUNT field.

3. **On the Data tab, click in the Validation Rule text box to select it.**

4. **Click the Build button.**

   The Expression Builder dialog box, shown in Figure 11-3, appears. You can also type the rule directly in the Validation Rule text box if you prefer.

5. **Enter the validation rule, using the various tools in the dialog box.**

   In my example, I entered >99.99 in the upper box to specify that the value must be at least $100.

6. **Click OK to close the dialog box.**

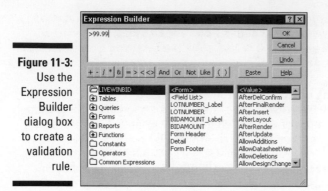

Figure 11-3:
Use the
Expression
Builder
dialog box
to create a
validation
rule.

7. **Enter the text that you want to appear on-screen if (when) a user enters an invalid value in the Validation Text text box.**

   In my example, I entered Bids must be at least $100. See Figure 11-4.

Figure 11-4:
Enter the
validation
text to
ensure that
users
understand
the rule.

8. **Switch the form to Form view and enter a value that does not meet the validation rule in the field where you just created the validation rule.**

   If everything's been done correctly, Access displays a message box with your Validation Text message as soon as you attempt to move to a different field or to a different record. See Figure 11-5.

Figure 11-5:
Access
displays a
message
telling users
that they've
entered
an invalid
value.

You can also specify validation rules by using expressions that check the values contained in other fields. For example, you can specify a rule that won't allow a bid to be accepted if it it's below the reserve price for an item. Or, you can specify a rule that won't allow a user to enter a date that hasn't occurred yet or doesn't exist (say, November 31, 200-never).

Whenever you create a validation rule, be sure to also specify a validation text message so that users see a message they can understand. If you don't create a text message, Access displays a generic message (see Figure 11-6). This generic message is enough to confuse even experienced Access users, so you can imagine the effect it has on ordinary users!

Figure 11-6:
You really
don't want
your users
to see a
message
like this
one!

To get help, or to view the complete contents of one of the properties, such as validation text that is too long to fit the text box, press Shift+F2.

Remembering Access validation rules

Creating your own expressions can be a bit confusing — especially if you can't quite get over what you've learned about creating formulas in Excel. One reason for this difficulty is that there are separate rules for *validation rule expressions* and expressions that you create to produce results in calculated controls:

 ✓ **A validation rule expression must not begin with an equal sign.** This type of expression is closer in concept to a conditional statement inside an Excel formula such as = IF (*conditional statement,* value if true, value if false).

 ✓ **An expression that calculates the value for a calculated control must begin with an equal sign (=).** This is essentially the equivalent of a complete formula in Excel.

Although I don't have room for a complete discussion of expressions, here are some points that can help you create expressions for validation rules with just a bit less frustration:

- ✔ **Use square brackets for field names, controls, and properties.** Place square brackets [] around the names of fields, other controls on a form, or any properties. This is a mandatory part of the process if the name includes any spaces, but good practice any time.

- ✔ **Use quotes for text strings.** Place double quotes (") around any text strings.

- ✔ **Use number signs for dates.** Use number signs (#) to enclose any date values.

- ✔ **Use periods to separate tables.** Place a period (.) between the names of tables and fields.

- ✔ **Use an ampersand (&) to combine the value of a field with a string value.**

- ✔ **Use *or* and *and correctly.*** Use *or* to specify that either of the conditions can validate the entry, and use the word *and* to specify that both of the conditions must be met to validate the entry.

Quick validation rules you can use

Here are a few quick examples of validation rules to get you started.

To specify that a date must be June 26, 2006, or later, use the following rule:

```
>=#6/26/2006#
```

To specify that a numeric value must be between 75 and 99, use this rule:

```
>74 and <100
```

To specify that an entry must have exactly five characters, use this rule:

```
Like "?????"
```

Finally, to specify that the entry must consist of three characters, and that the last two of these characters must be numbers, use this rule:

```
Like "?##"
```

Preventing Users from Changing Records

You may want to prevent users from making certain changes to complete records in your database. For example, perhaps you don't want users to delete records, or maybe you don't want them to add new records. To exercise this type of control over what users can do, you use the Properties dialog box for the form, as shown in Figure 11-7.

Figure 11-7:
You can control how users can modify records in a form.

The three options in question are:

- ✔ **Allow Edits:** Set this option to No to prevent users from modifying existing records.

- ✔ **Allow Deletions:** Set this option to No to prevent users from deleting existing records.

- ✔ **Allow Additions:** Set this option to No to prevent users from adding new records.

Even though the Allow Filters option appears just above these other three options, it has no effect on whether a user can modify the records in the database. The Allow Filters option simply controls whether users can apply a filter so that only specified sets of records can be viewed through the form. If you're dealing with inexperienced and easily confused users, setting this property to No might be useful in preventing panicked calls about how a whole bunch of records suddenly disappeared all on their own. Otherwise, you probably want users to have as much freedom to sort records as possible.

You can also use the Data Entry property to Only Allow a User to Add New records by setting the property to Yes. See Chapter 9 for information about how to lock individual controls on a form.

Looking Out for Poorly Formatted Data

Have you ever encountered information that was possibly accurate but so poorly presented that it was nearly impossible to understand? Almost anyone who has tried to read a badly translated user manual for a cheap piece of imported electronic gear has experienced this problem firsthand. Sure, the information is there, but unless you can figure out how to understand it, do you push this button or that one to adjust the volume, and which one is it that deletes all of your files?

Okay, so maybe your Access forms aren't quite that bad, but presenting information in a clear and understandable format is crucial to helping reduce the number of errors people will make when using those forms.

Knowing what not to do

Although I'm sure you would never make such mistakes on the forms you design, a few examples can give you an idea how poor presentation of data on a form can be awfully confusing. I'm using the term *formatting* in this context to mean more than simply choosing the proper Format property for a field. The broader definition also encompasses several other layout sins such as making text boxes too small to properly show the data.

Poor formatting could also include using text colors that are too close to the background color for easy readability, but those types of problems are extremely difficult to demonstrate in a figure. When in doubt, use common sense and not try to use pink text over a fuchsia background in your forms. Believe me — no matter how much you like those two colors, they won't work out!

In Figure 11-8, the DateReceived, Text4, Text6, and Text8 fields all show the same information even though it's very difficult to tell that from what is displayed on the form. The labels to the right of the four fields in question show the Format property for each of the text boxes. Here's a rundown of the errors shown in the figure — all of which you should avoid:

✓ **Wrong field format:** The underlying field is a `Date` field, so choosing one of the time formats is clearly an error (using a time format could be the correct choice in some instances, but not if you want to display a date).

✓ **Yucky text box sizing:** The `Text8` field shows that the `Long date` format isn't a very good option, either, because in an attempt to make the form look neat, I set the size of all the text boxes to that of the narrowest one, cutting off a good section of the month name. But this also hints at another potential problem with the form. The `DateReceived` field is too narrow, too. Suppose that the date that was displayed in this field appeared as `2/28/2004` — would you be able to tell for certain if the date was February 28 or December 28?

Figure 11-8:
It's difficult to under-stand the data in some of this form's fields because of formatting problems.

Date fields aren't the only ones that suffer from poor formatting choices. Figure 11-9 shows a form that has five variations of the same field included on the form. Each copy of the field has a different numeric formatting property.

Figure 11-9:
Varying numeric formatting can produce confusing results.

In Figure 11-9, the first copy of the field at the top of the form uses the default general number format. At first (and second, and third) glance, you may not notice whether the value shown in this copy represents a financial sum because there's no indication if this is in dollars, cents, or cow chips.

The second copy of the field is set to currency with two decimal places, so determining that the value estimate is $50.00 is much easier. The third copy is formatted as Euros, but with one decimal place, so this value is also confusing. The fourth copy is set to percentage and the last is displayed in scientific notation — clearly very bad choices to represent currency values.

I could go on, but I think you get the picture by now. Consider the type of information that you want to convey and apply proper formatting choices so that anyone using the form can easily understand what the data represents.

Formatting data on forms

You use the Format tab of a field's Properties dialog box to set the display format for the field, as shown in Figure 11-10. The options available from the Format drop-down list depend on the data type of the associated field.

Figure 11-10:
Use the
Format
property to
set the
display
format.

Text Box: Text8	
Format	Data	Event	Other	All
Format	
Decimal Places	Auto
Visible	Yes
Display When	Always
Scroll Bars	None
Can Grow	No
Can Shrink	No
Left	1.125"
Top	0.125"
Width	0.625"
Height	0.1771"
Back Style	Normal
Back Color	-214748364

You may need to resize the Properties dialog box so that when you click the Format List Box drop-down list, the dialog box is wide enough to display the format samples that appear to the right of the selected property's name.

Numeric formats have an associated Decimal Places property. By default, this value is set to Auto, but often you can choose a different value for better results. For example, if you choose the Currency format, you ought to select 2 (to tell Access to format numbers with two decimal places) as the number in the Decimal Places property.

The display formats you choose for the form fields have no effect on how the data is stored in the database. These formats only modify the way that the information is shown on the form.

Part IV
Designing Great Reports

The 5th Wave   By Rich Tennant

©RICHTENNANT

"The top line represents our revenue, the middle line is our inventory, and the bottom line shows the rate of my hair loss over the same period."

In this part . . .

Reports enable you to present the information from your databases to the world. Whether the viewer is your banker, your boss, or a customer, a great report makes that information far more useful and easy to understand. This part shows you how to create great reports that look good and that provide a wealth of understandable information.

Chapter 12

Adding Fancy Touches to Reports

• •

• •

*I*f forms are the objects that Access users probably see the most often, reports are what Access users are most likely to share with others. You aren't likely to haul your laptop to your bank to show your banker an Access form when you want to demonstrate that your business is worthy of an increased credit line; you'd probably create (and print) an Access report that shows how well things are going.

Standard reports are just that — standard, ordinary, or even boring. If you want to make an impact, there's nothing like adding a little pizzazz. With a fancy touch here and there, your reports can display the professional appearance that gets noticed and tells viewers that you're serious about what you're doing. This chapter shows you how to add just the right bits and pieces to your Access reports without going overboard about it.

The Access Report Wizard adds some elements to reports that at least attempt to make the reports a little more presentable than a plain old printout of raw information, but those wizards certainly don't have art degrees. By understanding the options that are available you can easily surpass the results that are produced by the wizards.

Adding Descriptive Titles to Your Reports

A good title says a lot about a report. A title should tell busy viewers enough about the report that they know instantly whether they need to read it. A poor title leaves people wondering about both the content of the report and also about the amount of effort the report's designer put into it.

Chapter 4 covered the basics of creating Access reports. Here's a brief review of the basics. There are three primary types of titles on Access reports:

- ✔ Report titles appear once, at the beginning of a report.
- ✔ Page titles appear once per page on the report.
- ✔ Group titles appear at the beginning of each grouping of similar records in a report.

Each of the title types is optional, and you can vary their placement by using the associated header to make the title appear ahead of the information or by using the footer to make the title appear after the information. Even the term *title* can be a bit deceptive, because you can include items (such as dates and page numbers) that don't ordinarily fit the strict definition of a title. But, hey, this is your report, so you can do what you want with it.

Getting title basics down

By default, the Access Report Wizard gives a report the same name as the table or query that is the basis for the report. Figure 12-1 shows a very basic report design with the totally unimaginative name, ItemsTable — which, of course, is also the name of the table.

Figure 12-1:
Access
isn't very
imaginative
in naming
and titling
reports.

The titles that the Report Wizard places on a report are *unbound controls* (see Chapter 9 for more about controls). They're not connected to any database fields or other objects. As a result, you can easily modify the titles as much as you want without worrying about hurting anything else in your database.

You can probably come up with good report titles without much help from me. After all, it doesn't take too much imagination to realize that "Items in Inventory" is a better, more descriptive title than "ItemsTable."

Modifying existing titles

Access gives a pretty ordinary default title to all your reports that corresponds with the name of your table. If you don't like the default title, you're by no means bound to keep it. You can modify a title by double-clicking the label and typing directly in the label itself, or you can right-click on the label and choose Properties from the pop-up menu to open the Properties dialog box for the label. In the Properties dialog box, click the Format tab and type the new title into the Caption text box (see Figure 12-2).

Figure 12-2:
The Caption property stores the text for the report title.

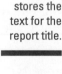

Even the Caption text box can be kind of restraining, so I like to press Shift+F2 to open the Zoom dialog box, as shown in Figure 12-3. The Zoom dialog box provides far more room to work than any of the property text boxes possibly can. Simply delete the boring default title in the Zoom dialog box and start typing your new title. Click OK when you're done.

Figure 12-3:
Use the Zoom dialog box to greatly expand your working area.

Although the Zoom dialog box is great, it doesn't do everything. In fact, despite all indications, it doesn't do formatting — at least not in your report. Don't waste your time trying to format the title by using the Font button in the Zoom dialog box. Any changes you make with that button only apply to how the text is displayed in the Zoom dialog box and they aren't carried over to the title in your report.

Formatting your report titles

You can greatly modify the appearance of a title by using the various formatting options that are available on the Format tab in the Properties dialog box. You can find many of the formatting options on the Formatting toolbar, as well.

The Font list box on the Formatting toolbar displays the font names, and on most systems it uses the actual font, so getting a feel for the font you're choosing is pretty easy without having to go to the extra trouble of using the Properties dialog box. The fonts may not appear in the actual font on some older versions of Windows.

Most of the formatting options are pretty familiar, but a few may not be. For example, the property called Fore Color is the color of the text. Colors in Access are expressed with a really strange numbering system that won't make any sense no matter how long you work at it, so I'd suggest you simply click the Build button after you select the Fore Color property and pick either an existing color or a custom color from the Color dialog box that appears.

Another property that might seem a little odd is the Font Weight property. Font weight is usually a choice between normal and **bold**, but the Font Weight property list box gives you nine different choices ranging all the way from Thin to Heavy. You just have to experiment with this property to see what works best for your titles.

Getting Dynamic with Your Titles

For a completely different type of report title you aren't likely to read about anywhere else, you might want to consider a *dynamic* title — that is, a title that you build by using an expression. This type of title can include information that you probably never knew was available, let alone put into a report title.

Understanding how to use expressions in your titles

Before you can create dynamic titles (see "Using expressions to create dynamic titles," later in the chapter), you need to understand how expressions work.

Dynamic report titles require you to use a *calculated* control, which returns the value of an expression instead of simply displaying fixed text. Using an unbound text box, you can create a calculated control that looks like this:

```
="Inventory Item Report for "&[CurrentProject].[Name]
```

Here's the basic anatomy of an expression:

- ✔ First, the expression begins with an equal sign (=). The equal sign is necessary to set the value of the calculated control equal to the result of the expression.

- ✔ Next, the expression includes a text string that's enclosed in double quotes. Notice that there is a space before the closing double quote mark to ensure that the result of the rest of the expression is spaced properly.

- ✔ To concatenate the text string and the calculated result you use an ampersand (&).

- ✔ The CurrentProject item is a built-in Access object that refers to the current database. This object name is enclosed in square brackets for consistency because the square brackets would be required if the object name included any spaces (and Access would automatically add them if you forgot to type them).

- ✔ The period between the two sets of square brackets tells Access that the next item in the string is a child of the previous item (CurrentProject).

  In programmer-speak, this period is what is known as *dot notation* and it is common in all modern *object oriented* programming languages.

- ✔ Finally, Name is a property of the CurrentProject object, and it refers to the name of the currently open database.

For more information on the various properties in the CurrentProject object, see the later section, "Using properties to control your expressions," later in this chapter.

Using expressions to create dynamic titles

To create a dynamic report title you need to use a different type of control than the ones you're probably used to. You need a *calculated* control because this type of control returns the value of an expression instead of simply displaying fixed text. You create this calculated control by using an unbound text box (just ignore any warnings Access tries to give you about the fact that the text box is unbound — that's exactly how you want it to be, unbound).

For example, say you want to create a dynamic title that combines some static text with the name of the database file so that the report title shows both the purpose and the source of the report. Although you could just enter the name of the database when you create the report, using a calculated control offers a great advantage. The name of the report is automatically updated if the database file is ever renamed.

To create a dynamic report title, follow these steps:

1. **Open the report in Design view.**

2. **Click the Text Box tool in the Toolbox to select it and then drag out a large rectangle in the report header area of the report design.**

   The rectangle should be large enough to hold the complete title, but you can always resize the text box later if necessary.

3. **Right-click on the Title text box and choose Properties from the pop-up menu.**

   Alternatively, click the Properties button on the toolbar to display the Properties dialog box.

4. **Click the Data tab to display it.**

5. **Click the Control Source text box to select it.**

6. **Press Shift+F2 to display the Zoom dialog box. You need the extra space it affords to easily enter the expression.**

7. **Enter an expression.**

   I entered

   ```
   ="Inventory Item Report for "&[CurrentProject].[Name]
   ```

   for my example, as shown in Figure 12-4.

8. **Click OK to close the Zoom dialog box.**

9. **Click the Close button to close the Properties dialog box.**

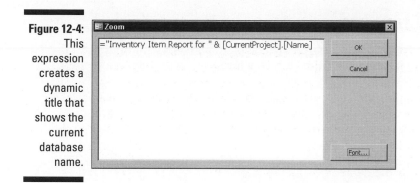

Figure 12-4:
This
expression
creates a
dynamic
title that
shows the
current
database
name.

10. **In the Report design, click the label for the text box to select just the label and then press Delete to remove the label.**

11. **Save your work and then switch the report to Print Preview view to view the results.**

    The result of your expression looks something like Figure 12-5.

Figure 12-5:
This is the
title that
results
from the
expression.

You can spice up the appearance of your dynamic title, using the same formatting options that you use on any ordinary title.

Using properties to control your expressions

There are additional properties of the CurrentProject object that you can use in addition to the Name property. To use any of these properties, simply replace Name with the name of the property you want:

✓ **FullName:** This property returns the complete name of the open data-base file including the path with the drive letter and all folder names.

✓ **Path:** This property returns the complete path but without the database name. It is identical to the `FullName` property with the `Name` property stripped off the end.

✓ **FileFormat:** This property returns a number that refers to the Access file format of the open database file. This number is equivalent to the internal Access version number, so the Access 2002-2003 file format returns a value of 10. This property probably isn't too useful in most cases, but it's there if you're curious.

The CurrentProject object has quite a few other properties, but they're not available in a calculated control. Those additional properties are only useful in VBA procedures.

Getting rid of the .mdb document extension

Even though I don't find the .mdb extension on the end of the calculated title (refer to Figure 12-5) objectionable, you may. If so, you can use a couple of the functions that are built into Access to strip that off the end of the result. The two functions are the `Left` function, which returns a specified number of characters from the beginning of a string, and the `Len` function, which returns the length of the string.

To apply this fix to the example, replace the calculation in the expression

```
[CurrentProject].[Name]
```

with the following:

```
Left([CurrentProject].[Name],Len([CurrentProject].[Name])-4)
```

This expression uses the `Len` function to determine the number of characters in the current database name, and then uses the `Left` function to return the name minus the last four characters — which happen to be .mdb. Your title now appears without the extension at the end of the result.

Coming up with Page Title Ideas

Page titles help readers keep track of multiple report pages. As with report titles, page titles can appear at the top of the page in the page header or at the bottom of a page in the page footer. Most often, you place page numbers, dates, or even a brief report name in a page title. Page numbers and dates are covered in the section "Adding Dates and Page Numbers," later in this chapter.

You can use the same types of formatting options to spruce up your page titles that you use with report titles, but because page titles typically appear on each page of the report, you may want to be a bit conservative on the size of page titles to cut down on wasted paper.

By default, any page headers or page footers you define appear on every page of the report. However, you can choose other options to control where these items appear. You use the Page Header property (see Figure 12-6) or the similar Page Footer property of the report to adjust these settings.

Figure 12-6:
The Page Header and Page Footer properties control where the page titles appear.

These two properties are just a bit cryptic, so a brief description is in order:

- **All Pages:** Choosing this option prints the page header (or footer) on every page of the report, and is the default setting.
- **Not with Rpt Hdr:** Choosing this option prints the page header (or footer) on every page except the first page where the report header appears.
- **Not with Rpt Ftr:** Choosing this option prints the page header (or footer) on every page except the last page where the report footer appears.
- **Not with Rpt Hdr/Ftr:** Choosing this option prints the page header (or footer) on every page except the first page where the report header appears and the last page where the report footer appears.

If you don't want to include the database name in the report title, you might want to use the calculated control idea that I discuss in "Getting Dynamic with Your Titles," earlier in this chapter to add the database name to the page title.

Adding Dates and Page Numbers

Date and page numbers are important report elements that probably seem like kind of a throwaway piece. But if you've ever dropped a big stack of report pages and had to figure out how to put the pages back in the proper order, you can easily understand the importance of page numbering. Likewise, if you've ever been faced with a situation where you ended up with several different copies of a report, you know that having the date and possibly even the time that the report was produced is the only way to be sure which copy is the current copy.

Choosing the right place for dates and numbers

Where's the best place for dates and page numbers? Well, the flip answer would be somewhere on the report, but that wouldn't be a very helpful thing of me to say, would it?

Page numbers can only go in the page header or the page footer. There's simply no other place on a report for them. Your choice of placing them at the top or the bottom of the page is simply a matter of personal preference.

The report date, on the other hand, could easily be placed on the report header or footer in addition to the typical location on the page header or footer. I find that adding the date to the report header is a good way to start off a report, but that displaying the date along with the page numbers is also valuable.

Getting fancy with date displays

It's very easy to add a date and time to a report. The simplest method is to choose Insert⇨Date and Time to open the Date and Time dialog box, as shown in Figure 12-7. Then you use the options in the dialog box to choose what you want to include.

You can also add the date to a report manually by using an unbound text box that is a calculated control. Generally you use the expression =Now() to return the current date and time, but you can modify the expression if necessary. For example, if you need to print a number of reports in advance of a meeting and want all the reports to display the same date, you can adjust the date easily. For example, the following expression will display tomorrow's date on the report:

```
=Now()+1
```

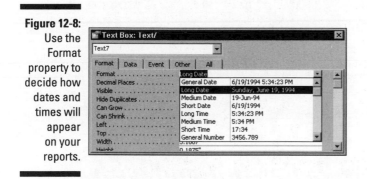

Figure 12-7:
You can add
a date and
time by
using the
Date and
Time dialog
box.

You could also backdate a report with this technique, of course.

The Now() function returns a date and time serial number (if you use Excel, you probably are already familiar with the function). You can display the result as a date, as a time, or as a combination of the two, depending on the format you choose. Figure 12-8 shows the date and time format options that are available on the Format tab of the Properties dialog box.

Figure 12-8:
Use the
Format
property to
decide how
dates and
times will
appear
on your
reports.

In the Access date and time numbering scheme, a *time serial number* of 0 represents 12:00 AM, Saturday, December 30, 1899. If you need to represent a specific date and time on a report, add 1 for each full day and a decimal fraction representing the fraction of a day equal to the time you want. For example, if you want to show the date as June 26, 2006, and the time as 12:00 PM, use the following expression:

```
=38894.5
```

Discovering some neat page number tricks

Page numbers are similar to dates and times in many ways. You can use the Insert⇨Page Numbers command to add page numbers to a header or to a footer, or you can add page numbers yourself by using calculated controls. You can also use any of the formatting options to make the page numbers as fancy or as unobtrusive as you like.

Access has two built-in objects you use to create page number expressions:

- **Page:** This object represents the current page number.
- **Pages:** This object represents the total number of pages in the report.

You might notice a very slight delay before a report begins printing when you have page numbers included in your report. That's because Access has to make two passes through the report in order to first determine how many pages it contains so that the Pages object holds the correct value.

Even though page numbers are usually used only in page headers or page footers, you can show the total number of report pages on the report header by adding an unbound text box to the report header and entering the following expression into the Control Source property for the text box:

```
="Total Report Pages: "&[Pages]
```

If you're the type of person who always wants to know how much work you still have in front of you, try using the following expression in an unbound text box in the page header or footer:

```
="Pages Left in this Report: "&[Pages]-[Page]
```

Making Records Easier to Read with Alternating Bands of Color

The following sections offer some ways you can make the main parts of your reports a bit fancier. In the following sections you discover some techniques that are quite a bit different from the old tried-and-true methods that most Access users know. You can create some really unusual results.

You've probably seen reports that were printed on paper that has alternating bands of color. Those bands of color make it a bit easier to follow a line of data across a page, but they often don't line up very well with individual records. These steps show you how you to add alternating bands of background color that automatically line up perfectly with each record.

You already know that you can use the various formatting options to spruce up your reports, but you may not have considered using the color options, despite the fact that you may use a color printer. You don't have to do everything in plain old boring black text against a white background, and you can do color without *overdoing* color.

Step 1: Picking colors and translating them to hex

There are a couple of ways you can set colors in Access. The most common method is also the least complicated. First, you select the object whose color you want to change, open the Properties dialog box, select the color property you want to adjust, and then click the Build button to display the Color dialog box. Figure 12-9 shows the Color dialog box after clicking the Define Custom Colors button so that the whole dialog box is visible.

Figure 12-9:
Use the Color dialog box to choose colors for objects.

After you choose a color, Access throws a really strange-looking number into the selected color property in the Properties dialog box. In the case of pure white, for example, the color is shown as 16777215.

Computers use a color model known as *RGB* — for red, green, and blue. Every color is measured by how much red, how much green, and how much blue is in the color. But computers use a different form of measurement called *hexadecimal* (often shortened to *hex*) rather than the decimal (or base-10) system most humans use. Hexadecimal is a base-16 system. The first 10 numbers are 0 to 9, and the numbers we think of as 10, 11, 12, 13, 14, and 15 are shown as A, B, C, D, E, and F in hexadecimal.

So why is this important? It's because you need to use the hexadecimal numbers to figure out the equivalent decimal values that Access shows in the Properties dialog box so that you can tell Access what colors you want it to use.

To further complicate things, the Color dialog box shows the red, green, and blue values in decimal, and you need to first convert those numbers to hex in order to create the alternating colored records. Fortunately, this all sounds a lot worse than it really is.

To figure out a color number manually, follow these steps:

1. **Open the Windows Calculator application.**

   You can find it under the Accessories submenu on your Start menu.

2. **Make sure the Calculator is in Scientific view by checking the View menu.**

3. **In Access open the Color dialog box.**

   Click the Build button in the Properties dialog box for one of the color properties you want to set.

4. **Make sure that the Color dialog box is fully expanded so that you can see the red, green, and blue values.**

5. **Choose a color you want to use.**

6. **With the Calculator in Dec (decimal) mode, enter the red value.**

7. **Click the Hex option button to convert the decimal value to a hexadecimal value.**

8. **Write down the value shown in the Calculator display.**

9. **Repeat Steps 5 through 8 for the green and then the blue values.**

10. **Clear the entry in the calculator and then enter the red, green, and blue values as a single hexadecimal value.**

    In the example shown in Figure 12-9, the value is FFFFFF.

11. **Click the Dec option button to display the equivalent decimal value.**

    My example happens to be the same number that appears in the Properties dialog box, 16777215.

Go ahead and try several different color values by changing the color selection in the Color dialog box and then calculating the value that should appear in the Properties dialog box. The numbers should match in every case if you don't make any mistakes entering the values.

So, now you know how Access comes up with those strange numbers, and you also know how to calculate the correct color number for a selected color. Is that better than simply choosing a color and writing down the color number that appears in the Properties dialog box? Probably not, but at least the color numbers make a bit more sense to you now and you have a better understanding of what's going on in the next exercise.

Step 2: Writing code to apply your color bands

In the previous section I show you how to find colors that look good as alternating backgrounds for the records in your reports. In this section, I show you how to achieve this by creating an *event procedure* — which actually is a bit of VBA code — in Access. Don't worry, though; even if you're not a programmer, this is a pretty painless process.

Here's what you need to do to add alternating bands of color to your report:

1. **Open the report that you want to modify in Design view.**
2. **Click the Detail band to select it.**
3. **Open the Properties dialog box and click the Event tab to make it visible.**
4. **Click the On Format property box to select it.**
5. **Click the Build button.**

   The code editing window in Microsoft Visual Basic appears, as shown in Figure 12-10.

Figure 12-10: Use this window to create the event procedure.

```
Holabird Americana - Report_ItemsTable (Code)

Detail                              Format

Option Compare Database

Private Sub Detail_Format(Cancel As Integer, FormatCount As Integer)


End Sub
```

6. **Move the insertion point to the blank line just below the top line and enter** Private RowNumber As Long.

   This is a necessary step because in VBA you need to *declare* a *long integer variable* before you can use it in the procedure.

7. **Move the insertion point to the line below the one that begins with** `Private Sub Detail_Format`.

8. **Enter the following lines exactly as shown here:**

```
RowNumber = RowNumber + 1
If RowNumber / 2 = CLng(RowNumber / 2) Then
Me.Detail.BackColor = 16777088
Else
Me.Detail.BackColor = 8454143
End If
```

TIP

The numbers used in my example give alternating yellow and aqua bands. If you don't care for these colors, you can easily specify different colors by changing the two values 16777088 and 8454143 in Step 8. Use the procedures mentioned in the previous section to determine the values to use.

9. **Close the Microsoft Visual Basic window to return to your database.**

10. **Save your work and then switch the report to Print Preview view.**

   Switching to Print Preview view takes a bit longer than usual because Access is applying the formatting you asked it to add. Figure 12-11 shows how your report should appear.

Figure 12-11: Each record is now displayed with alternating color backgrounds.

ItemsTable		

Inventory Item Report for Holabird Americana.mdb

ItemID Title

```
        7  Map of the Bimetal Mine
        8  Leonita Development Company
        9  57th Annual Session I.O.O.F Ribbon, 1909.
       10  Manhattan Higgins Mining Co.
       11  Exchequer MC.
       12  Hale & Norcross MC
       13  Shoshone National Bank MC
       14  Greenwater Copper Mines Smelter Co.
       15  Oriental Gold Mining Co.
```

Page: 14 ◄ 1 ► ►| ◄

You can modify the event procedure by once again clicking the Build button to open the code editing window.

You can probably figure out most of the event procedure on your own, but there are a few things that might throw you:

- ✔ The CLng function in the second line rounds a number to the closest integer value. This is how the procedure determines whether the current record is an even- or odd-numbered record, so this function controls whether the next line or the line following Else is executed.

- ✔ Me.Detail.BackColor is a programmer's method of referring to the background color of the current record in the Detail section.

- ✔ The procedure uses an If *condition* Then *statement if true* Else *statement if false* structure to control which statement is executed. As the RowNumber value is incremented, the two statements that set the background color are alternately executed as a result.

Making Records Stand Out

One cool way to make certain records stand out is to use *conditional formatting* to apply special formatting to records that meet certain conditions. Bonus: This method doesn't involve any VBA programming. For example, you could color all orders for a particular state by using a different color or you could use colors to flag records relating to products that are on sale.

To apply conditional formatting to a report, follow these steps:

1. **Open the report that you want to modify in Design view.**

2. **In the Detail section of the report, select the fields to which you want to apply the conditional formatting.**

   If you want, you can test the conditional formatting option with just one field. Building the conditional test is a little easier, of course, but only that field will have conditional formatting applied.

3. **Choose Format⇨Conditional Formatting from the Access menu.**

   The Conditional Formatting dialog box appears, as shown in Figure 12-12.

4. **From the first drop-down list in the Condition 1 section, select Expression Is.**

   Making this selection hides two of the three remaining boxes on the same line.

5. **In the blank text box, enter the expression that defines the condition you want to test for.**

In this example, I entered [State] = "CA" Or [State] = "California" to apply the conditional formatting if the value in the State field is CA or California.

Figure 12-12:
Use the
Conditional
Formatting
dialog box
to specify
conditions
and
formatting
options.

Conditional Formatting	? X
Default Formatting	
This format will be used if no conditions are met:	AaBbCcYyZz B *I* U ◌▾ A▾ ▭
Condition 1	
Field Value Is ▾ between ▾ _____ and _____	
Preview of format to use when condition is true:	No Format Set B *I* U ◌▾ A▾ ▭
	Add >> Delete... OK Cancel

6. **Select the formatting options you want to apply if the condition is met.**

In this case, I chose a red background color. The dialog box looks similar to Figure 12-13.

Figure 12-13:
The
conditional
formatting is
defined and
ready to
apply.

Conditional Formatting	? X
Default Formatting	
This format will be used if no conditions are met:	AaBbCcYyZz B *I* U ◌▾ A▾ ▭
Condition 1	
Expression Is ▾ [State]="CA" Or [State]="California"	
Preview of format to use when condition is true:	AaBbCcYyZz B *I* U ◌▾ A▾ ▭
	Add >> Delete... OK Cancel

7. **If you want to specify any additional conditional formatting, click the Add button and repeat Steps 4 through 6. Click OK after you specify all the conditional formatting you want to apply.**

The Conditional Formatting dialog box closes.

8. **Save your work and then switch the report to Print Preview view to view the results.**

Access takes a bit longer to display the report when conditional formatting is applied. Figure 12-14 shows the results for my sample report.

Figure 12-14:
Access
applies the
conditional
formatting
to the
records that
meet the
specified
conditions.

ItemsTable-Basic

Items Table List

ItemID	State	Title
7	Arizona	Map of the Bimetal Mine
8	Arizona	Leonita Development Company
9	California	57th Annual Session I.O.O.F. Ribbon, 1909.
10	Nevada	Manhattan Higgins Mining Co.
11	Nevada	Exchequer MC.
12	Nevada	Hale & Norcross MC
13	Nevada	Shoshone National Bank MC

Page: 1

Conditional formatting is only applied to the actual area occupied by the selected fields. If you don't want the color gaps between the fields to appear, either make the fields large enough so they're against each other or add an empty control like a blank label behind the other fields and apply the conditional formatting to the empty control.

It's not necessary for the field that you're testing in the conditional formatting expression to actually appear on the report, as long as the field is a part of the table or query that supplies the data for the report. You could, for example, test the value in the State field even if the state never appeared on the report. This might cause some confusion among people reading the report, however, so you would want to explain the conditional formatting somewhere on the report — perhaps in the report footer.

If you print your reports in black and white, you can still use the color options discussed in the last two examples in this chapter. Just make sure that you substitute colors that appear as a light gray background in the print-out so that the text is readable in print.

Chapter 13

Creating Reports that Summarize Data

. . . .

In This Chapter

▶ Grouping records

▶ Adding everything up

▶ Working with advanced summarizing methods

. . . .

All Access reports show data, of course, but sometimes that's all a report does — show raw data. In many instances, reports could be more useful if they went a bit further to analyze information and provide helpful summaries. Fortunately, Access offers a number of different options that enable you to create various types of summary reports.

Access offers a lot of tools for creating reports that summarize data. Many of them are fairly well hidden by the Report Wizards, but there's no reason why you can't take control and create your reports the way you want.

This chapter shows you how to group data to help organize your reports, how to add totals and subtotals to reports, and how to apply some more advanced report summarization techniques. Using the methods presented in this chapter, you can analyze the information that is contained in your databases so that the data is even more useful to you (and to others) than it already is. Do I smell a raise in your future?

Discovering How to Group Records

Organization is absolutely vital in making information useful. Imagine how useless a large city's telephone book would be if the listings were simply added randomly without alphabetizing the records? Or consider how difficult shopping in a supermarket would be if the groceries weren't grouped into general categories such as produce, meats, dairy products, and so on. Just because information exists doesn't mean that it has much value unless it's organized in some way.

Access offers several ways for you to organize your data. Simple record sorting (see Chapter 12) is one of the most basic methods of organization, but record grouping bumps up the utility to the next level.

Understanding your record-grouping options

When you *group* records in a report, Access arranges the records according to your specifications; but that's just the beginning of what's going on. Each group of records acts almost like a report within a report, meaning that you can create record subgroups using another field within the database. You can also create multiple groups within the same report. In addition, you can tell Access to summarize the records within each group so that you can view information, such as group totals, group record counts, or other more advanced forms of analysis.

Here's a look at the grouping methods available to you:

- ✔ You can group records based on an exact match of alphabetized values. People typically think of record grouping this way, but that's only one of the available options.

- ✔ You can group records that have similar but not precisely the same values in a field.

- ✔ You can group records based on date or time ranges.

In most cases you use a group header (and sometimes a group footer) to show how the records are being grouped. Generally, you place the field that is being used for the grouping in the group header so that the user can easily tell which group of records they're seeing. For example, if you group the records in a report by state, each group header shows the name of the state for the following group of records.

You might want to include a visual element such as a horizontal line in the group header or in the group footer to make the groups stand out from each other.

Creating your first report grouping

The simplest way to set up report grouping is to use the Report Wizard and specify that you want to group the records as you're building the report.

As you've seen in earlier chapters, the wizards aren't always as flexible as you might like. In addition, the wizards really only give you one shot at getting things correct — if you don't like the results, you must either start over from scratch or make the changes you want in Design view. Because of these limitations, I say you should bypass the wizard and instead create useful report groupings with the tools that you find in Design view.

Grouping by date range

If you run a business, one thing you're always trying to find out is how your business is progressing. You may know it's progressing nicely, but a little evidence would be nice, wouldn't it? Are you getting more orders or making more profit as time goes along? Can you demonstrate to your banker that your business is growing steadily over time? These are some of the types of questions you can answer with a report that groups records by date.

Figure 13-1 shows an example of a report that shows the number of items received for an auction each month, along with the estimated total value of the items. This type of report uses grouping by a date range, so it can give you a good picture of how your business is doing on a monthly, quarterly, or yearly basis. If you really want to get an up-close look at progress, you can even track inventory, sales figures, and more on a weekly or daily basis.

Figure 13-1: This report groups the records by month.

DateReceived by Month	DateReceived	LowEst
October 2001		
7 detail records		
Sum		$650
November 2001		
43 detail records		
Sum		$1,995
December 2001		
88 detail records		
Sum		$2,140

Summary of Items by Date

Summary of Items by Date

Page: 1

To add date grouping to a report, follow these steps:

1. **Create your basic report and open it in Design view.**

   Make sure that the underlying table or query includes a field with dates that you want to use for grouping the records.

2. **Choose View⇨Sorting and Grouping or click the Sorting and Grouping button on the toolbar.**

   The Sorting and Grouping dialog box appears.

3. **Select the field that you want to use for grouping from the drop-down Field/Expression list box.**

   This drop-down list is in the top row of the dialog box. In this example I selected the `DateReceived` field.

4. **Select the sorting method you want to use by choosing Ascending or Descending from the Sort Order list box.**

5. **With the first row still selected, choose Yes from the Group Header list box.**

   Adding a group header or a group footer changes the associated field from simply being used for sorting to being used for grouping.

6. **If you want to include a group footer, choose Yes from the Group Footer list box.**

   In this example, I used a group footer to add the summary information, but I could have made the report even more compact by adding the information shown in the detail section to the group footer and eliminating the detail section.

7. **Select the grouping range that you want to use from the drop-down Group On list box.**

   In this example, I selected `Month` to group the records by dates in the same month. Figure 13-2 shows how the Sorting and Grouping dialog box should appear at this point. In the following sections you see how to use the group interval options.

Figure 13-2:
Use the Sorting and Grouping dialog box to set up the grouping for your report.

Specifying how groups are formed with the group interval

The Sorting and Grouping dialog box includes an option labeled *Group Interval* that you may find just a bit confusing at first. This option operates differently depending on the type of data that is contained in the field that you're using for grouping:

- **If the data type is text, the Group Interval value specifies the number of characters at the beginning of the text string to use to group the records.** For example, if you set the value to 3, the report groups all records where the first three characters in the grouping field match; *Undercover* and *Underdahl* would be grouped together, but *United* would be in a different group.

- **If the data type is a numeric or date type, the Group Interval value specifies the number of values that will be consolidated.** For example, if you set the Group Interval value to 3 and the Group On value is Month, the report consolidates records for sets of three consecutive months.

Keeping records together

You've probably seen plenty of reports that used grouping but were still difficult to understand because the grouping simply wasn't very obvious. For example, it's simply not very intuitive to try to figure out what's going on in a report if a group header prints at the bottom of a page, but none of the records in that group appear until the next page.

The Keep Together option in the Sorting and Grouping dialog box is intended to help you control the location of the group headers, footers, and the related detail records. This option includes the following choices:

- **No:** Access makes no attempt to keep the group header, detail records, and group footer together on the same page. This is the default setting.

- **Whole Group:** Access tries to keep the group header, detail records, and group footer together on the same page.

- **With First Detail:** Access starts a new page before starting the group if at least one detail record can't follow the group header on the page.

Unfortunately, the Keep Together option is somewhat less than perfect in execution. Alas, that's just the nature of reports. Depending on the data that you're including in a report, it might simply be impossible to keep the group header, detail records, and group footer together on the same page. For example, if you have a report in which a single group of detail records needs several pages to print, there's really no way that Access can fit the group header, detail records, and group footer together on the same page.

If the number of records in your database simply makes the Keep Together options unworkable, consider adding the field that you're using for grouping to the detail band on the report to help identify which group each detail record belongs to.

Fortunately, Access does provide another option that you can use to improve the layout of your grouped reports. You can set the Force New Page property for the group using the Format tab of the Properties dialog box, as shown in Figure 13-3.

Figure 13-3:
Use the
Force
New Page
property for
additional
control
over how
grouped
records
print.

The Force New Page property has four options:

- ✓ **None:** No extra pages are added and the new group simply begins after the previous group ends.
- ✓ **Before Section:** Always starts each group at the top of a new page.
- ✓ **After Section:** Always starts the next group on a new page.
- ✓ **Before & After:** Begins each group at the top of a new page and forces the next group to advance to a new page.

All these options other than None should cause each group to begin at the top of a new page. You can set this property for any report section except for page headers and page footers.

Making sure you get the right groups

Unfortunately, you may not always find determining how to create the right type of grouping is not always easy. Making a report return the type of results that you want can be a tricky process. This is especially true if you want to summarize results using date or time intervals that are just a bit offbeat.

For example, suppose that you want to analyze your sales results from a number of years. Instead of showing the trend over time, you may want to know the number and amount of sales for each season or fiscal quarter. You could have your report show the total of all Quarter 1 results, the total of all Quarter 2 results, the total of all Quarter 3 results, and the total of all Quarter 4 results, regardless of the year. Getting this type of summary can be pretty tricky because even though you can group dates by quarter, you end up with four individual quarter groups for each year that's represented in your database. What you really want are four quarterly summaries where each summary totals all of the results by quarter regardless of the year. Figure 13-4 shows an example of this type of report. In this case, the results for several years are combined into four quarterly summaries, and users can easily determine that demand for the business has been pretty seasonal.

Figure 13-4:
This report groups the records by quarter, regardless of the year.

Summary of Items by Quarter	
Quarter Received	**LowEst**
Quarter 1	
1879 records Sum	$79,761
Quarter 2	
2205 records Sum	$373,043
Quarter 3	
4397 records Sum	$550,015
Quarter 4	
423 records Sum	$67,557
Grand Total	$1,070,376

The key to creating this type of summary is to use one of the functions that are built into Access. The DatePart function enables you to group records based on specific pieces of date information without the chronological constraints that are imposed by the normal grouping options.

To use the DatePart function, you create an expression in the Field/Expression list box in the Sorting and Grouping dialog box, as shown in Figure 13-5. The expression takes the place of the field name that you usually select from the drop-down list.

If you change from grouping on a field to grouping using an expression with the DatePart function, be sure to set the Group On option to Each Value.

Figure 13-5:
The
DatePart
function
provides
additional
grouping
options
compared
to simply
grouping on
a field.

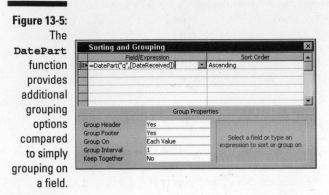

An expression using the `DatePart` function uses the following syntax:

```
=DatePart("date code",[fieldname])
```

Table 13-1 describes the date/time codes you can use with the `DatePart` function.

Table 13-1	Date/Time Codes for the DatePart Function
Code	*Meaning*
d	Day
h	Hour
m	Month
n	Minute
q	Quarter
s	Second
w	Day of the week
ww	Week of year
y	Day of year
yyyy	Year

If you want to analyze your sales by month instead of by quarter, you replace the q with an m in the expression.

Adding Subtotals and Totals

One of the big advantages of grouping records is that you can generate subtotals for each group in addition to overall totals for the entire report. In the report examples shown earlier in this chapter, you see how creating groupings can enable you to view the subtotaled results by month or by quarter.

You can use the Report Wizard to add subtotals and totals to your reports automatically. But, as is the case for everything that you can add to an Access report, adding these items yourself is also very easy.

Understanding how subtotals and totals work

Totals and *subtotals* are actually the same thing. The only difference between the two has to do with where they're placed in a report. That may sound a little strange, but it's actually true, because of the way Access groups records.

You can add a total or a subtotal to any footer on a report. (You can also add them to headers, but doing so tends to be a bit confusing for someone viewing the report.) When you run the report, Access calculates the totals and subtotals based on the report section where you placed the expression.

If you place the expression on the report footer, the result of the expression is a total of all matching records in the entire report. If you place the expression on the page footer, Access totals the records for each page individually. And if you place the expression on a group footer, Access creates the subtotals by group.

Essentially, Access treats totals and subtotals as (in programming parlance) *private* or *local* variables. That is, a subtotal for a group can only include the items that are contained within the single group. Any items that are in another group simply don't exist as far as the subtotal is concerned.

Adding totals to groups and reports

You use the Sum function to create totals and subtotals. The following expression placed in an unbound text box control would create a group subtotal, a page subtotal, or a report total for the values in the LowEst field, depending on where you placed the expression:

```
=Sum([LowEst])
```

Figure 13-6 shows a report design that includes both a group subtotal and a report total. The same expression is clearly used in both instances, but because the group subtotal only includes the items within each group, the expression produces very different results in each instance.

Figure 13-6:
The same
expression
produces
both the
group
subtotal and
the report
total.

Summary of Items by Quarter : Report

Report Header

Summary of Items by Quarter
=Now()

Page Header

Quarter Received   LowEst

=DatePart("q",[DateReceived]) Header

="Quarter " & DatePart("q",[DateReceived])

Detail

=DatePart("q",[DateReceived]) Footer

=Count(*) & " " & IIf(Count(*)=1,"record"," records")

Sum   =Sum([LowEst])

Page Footer

Report Footer

Grand Total   =Sum([LowEst])

Group subtotal

Report total

Be sure to set the Format property for any totals or subtotals appropriately (such as to Currency) so that the meaning of the total is easier to understand in the printed report. Figure 13-7 shows how different the results of the expression can be.

Summary of Items by Date

Summary of Items by Quarter

Tuesday, June 07, 2005

Quarter Received	LowEst
Quarter 1	
1879 records	
Sum	$79,761
Quarter 2	
2205 records	
Sum	$373,043
Quarter 3	
4397 records	
Sum	$550,015
Quarter 4	
423 records	
Sum	$67,557
Grand Total	$1,070,376

Page: |◄ ◄ 1 ► ►| ◄

Figure 13-7:
The same expression produces different results in different places in the report.

Using Some Advanced Summarizing Methods

Just as Excel really isn't much of a database application, Access isn't the best spreadsheet, either. Even so, Access does include a very large number of built-in functions that you can use in your reports. The latest version of Access actually includes more functions than most spreadsheet programs did a few years ago — although not all of those functions are useful outside of VBA procedures.

Different versions of Access include varying numbers of built-in functions. Probably the easiest way to get a feel for the functions that are included in your version is to search the help file for *Functions by category*. This listing is far more useful for you than an alphabetical listing of functions because you can find related functions based on their purpose instead of trying to figure them out by name. You can also view the list on the Web at office. microsoft.com/en-us/assistance/HP011359591033.aspx.

Going beyond simple math

Even though Access has several built-in functions, you probably won't use more than a few of them in your reports. Still, if you don't know they're available, you could miss many of the functions that you might find awfully useful.

Although I can't list all the functions you might find useful, Table 13-2 shows a number of functions that you might want to use when you want a little more than just a simple sum. This table is far from comprehensive. For example, I have left out various financial functions that you're more likely to use in Excel than in Access.

Table 13-2	Some Useful Access Functions
Function	*Description*
Abs	Returns the absolute value of a number.
Avg	Calculates the arithmetic mean.
Count	Calculates the number of records.
DateAdd	Returns a date to which a specified interval has been added.
DateDiff	Calculates the number of time intervals between two dates.
DatePart	Returns a specified part of a given date.
Fix	Returns the integer value of a number. If the number is negative, Fix returns the first negative integer greater than or equal to the number.
Hex	Returns a string representing the hexadecimal value of a number.
IIf	Returns one of two values depending on the evaluation of an expression.
InStr	Returns the position of the first occurrence of one string within another.
Int	Returns the integer value of a number. If the number is negative, Int returns the first negative integer less than or equal to the number.
LCase	Converts a string to lowercase.
Left	Returns a specified number of characters from the left side of a string.
Len	Returns the number of characters in a string.

Function	Description
Log	Returns the natural logarithm of a number.
LTrim	Removes extra spaces from the beginning of a string.
Max	Returns the maximum value.
Mid	Returns a number of characters from a string.
Min	Returns the minimum value.
Now	Returns the current system date and time.
Nz	Converts a Null value to zero, an empty string, or a value you specify.
Replace	Replaces part or all of a string with a different string.
Right	Returns a specified number of characters from the right side of a string.
Rnd	Returns a random number between 0 and 1.
Round	Rounds a number to a specified number of decimal places.
RTrim	Removes extra spaces from the end of a string.
Space	Creates a string consisting of the specified number of spaces.
Sqr	Calculates the square root of a number.
StdDev	Calculates the standard deviation for a population sample.
StdDevP	Calculates the standard deviation for a population.
StrConv	Converts string values to other forms.
StrReverse	Reverses the character order of a string.
Sum	Returns the sum.
Time	Returns the current system time.
Timer	Returns the number of seconds elapsed since midnight.
Trim	Removes extra spaces from both ends of a string.
UCase	Converts a string to uppercase.
Var	Calculates the variance for a population sample.
VarP	Calculates the variance for a population.

Okay, so I'm the first to admit that your eyes probably glazed over at the sight of Table 13-2. Nothing's quite as boring as a list full of strange looking functions — especially if you have no clue about how you might use them. The following sections pick out a few of the functions to show you how you can put them to use in a report.

Converting string values

Refer to Table 13-2 to see a list of several functions that process string values in some way. The LCase function converts all of the characters in a string to lowercase, while the UCase function converts everything to uppercase. But suppose you're dealing with a database where some users have carelessly entered customer names in a variety of styles. Some names are properly capitalized, some are all lowercase, and some are simply weird.

Now imagine that you need to create a set of reports to send to your customers so that they can see a year-end summary of their orders. You wouldn't want to have the reports look sloppy, with all of that strange capitalization in the customer names, would you?

Well, the StrConv function (refer to Table 13-2) has several options, but its ability to convert strings so that the first letter of each word is capitalized (also known as putting words in *proper case*) is a real life-saver in this scenario. Although this function isn't perfect — names like O'Reilly and McDougal are still problematic — it works wonders for most of the messed up names in your database.

To convert strings to proper case, all you need is to create an expression like this one (substituting the name of the field containing your customer names for *FullName*):

```
=StrConv([FullName],vbProperCase)
```

In the example, *vbProperCase* is a Visual Basic *constant* that tells the StrConv function the type of conversion you want to make. You could replace vbProperCase in the expression with the number 3 because that's the actual value of the constant, but using the constant makes your expression a little easier to understand. The Access help file lists several other constants you can use with the StrConv function.

Finding the largest, smallest, and average values

You can probably think of several instances in which you'd like a report to show the largest, smallest, or average values — either in the report as a whole or in each record group. If so, some of the built-in functions can help here, too. The following expressions show the maximum, minimum, and average values in a field named LowEst:

```
=Max([LowEst])
=Min([LowEst])
=Avg([LowEst])
```

Where you place the expression is the key to how many records are analyzed. Place the expression in the group footer to give group results or in the report footer to give results for the entire report.

Trimming off extra spaces

Extra spaces can creep into strings pretty easily. A user might accidentally press the Spacebar or you might concatenate some values and inadvertently add some extra spaces along the way. Access offers several functions to get rid of the excess so that your reports look a bit neater.

The LTrim, RTrim, and Trim functions all seem like excellent candidates for this task — and they are, if the extra spaces you want to remove are at the beginning or end of the string. But if you want to tighten up a report by removing extra spaces somewhere in the middle of a string, you need to use the Replace function. The following expression looks in a field named Description for instances of two spaces; it replaces the two spaces with a single space:

```
=Replace([Description],"  "," ")
```

In order to make this expression work correctly, make sure that you include two spaces between the first set of double quotes and only one space between the second set. Separate the two sets of quotation marks with a comma (and no spaces).

Having some fun with functions

The function I mention here probably won't be very useful on most of your reports, but it can provide a few moments of fun. You might find it especially handy for reports you print on April Fool's Day.

Of course, I'm talking about the `StrReverse` function. You can use it to reverse all of the characters in a string so that *Underdahl* becomes *lhadrednU*. If you play this trick correctly and can keep a straight face, you might even be able to get the day off by claiming that you have to go and get some recharge fluid for your printer's "character order generator." After all, without a refill, everything comes out backwards.

Here's the expression to reverse the characters in the `Description` field:

```
=StrReverse([Description])
```

To pull off this trick successfully, you may also want to use the function on all of the titles in the report, too.

Rounding numbers

If you have values in your database that are the result of calculations, you need to be aware that setting the display format of a number doesn't change the underlying value, and sometimes the underlying values don't quite match what's shown in a report. For example, suppose you create a report that generates customer invoices and the invoices include a 15% buyer's premium on each item.

It's entirely possible that the order total shown on the report won't exactly match the individual item amounts shown on the report because numbers have been rounded. For example, if the bid is $125.75, a 15% buyer's premium is exactly $18.8625, but appears as $18.86 on the invoice. If you have three items like that, the total on the invoice won't precisely match the totals of the individual items as shown on the invoice. To fix this problem, use the `Round` function. This function rounds the values displayed on the report according to your specifications (to the nearest integer, to two decimal places, and so on). The following expression rounds the values to two decimal places for the `WinningBid` field after the buyer's premium is added:

```
=Round(([WinningBid]*1.15),2)
```

The `Fix` and `Int` functions convert values to the nearest integer and can be useful in some instances. As noted in Table 13-2, these two functions differ in the way they treat negative numbers. The `Abs` function doesn't round numbers, but it strips off a negative sign if it's there and makes all numbers into positive values.

Chapter 14

When Reports Go Wrong . . .

A report that has problems can be a real nightmare. You depend on reports to be accurate, but if something does go wrong with the report you're lucky if it's only a small inconvenience. Remember, if you find an error, that things could always be worse — you could have sent out printed copies of a really messed up and incorrect report without knowing it!

A few miscues such as poor layout, bad formatting choices, and even too many labels can mess up your carefully created report designs if you aren't careful. It's important to take an objective look at your reports before you inflict them on anyone else so that you don't mislead readers or look like you haven't got a clue.

This chapter focuses on helping you find and correct various types of report problems. These issues can range all the way from missing data to poor, confusing, or paper-wasting layouts. Even if you aren't having any report problems right now, read this chapter so that you can avoid problems in the future.

Troubleshooting Reports

Troubleshooting is a process that requires a different type of thinking than you use when you're creating reports. When you're involved in the creative process, you're thinking about what you can do to make the report useful and attractive. But when you're troubleshooting, you're probably at least a little frustrated because things don't seem to be working quite the way you expect.

Figuring out whether the report is really wrong

Keep one fact in mind when a report doesn't give you quite the results that you expected — perhaps there's nothing at all wrong with your report. Maybe you're expecting results that simply aren't supported by the data. For example, I'd love to have a report tell me that my business made a couple of million dollars in profits last month, but the report would have to be based on totally bogus data to show those kinds of results!

Before you set off to find out what's wrong with your report, step back and consider whether the report is correct, but your assumptions aren't. One way to do this is to open the underlying table in Datasheet view and then look to see what you find there. Alternatively, you might need to open a query (if your report is based on a query) and switch the query to Datasheet view. After you've verified the accuracy of the data you're in a better position to determine whether you really need to do some report troubleshooting.

Figuring out what's wrong with the report

If you've determined that there's nothing wrong with the data but your report isn't producing the results that you expect, it's time to figure out what is actually wrong with the report. You can break the problem down into one of two areas — report layout errors or missing data.

Correcting layout problems

Any number of layout problems can afflict your reports. You can end up with a report that is hard to understand, misleading, or even incomplete. Here are just a few of these types of layout problems:

- **Using the field names for labels:** This is fine if you've created field names that are a single, real word that accurately describes the contents of the field (something like `Name` is a fine label). But using labels like `LowEst`, `CustName`, or `OrdDt` probably isn't a very good idea — especially if you plan on showing the report to someone else (like your banker).

- **Using unlabeled fields:** This practice is a good way to save paper, but unless it's obvious which data is being displayed in each of the fields, expect that people reading the report will make errors and incorrect assumptions.

- ✔ **Not lining up field boxes with the correct labels:** If you've gotten creative in rearranging the report's layout, make sure that related field boxes and labels line up properly. Otherwise it's easy to associate the wrong label with a field. And don't forget that subtotals and totals should almost certainly be aligned with the data that they're summarizing in the detail section.

  If you have many summary fields, you can always number them so that readers can tell at a glance what material is being summarized, and where the summary falls in the sequence.

- ✔ **Making field boxes that are too narrow to fully display the data:** You can mislead readers if data doesn't fit completely in the boxes meant to contain it. For example, if you have a text box that's only wide enough to show values under 100, readers won't know when there are values above 100 in the report.

- ✔ **Putting fields too close to the edge of the paper:** Most printers cannot print to the edge of a sheet of paper, so fields that are too close to the edge can be truncated. Access warns you if you try to print and some fields are too close to the edge, but most computer users are pretty good about ignoring warnings!

See the section, "Avoiding Bad Report Layouts," a bit later in this chapter, for some help resolving report layout problems.

Correcting missing data problems

If you have a report that appears to be correct, but which simply isn't showing certain data when you run the report, there are a number of possible causes. If you've already checked the obvious one — that the data doesn't really exist, you might want to check the properties for the field, as shown in Figure 14-1. (You can display the Properties dialog box by right-clicking the field and choosing Properties from the pop-up menu or by selecting the field and clicking the Properties button on the toolbar.) What you want to see is that the field is visible.

You should make certain that the Visible property is set to Yes, of course. This setting can be a little confusing because even if the Visible property is set to No, the field still appears in Design view. It's only when you switch to Report view that the field disappears if the property is set to No.

The label for a field and the field itself both have a Visible property. As a result, the field label can appear when you run the report, but the data can be hidden.

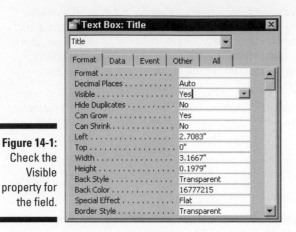

Figure 14-1:
Check the
Visible
property for
the field.

Avoiding Bad Report Layouts

Throughout this book, I mention on numerous occasions the various report layout issues that you need to be aware of. In the following sections you get a quick look at a few points that you might have missed along the way.

Considering the purpose of your report

Sure, it's pretty obvious that the primary purpose of any report is to present some data. After all, why even bother going to all the work to create and print a report if the report doesn't say anything?

What I'm talking about here is something beyond simply presenting some data in a report. That is, I'm suggesting that you consider both the ultimate goal of producing your report *and* the target audience.

Here are some examples of what I mean:

✔ **Going overboard with formatting and style is a bad idea.** If you're creating a report that will serve a very formal function, don't create a report that uses a different page layout than the rest of your proposal. Perhaps the report is just a single component of a business plan that you plan on presenting to your banker or other potential backers. If you have a cover letter that's printed in standard portrait mode, format your Access report so that it fits into portrait mode, too.

✔ **Orienting the page layout to landscape can make all the difference.** A report that you create for a business brainstorming session might need to include more information than many other types of reports, so using the landscape printing option could be your best choice. This layout also enables better note taking (or doodling) during the meeting.

✔ **Cutting to the chase is usually a good idea.** Remember that people are often busy, so you might want to create a summary report that skips most of the fine details. This is especially true if you're dealing with the type of executive who just wants to know the bottom line without being bothered with the trivia.

The real point here is simply that a report layout that is perfect in one case could be a bad choice in another. Consider your audience when designing your reports.

Avoiding text box data overflow

As I mention earlier in this chapter, creating an otherwise perfectly good-looking report that contains deceptive field boxes can be a disaster. Figure 14-2 shows an example of a report that contains two text boxes that are both bound to the same database field. You've got two very different views of the same record.

Figure 14-2:
Both text boxes are bound to the **Description** field.

In this example, the upper text box can display the entire contents of the field, but the lower text box can't. Figure 14-3 shows why the lower text box cannot show the entire value.

Figure 14-3:
The Can
Grow
property
controls
vertical
expansion
for a report
field.

If the Can Grow property is set to the default of Yes, the text box (or any report control or section) automatically expands vertically if necessary to display the entire contents of the field. The related Can Shrink property allows the text box to contract vertically.

There is no property that allows a control to grow or shrink horizontally. As a result, fields with numeric values can be truncated even if the Can Grow property for the field is set to Yes.

Avoiding page overflow

You can have problems with data overflowing the edges of the report if your design is too wide to fit the paper. As Figure 14-4 shows, getting too close to the edge is easy to do if you try to fit too many fields into a tabular report design — even if you switch to landscape layout. In many cases this can also result in blank pages when you print, too.

If you use the Report Wizard, be sure that the Adjust Field Width So All Fields Fit on a Page check box is selected to reduce the chances of your report design being too wide.

One way to avoid making your report design too wide to fit the paper is to stack fields vertically. Unfortunately, this solution can create more problems if you're not very careful with the layout. Here are some considerations:

✔ If you have fields that might need to expand vertically to fit the data, place those fields so that no other fields are directly below them in the design.

✔ If you need to allow several fields to grow vertically, be sure to place them across the page so that none of them will interfere with each other.

The ruler shows that this report is too wide to fit the paper.

Figure 14-4: This report design is too wide to print properly.

Formatting data in reports

Your Access databases can contain a number of different types of data, of course. In most cases, this diversity causes no problems, but because a few of the data types have alternate formatting options, it's possible to cause real confusion by choosing inappropriate formatting.

Here's the rundown on the properties to keep an eye on:

✔ **Format property:** The Format property's most confusing data types are Number, Date/Time, and Currency. If you choose the wrong format for a text box that displays one of these data types on a report, you could confuse or even mislead anyone who reads the report.

Figure 14-5 shows the formatting options that are available in the Format Property drop-down list on the Format tab of the Properties dialog box.

✔ **Decimal Places property:** This property controls the number of digits that are shown to the right of the decimal point. Here, too, an inappropriate choice can be awfully confusing.

Figure 14-5:
Choosing
the wrong
number
format can
cause real
confusion.

Although you can specify up to 15 decimal places, if your values are set to the Currency data type, your numbers are only accurate to 4 decimal places. Displaying more than 4 digits to the right of the decimal point for Currency values could imply that values are being calculated to a higher degree of accuracy than is actually the case.

Eliminating Unnecessary Labels for Tighter Reports

Labels are report elements that you can love and hate at the same time. Sure, labels do help people to understand what they're seeing in a report, but labels can also eat up an awful lot of space, making reports use far more paper than is really necessary.

By default, Access labels all the fields you add to a report. The field names are used as the labels, but you can easily change the text to suit your needs. If you use a Report Wizard to create a report that uses grouping, the wizard places the labels in the group header directly above the position of the field box in the detail section.

Deciding whether you really need all those labels

Labels aren't always necessary, and in some cases they're downright undesirable. On the left side of Figure 14-6, you can see the default, labeled layout created by the Report Wizard; a much more compact, unlabeled layout appears on the right side. As long as the data is readily understandable, most readers won't have any difficulty understanding the unlabeled data.

Labeled and Unlabeled

OWNERID	Undl
OWNERFIRSTNAME	Brian
OWNERLASTNAME	Underdahl
COMPANYNAME	Underdahl Computing
ADDRESS	123 Dirt Road
CITY	Bodie Flats
STATE	NV
ZIP	89889

Undl
Brian   Underdahl
Underdahl Computing
123 Dirt Road
Bodie Flats   NV   89889

Page: |◄ ◄   187   ► ►| ◄

Figure 14-6:
This report
shows that
labels aren't
always
necessary.

Deleting labels

You may be surprised to discover that Access doesn't have a property that controls whether a field is labeled on a report. This means that deleting labels can be just a bit tricky. Because the field's label and the field's text box display the same text in Design view (unless you've modified the label, of course), you need to make sure you delete the right thing. To delete a label (and leave the text box), you must first click within the label (which is to the left of the text box) and then choose Edit⇨Delete or press the Delete key.

Moving labels to headers

In some cases, you can save some space on a report by moving the labels to one of the headers. The page headers and any group headers are certainly good candidates for placing the labels in many types of reports. Both locations offer certain advantages. Determine which location works best by experimenting with the possibilities.

Your decision should be based on the functions of your report and the needs of your audience.

If you're used to rearranging your report designs by using drag-and-drop methods, you'll quickly discover that you're out of luck when you try this method to move labels from the detail section to one of the headers. That's because Access automatically moves the entire field — the label and the text box — as a unit when you use drag and drop.

To move a field to the header without taking the text box with it, you need to use the cut-and-paste method.

Part V

Way Cool
Advanced Queries,
Forms, and Reports

The 5th Wave   By Rich Tennant

"No it's not a dip in sales. It's just a corn chip that
got photocopied into the document."

In this part . . .

This part takes your Access skills and bumps them up to a whole new level by showing you advanced techniques for queries, forms, and reports. Here you discover some really cool tricks that take Access well beyond the ordinary. In addition, this part shows you a number of Access add-ons that can solve many of the problems you may encounter while putting Access through its paces.

Chapter 15

Tricks for Finding Data with Queries

. . . .

. . . .

Queries can be almost magical things in the ways that they enable you to almost instantly find data that's hidden somewhere in a database. The old saying about finding a needle in a haystack really does describe the kind of power that you can wield if you know the right query tricks. For example, by moving beyond ordinary query techniques, you can find records that fall within a range of values, locate records that are similar, and create queries that politely ask you what you want to find instead of always returning the same set of records. You can even create queries that toss out the junk so you can focus on the truly meaningful results.

A few new tricks can help turn ordinary queries into powerhouses that do far more than you might expect. From returning a range of records, to asking what you want, and finally to paring down the results so you're not swamped with useless information, bumping your queries up to the next level makes you far more efficient.

This chapter shows you how to use these advanced techniques to create queries that can find those lost needles in your haystack of data. You are sure to find that these tricks end up saving you a whole lot of time and frustration in the future.

Finding Just the Data You Need

Plain-vanilla, everyday queries are fine when your needs aren't very complex and you just want to find a simple set of records. But sometimes, your needs are more complex and a simple query simply isn't going to do it. In the following sections, you see how to create more complex queries that return a range of records instead of simply delivering a set of records that match a specific criterion. You also discover how to tell Access that you want to find records based on some inexact criteria.

Getting to know the operators

You can use a number of *operators* in expressions. Unfortunately, Access doesn't exactly make it easy for you find the operators that you can use (or understand how they work). Table 15-1 explains several of the operators that you may find useful in your queries.

Table 15-1	Some Useful Operators for Queries
Operator	*Description*
–	Subtracts one value from another or makes a value negative.
&	Concatenates two strings.
*	Multiplies two numbers.
/	Divides one number by a second number.
\	Produces an integer by rounding both numbers to integers and then dividing the first number by the second number, and dropping any fraction.
^	Raises a number to a power.
+	Adds two values.
<	Less than.
<=	Less than or equal to.
<>	Not equal.
=	Equal to.
>	Greater than.

Operator	Description
>=	Greater than or equal to.
AND	Returns True when both expressions are true.
Between	Determines whether a numeric or date value falls within a range.
Eqv	Returns True when both expressions are true or both expressions are false.
In(string1, string2...)	Determines whether a string value is one of a set of string values.
Is Null	Returns True if a value is Null.
Like "pattern"	Matches string values by using the wildcards ? and *.
Mod	Divides the first number by the second number and returns the remainder.
Not	Returns True when the expression is not true.
OR	Returns True when either expression is true.
Xor	Returns True when either expression is true and the other expression is false.

You probably won't use all the operators shown in Table 15-1, but they certainly do give you many options. You can see a number of these operators in action in the examples that follow in this chapter.

Selecting a range of records

You already know how to create a query that finds records that are an exact match for a specific value. But what if you want to find a range of records, such as all the orders you received between July 1 and the end of December? You can use several different methods for finding these records, but most of them are simply too much work and you run the risk of accidentally missing some of them if you try to locate them manually. Besides, why not let your PC do the work? That's what it's there for.

To find a range of records, you need to use an *expression*. You place this expression in the Criteria text box in the Query Design window. That is, your expression takes the place of the single value that you ordinarily place in the Criteria text box.

Selecting a range of records with greater than and less than operators

As you might guess, there often is more than one way to create an expression to select a range of records. Figure 15-1 shows two different methods for specifying a range of values in expressions.

Figure 15-1:
This query
uses two
different
methods to
specify a
range of
values.

In Figure 15-1, the expression for the selection criteria for the ItemID field uses the greater than (>), And, and less than (<) operators:

```
>16008 And <16020
```

In English, this expression means "the value must be greater than 16008 and less than 16020."

Selecting a range of records with Between operators

The expression for the DateReceived field selection criteria uses the Between and the AND operators:

```
Between #7/1/2004# And #12/31/2004#
```

This second expression is easy to understand, but you need to be clear about a couple of items:

- ✔ **Date values must be enclosed in pound signs (#).** Otherwise, Access won't think you're entering a mathematical expression.

- ✔ **The Between operator works like the greater than or equal to (>=) and less than or equal to (<=) operators.** That is, the values that you specify with the Between operator are included in the range of values that are selected when you run the query.

Figure 15-2 shows the results of running the query shown in Figure 15-1. Notice that all the 11 selected records satisfy both the sets of criteria (the final row that shows `AutoNumber` in the `ItemID` field is not a record in the table — it is a placeholder for a new record with the default value of the current date).

Figure 15-2:
Running
the query
selects a
range of
records that
match both
criteria.

Switching between the **AND** *operator and the* **OR** *operator*

In the previous example, both sets of criteria have to be met in order for a record to be selected. That's the nature of the AND operator; both criteria expressions are on the same row of the design grid, so the two expressions are combined by using the AND operator. The equivalent SQL statement shows how the two are combined:

```
SELECT ItemsTable.ItemID, ItemsTable.DateReceived
FROM ItemsTable
WHERE
    (((ItemsTable.ItemID)>16008
    And (ItemsTable.ItemID)<16020)
AND
    ((ItemsTable.DateReceived)
    Between #7/1/2004#
    And #12/31/2004#));
```

If you move the second expression down a row, as shown in Figure 15-3, you change the query to an OR query, where records that meet either criteria are selected.

Figure 15-3:
Moving the
second
expression
down a row
turns the
AND query
into an OR
query.

This seemingly small change makes a big difference in the final results. As Figure 15-4 shows, the record counter now indicates that instead of 11 matching records, 3,003 records now meet one or the other of the two criteria.

Figure 15-4:
Running the
OR query
results in
many more
matching
records.

Here's what the modified query looks like. I've made only one small change — the AND in line 6 is changed to OR:

```
SELECT ItemsTable.ItemID, ItemsTable.DateReceived
FROM ItemsTable
WHERE
    (((ItemsTable.ItemID)>16008
    And (ItemsTable.ItemID)<16020)
OR
    ((ItemsTable.DateReceived)
    Between #7/1/2004#
    And #12/31/2004#));
```

You can, of course, continue to add additional sets of criteria as needed. For example, you can add another OR clause that also includes one or more AND clauses.

Selecting the top set of records

Say you want to see a list of the top 25 orders for the year. The following SQL query statements can do the trick:

```
SELECT TOP 25
  Customer, OrderNumber, OrderDate
FROM OrdersTable
WHERE OrderYear = 2005
ORDER BY OrderAmount DESC;
```

This example uses a few SQL keywords you may not be familiar with. TOP tells Access that you want to see the top matching records, and 25 is a parameter that says how many of the top records to display. ORDER BY tells Access to sort the results, and DESC says to use descending order (you can use ASC to sort in ascending order).

You can add another SQL keyword, PERCENT, to tell Access that you want to see a *percentage* of the records instead of a *specific number* of them. The following modification to the query returns the top 10 percent of the orders:

```
SELECT TOP 10 PERCENT
  Customer, OrderNumber, OrderDate
FROM OrdersTable
WHERE OrderYear = 2005
ORDER BY OrderAmount DESC;
```

To find the bottom set of records, change the sort order to ascending.

Finding data that's close but not exact

Maybe you've heard the old saying that goes something like, "Close only counts in horseshoes and hand grenades." Whoever made that one up didn't know much about finding information in databases, because I can think of many occasions when you might need to find data that's close, but not necessarily right on target.

Understanding why close may be what you need

This may come as a bit of a shock, but many people are poor spellers, bad typists, or both. Well, okay, so maybe this is no big surprise to you, but the end result can be errors in your databases; as a result, your queries that depend on exact matches may fail to find all the records that you want.

For example, suppose you have a customer named Dee Anderson, and she's asked for a listing of all of her orders for an insurance estimate. You may know that her orders were entered by several people over the years, and you may not be sure that everyone always spelled her name the same way. What if some of the orders were listed under Dee Andersen, De Anderson, or even D Andersen? That's why you need to be able to find close matches — so that you can be sure to find all the possible variations.

Using the Like operator with wildcards

To find close matches that don't necessarily make an exact match, you can use the `Like` operator along with the asterisk (*) and question mark (?) wildcards. To find the variations on Dee Anderson, use the following criteria expression:

```
Like "D* Anders?n"
```

In this example both the asterisk and question mark wildcards help you create an inexact match. Here's how each of the two wildcards function:

✔ The asterisk matches any number of characters. All these names would be caught by the asterisk: Dee, Deborah, Deeana, Derek. It doesn't matter how many letters are in the name.

✔ The question mark matches exactly one character. In this instance, it catches any record that has the last name Anderson, Andersen.

✔ Together, however, the two wildcards work like the AND operator. All the Deborahs, Deeanas, and Dereks are eliminated from the search if their last names aren't Andersen or Anderson.

Now, suppose you wanted to find every customer whose name included the word auction somewhere in the company name. The following criteria expression would do the trick:

```
Like "*auction*"
```

Access isn't *case sensitive*. When you run a query by using inexact matching, `Like "*auction*"` produces the same results as `Like "*Auction*"`.

Using other operators for inexact matches

You can use other operators to create inexact matches, too. For example, suppose you want to find all orders from customers whose company name doesn't include the word auction. The following expression does the trick:

```
Not "*auction*"
```

You could also find all customers whose last name starts with the letter U or later using the following expression:

```
>="U"
```

Notice that in this example you don't need to use a wildcard, because the expression already says *find all records that are greater than or equal to U,* automatically including any records where additional characters follow the first U.

Creating Queries That Ask What to Find

Creating a great query that finds the set of records you want isn't too difficult after you get the hang of it, but most queries suffer from one problem — they're set up to always return a set of records that match predefined criteria. After you create a query, that same set of criteria is used every time you run the query until you open the query in Design view and edit the criteria. That's probably not a very good option for queries that you're setting up for use by the average Access user. To get more flexibility in your searches, try parameter queries.

Understanding parameter queries

As an alternative to using a query that uses specific, set criteria to select a group of records, you can create a *parameter* query. As Figure 15-5 shows, when a user runs a parameter query, Access displays the Enter Parameter Value dialog box and prompts the user to specify the criteria to use in the query.

Figure 15-5:
A parameter query asks which records you want to find.

Enter Parameter Value	?	X

Enter Company Name

OK	Cancel

You aren't limited to asking the user to enter the criteria for a single field in a parameter query. You can request as many parameters as necessary.

Parameter queries enable you to make a query flexible, but this flexibility comes at a price. Parameter queries only accept exact, matching values, so they return empty results unless you enter a value that completely matches the value in the field for one or more records. You can't use wildcards or expressions in the Enter Parameter Value dialog box. Access won't display an error message if you do use wildcards or expressions — it simply won't return any records.

Building your very own parameter query

You can turn an ordinary query into a parameter query pretty easily. You may even have done so inadvertently in the past when you were experimenting with queries and wondered why that darn Enter Parameter Value dialog box popped up when you tried to run the query.

To make a query into a parameter query, enter the prompt that you want to display (enclosed in square brackets) in the Enter Parameter Value dialog box in the Criteria text box of the query design. Figure 15-6 shows an example of the query design that displays the prompt shown in Figure 15-5.

Figure 15-6:
Enter the prompt in square brackets in the Criteria text box to create a parameter query.

Field:	MailingListID	OrganizationName
Table:	Company List	Company List
Sort:		
Show:	☑	☑
Criteria:		[Enter Company Name]
or:		

If you want the user to specify multiple criteria, you can simply enter the additional prompts in the Query Design grid, but if you do, Access displays the prompts in the order that they appear (left-to-right) in the Design grid. You may want to display the prompts in a different order. To do so, you use the Query Parameters dialog box, as shown in Figure 15-7.

Figure 15-7:
The Query
Parameters
dialog box
enables you
to specify
the order for
the prompts.

Parameter	Data Type
[Company?]	Text
[Order Date?]	Date/Time

Query Parameters

OK   Cancel

To use the Query Parameters dialog box to specify the order for the prompts, follow these steps:

1. **First create the prompts in the Design grid.**

2. **Choose Query➪Parameters.**

   The Query Parameters dialog box appears.

3. **Enter the prompts in the Parameter column exactly as they appear in the Design grid.**

   Enter the prompts in the order that you want them to display when the query is executed.

4. **Choose the appropriate Data Type for each of the prompts.**

   This must match the data type that is used in the table.

5. **Click OK.**

   The Query Parameters dialog box closes and you're returned to the Query design.

Chapter 17 shows another technique that might be even more useful in some cases than parameter queries. *Lookup lists* enable users to select a value from a list, thus eliminating the possibility of typing errors.

Excluding Data You Don't Want

You've probably struggled with query results that were too inclusive. Sometimes having too many results is almost worse than not getting as many results as you might like. After all, when you're looking for a specific record, you probably don't want to have to wade through a couple of hundred of them that were returned by an overexuberant query.

Eliminating duplicates from results

Most Access databases use *indexes* to prevent tables from being loaded with duplicate records. As a result, queries that include all the fields from a table typically don't return results that are complete duplicates across every field. The problem arises when you create a query that uses only some of the fields — in particular, in the type of query that you're most likely to create.

You might decide to eliminate duplicate results when you run a query for any number of reasons. Here are just a few examples:

- ✔ If you're trying to figure out where it would be most effective to advertise, you might want your query to display a list of cities where you have customers. You probably are likely to find this type of list most useful if San Francisco is listed once rather than 392 times.

- ✔ If you want to know which customers have placed orders in the past six months, a list with one result for each active customer is probably what you want.

- ✔ If you're sitting down with a consultant to brainstorm about what to include in your upcoming TV advertisement, you may want to give the consultant a list showing each type of item that's currently available for sale. Here, too, you'd want one result for each type, not one for every item.

- ✔ Finally, if your club is going to hold an election soon and you need a list of potential candidates, you might want to create a list that shows the names of members who have attended at least one meeting in the past year. You don't want to sift through multiple listings for your most active members.

Finding duplicates with SQL queries

The easiest and most straightforward way to find the records you want without including all the duplicates is to use a SQL query. You can use two SQL keywords to eliminate duplicates from the results:

- ✔ **DISTINCT:** Use this keyword to examine the fields that you've included in the query to determine whether the records are duplicates. Generally, you should use DISTINCT to return the smallest set of records.

- ✔ **DISTINCTROW:** Use this keyword when you want to examine all the fields, not just those included in the query, to determine if records are duplicates. Use DISTINCTROW when your query uses multiple tables.

The following example uses DISTINCT to return a list of cities where you have customers:

```
SELECT DISTINCT
City
FROM Customers
ORDER BY City;
```

Here's an example that lists the active members in your club, using DISTINCTROW to look at two tables, Members and Events:

```
SELECT DISTINCTROW MemberName
FROM Members INNER JOIN Events
ON Members.MemberID = Events.MemberID
ORDER BY MemberName;
```

If your database doesn't use an index and you find that it's a real mess due to duplicate records, you might want to use DISTINCTROW to find one instance of each of the duplicates and then use a make-table query to create a new table by using the unique records. Be sure to apply an index to the new table to prevent it from becoming loaded with duplicates.

Modifying join properties to get the results you want

Sometimes you may need to modify the type of join that's used in a query in order to get the results you want. If you skipped over some of the earlier chapters, you might not realize why the type of join is so important to eliminating the records you don't want from the query results. See Chapter 8 for more on joins.

You can use any of the three types of joins in an Access query:

- *Inner joins* include all matching records from both of the joined tables. This is the default join.

- *Left outer joins* include all the records from the left-side table even if no matching records appear in the right-side table.

- *Right outer joins* include all the records from the right-side table even if no matching records appear in the left-side table.

Using the wrong type of join can lead to results that you don't want. You need to choose a join type that actually makes sense. If necessary, sit down and consider what results you want and see whether the join type that you specify returns those results. Access is perfectly happy to give you meaningless results if that's what you ask for.

Although you can use the Join Properties dialog box to change the relationships between tables, the most straightforward way to change the join type that is used in a query is to edit the SQL statements in SQL view. To do so, open your query in Design view and then switch to SQL view by choosing View➪SQL View or by right-clicking on the query and choosing SQL View from the pop-up menu.

When you have the query open in SQL view, simply replace the join type that is specified in the SQL statements with the join type you want to use. For example, the following shows the members and events example (see "Finding duplicates with SQL queries," earlier in this chapter) changed from an inner join to a left outer join:

```
SELECT DISTINCTROW MemberName
FROM Members LEFT OUTER JOIN Events
ON Members.MemberID = Events.MemberID
ORDER BY MemberName;
```

Chapter 16

Tricks for Updating with Queries

- -

In This Chapter

▶ Using queries to create new fields

▶ Changing default values

▶ Crunching numbers with queries

▶ Choosing the right query for the job

▶ Updating records with multiple tables

- -

Queries can do far more than simply find records that match specific criteria. You can also use queries to update data, add new fields, and fix certain problems in existing databases. You can even use a query to modify the data in a table, using information from another table. This chapter shows you the tricks and techniques you need to know to do all these tasks quickly and easily.

The queries I discuss in this chapter, action queries, make changes directly to your database. These changes can be to your data, to the structure of your tables, or both. Be very careful so that you don't put an important database at risk while you're trying out the tricks you discover in this chapter. In fact, why not back up your database right now.

Creating New Fields with a Query

If you've worked with Access for any length of time, you've no doubt encountered many instances when you discovered that a particular table would be far more useful if only it had another field or two. Maybe you forgot to include a field to indicate whether a club member was active, or maybe you discovered that your Items table really needed a field to indicate products that are considered hazardous materials. Whatever the case may be, you can use queries to add these fields.

Deciding whether using a query to add fields is worth it

If you've decided that a table needs a new field, the natural reaction is to simply open the table in Design view and add the field. That's easy enough to do, of course, but sometimes getting a bit creative and using a query instead is worth the effort.

For example, consider the following reasons why you might want to add the field by using a query instead of adding it in Design view:

✔ When you add a new field to an existing table in Design view, that field is empty for all the existing records. By using a query you can add default values to the field as you add it to the table.

✔ If the values in the new field will result from a calculation that is performed when a user opens the record in a form, you can save time and effort. Instead of opening every existing record after you've added the new field in order to update the field values, write your query to perform the calculations and load the proper values into the existing records automatically.

✔ If the values for the new field already exist in another table, you can use a query to extract the values from the other table and add them to the proper records in the existing table.

If none of these conditions apply in your case, you'll obviously spend far less time adding the new field in Design view. You're also far less likely to make an error adding the field in Design view simply because of the various prompts that Access provides when you're modifying a table in Design view. Sometimes the simplest way of doing something really is the best way!

Adding your first field with a query

To add fields to an existing table by using a query, you need to turn to SQL-specific queries. (If you need a bit of SQL review, take a look at Chapter 7 before continuing.)

Access SQL provides two different *Data Definition Language* statements that you can use to add fields to a table. The CREATE TABLE statement creates a whole new table and you use it for a make-table query.

You don't want to use the CREATE TABLE statement if the target table already exists because if you do, you'll destroy the existing table and any data that it contains — clearly not a move designed to make your day!

To add a field to an existing table, you use the ALTER TABLE statement, as in the following example:

```
ALTER TABLE ItemsTable
ADD COLUMN NewDesc TEXT(50) NOT NULL;
```

This SQL query tells Access to alter the table named ItemsTable by adding a field (column) named NewDesc. The new field will be a text field 50 characters long, and users must make an entry in the field when they add any new records.

See the section, "Adding Default Values by Using a Query," later in this chapter, to see how to add default values to the new field without overwriting any existing data.

Don't attempt to run the ALTER TABLE query more than once unless you remove the new field from the table's design between runs because you'll encounter errors if you try to run the query again. The reason for this odd Access activity is that you cannot apply the NOT NULL statement more than once to the same field.

Here are some other things you can do:

- **Make the new field a key field.** You can also use the CONSTRAINT statement to make the new field into a key field so that the new field can be used in table relationships. Adding a constraint can be a little tricky because you need to remember that a table can only have one primary key — although it can have any number of secondary keys. A primary key does not, however, have to be a single field. You can create primary keys that combine the values in several fields.

- **Build an index.** Instead of adding a constraint, you may want to add an index for the new field you've added to the table. Adding an index can make table lookups faster because Access doesn't have to search all the records to find a value in an indexed field.

    You use the CREATE INDEX statement to add an index. Here's an example of how to add an index that is sorted in ascending order for the new NewDesc field:

    ```
    CREATE INDEX Index1
    ON ItemsTable (NewDesc) ASC;
    ```

    You can also create a unique index by adding the UNIQUE keyword between CREATE and INDEX. However, this may not be a wise choice in many cases because a unique index requires that each record contain unique vales in the field. That's probably not what you'd want for a 50-character text field because you may have more than one item with the same description.

You can only add one field at a time with the ALTER TABLE statement. You'll need additional queries if you want to add additional fields — this might be an excellent reason to consider mastering a bit of VBA programming (see Chapter 7) so that you can combine several ALTER TABLE and UPDATE queries into a single procedure.

Adding Default Values by Using a Query

As you build upon your ALTER TABLE queries, you may reach a point at which you want to add default values to the new fields. By adding default values you can be sure that any rules you've established — such as requiring that the field not contain blank entries — are enforced.

Getting to know what you can add

You can't add just any old value to a field by using a query. You do have to follow the rules even if it is your own database. Before you create a query to add values to a table, consider the following factors that might affect what you can do:

- ✔ **The data must be the proper type for the field.** You can't, for example, add text to a Date/Time field.

- ✔ **If you've set any rules restricting the values that can be entered in a field, your query must also follow those same rules.** You can't add data that is outside the range of acceptable values.

- ✔ **If you've set a field as a primary key or as a unique index, your data must be different for each record.** Trying to set default values for these types of fields by using a query isn't a good idea, simply because generating unique values is going to be really hard.

Adding default values to your very first field

If you use a query to add a new field to a table, the new field will be empty in all the existing records, of course. So your next step is to add a default value to the field. To do so, you can use a simple update query, as shown in Figure 16-1.

Figure 16-1:
This query
sets the
default
value for the
new field.

If you prefer to work in SQL view, the following SQL statements are the equivalent update query:

```
UPDATE ItemsTable
SET ItemsTable.NewDesc = "Needs Description";
```

See Chapter 17 for tips on running queries by attaching them to buttons you add to forms. This can be an excellent way to ensure that both the ALTER TABLE and UPDATE queries are run consecutively.

Making sure you don't override real data

Unfortunately, the query example shown in Figure 16-1 presents one little problem in the real world — you're overriding real data. You can remedy this situation by modifying the update query as shown here:

```
UPDATE ItemsTable
SET ItemsTable.NewDesc = "Needs Description"
WHERE (((ItemsTable.NewDesc) Is Null));
```

In this second version of the query the NewDesc field in the table ItemsTable is given a value of "Needs Description" only if the existing field is empty. You might be wondering why this query even bothers with the WHERE clause. You don't really need to use the WHERE clause if you run this second query immediately after the ALTER TABLE query, but suppose you get distracted for a few minutes between running the two queries and someone else begins entering values in the NewDesc field. Oh, the horror! By including the WHERE clause you ensure that you don't destroy any existing values in the field.

Performing Calculations

When you think of performing calculations, you probably don't think of Access queries first. In fact, if you're anything like many Office users I know, you likely start thinking about ways to move your data from Access into Excel to do calculations and don't even give a moment's consideration to doing them in a query.

Determining whether to use a query for your calculations

So why should you buck the trend and use a query for calculations? Why not use your old tried-and-true method? Actually, I can offer several reasons why you might want to consider using a query:

- **Doing calculations by using a query is a lot less work than moving data to Excel and then doing the calculations.** Who needs extra work? And keeping your calculations in one application is so much faster.

- **Unless you're very careful, moving data between applications like Access and Excel increases the risk of errors.** This statement is especially true if you'll need to bring the calculated values back into Access.

- **If you're already comfortable with Excel, the expressions in Access are familiar.** In fact, the expressions you use for calculations in an Access query are almost identical to the formulas you create in Excel.

- **Finally, telling people that you're an Access expressions expert is just a whole lot cooler, isn't it?** Oh, the glory.

Writing your first query calculations

You typically use calculations in queries to either modify existing values in a database or to supply new values where none currently exist. You can create calculations to serve many different purposes.

Adding days to date values

Figure 16-2 shows an update query that uses an expression to add 90 days to the current date in the `ServiceDate` field if that last scheduled service date is earlier than the current date when the query is run. This type of query can be very useful if you run a business and you need to schedule periodic service calls with your customers. You could then run a query daily to produce a list of customers you need to call to set up appointments.

Figure 16-2:
This query
updates
values,
using a
calculation.

When you're working with dates in an expression, remember that integer values represent days and fractional (decimal) values are fractions of days — hours.

Modifying numeric values

Another common way to use calculations is to modify a numeric value. One example of this is to increase the prices of a certain class of products based on increased transportation costs. The following SQL query increases the price of all heavy widgets by five percent:

```
UPDATE Items
SET Items.Price = [Price]*1.05
WHERE ((Items.Class) = "HeavyWidgets");
```

Once again, this example uses criteria (the WHERE clause) to select the items to include in the calculation. Briefly switching to Datasheet view when you use criteria in a query is always a good idea. The switch helps you verify that your query will select the correct set of records. In fact, it's an order.

Summarizing values

In some cases, you may want to create a calculation that returns a summary report of the values in your database. That is also quite easy to do. The following example summarizes the values in the LowEst field of the ItemsTable table and shows both the total for each state and the maximum value for each state:

```
SELECT ItemsTable.State,
   Sum(ItemsTable.LowEst) AS [Sum of LowEst],
   Max(ItemsTable.LowEst) AS [Max of LowEst]
FROM ItemsTable
GROUP BY ItemsTable.State;
```

The following item:

```
Sum(ItemsTable.LowEst) AS [Sum of LowEst]
```

totals the values in the `LowEst` field and displays `Sum of LowEst` as the name at the top of the column. An `AS` clause always specifies how you want the information to be named in the output.

The last line in the statement:

```
GROUP BY ItemsTable.State;
```

tells Access to group the results based on the values in the `State` field. The two summary values are summarized by state. If you don't include the `GROUP BY` clause in the query, the summaries include all the values in the table. You can see what this query looks like in Design view in Figure 16-3.

Figure 16-3:
The summary query in Design View.

Updating Records by Using Data from Another Table

Relational databases are efficient for many different reasons, and one of those reasons is that the data is typically split up over several related tables. While this arrangement makes your Access database easier to maintain, it also makes sharing data with other applications, such as Excel, just a bit harder. So why not create a table that combines information from several tables if you intend to share that data?

Even if you don't need to share your Access data with other applications, you may well need to update records in one table with information from another table. Suppose, for example, that you sell a line of products that are manufactured by the Giant Kazoo Company and the good people at Giant Kazoo just sent you a new Access database containing the latest legal disclaimer statements for each of the company's products. To avoid problems, you have to add those statements to the product descriptions in your database, but because you sell several hundred different Giant Kazoo products, updating everything manually is going to be awfully tedious. Well, this, too, is a perfect place to use a query that updates records in one table by using information that's contained in a different table.

Choosing the right type of query for your updates

In order to update records in one table with data from another table, you need to use an update query, of course. But this query must include both of the tables, and the tables must be properly joined. If you aren't quite up to speed on using multiple tables in a query and making sure that they're properly joined, you may want to review Chapters 5 and 8 before you continue.

Updating data in one table with data from another without any conditions

The simplest example of updating data in one table with data from another table would be if you're just updating the records without applying any conditions other than that you update the correct records. Sure, this condition might seem obvious, but if you consider how the tables are joined, you realize that the join is the key to making sure that the correct records are updated.

To update records without any conditions, you create a query that adds the value from the `TypeName` field in the `TypeTable` table to the `NewItemType` field in the `ItemsTable` table. You might want to do something like this if you're creating a new table so that you can export the data for use in Excel or Word. Remember to link the two tables before you begin these steps.

To create the query, follow these steps:

1. **Double-click Create Query in Design View in the Queries list.**

   The Query editor and the Show Table dialog box appear.

2. **Add the** ItemsTable **and** TypeTable **tables to the Query design and then close the Show Table dialog box.**

   Make sure that the query design shows that the two tables are linked before you continue.

3. **Choose Query⇨Update Query to change the query from a select query into an update query.**

   You can also click the Query Type button on the toolbar and choose Update Query from the drop-down list.

4. **In the first column of the Query Design grid, select** ItemsTable. NewItemType **as the name of the field to update.**

   This action places NewItemType in the Field text box and ItemsTable in the Table text box.

5. **Enter the expression** [TypeTable].[TypeName] **in the Update To text box in the first column.**

   Your query now looks similar to Figure 16-4.

Figure 16-4:
The finished query updates one table with data from another table.

6. **Save and name the query.**

7. **Choose Query⇨Run or click the Run button on the toolbar.**

   Access displays a message box telling you how many records will be updated.

8. **Click Yes to update the records.**

This simple example updates all the records in the ItemsTable table, but that might not be what you want to do. Suppose that you only want to update the records where the State value is Nevada and the TypeName value is Mining. Now you have a slightly more complicated task because you need to specify two criteria that apply to two different tables. Because both criteria must be satisfied, you need to use an AND clause to join them.

The SQL statement equivalent of what you just saw

If you prefer to work in SQL view, you can create the query listed in the previous steps (see the previous section, "Updating data in one table with data from another without any conditions") by using the following SQL statement:

```
UPDATE TypeTable
INNER JOIN ItemsTable ON
   TypeTable.TypeID =
      ItemsTable.TypeID
   SET ItemsTable.NewItemType =
      TypeTable.TypeName;
```

If you're a little confused by the SQL statement, don't worry. The layout of this statement simply demonstrates that you can accomplish the same goal in more than one way. Here's what you probably expected:

```
UPDATE ItemsTable
```

```
INNER JOIN TypeTable ON
   ItemsTable.TypeID =
      TypeTable.TypeID
   SET ItemsTable.NewItemType =
      TypeTable.TypeName;
```

In reality, both SQL statements do the same thing. When you have a multiple-table update query like this one, the first part of the SQL statement (everything before the keyword SET) simply defines the join properties for the query. So it doesn't matter which of the two tables is listed first as long as you build the join in the same order as the tables are listed. The SET portion of the SQL statement is where the real work gets done, and the order in that portion of the statement is extremely critical!

Figure 16-5 shows how to modify the query to add the two criteria. Notice that in this case, the criteria expression must specify both the names of the tables and the names of the fields because the criteria aren't based on the field that's being updated.

Figure 16-5:
The query now has two criteria that must be satisfied before a record is updated.

If you prefer to keep the query design a bit simpler, you can specify each of the criteria in its own column, as shown in Figure 16-6. Either way, the query returns the same results when you run it.

Figure 16-6:
You can also specify the criteria like this.

In SQL view, the query now looks like this (it doesn't matter if you specify the criteria in the first column as shown in Figure 16-5 or in separate columns as shown in Figure 16-6 — the resulting SQL statement is the same):

```
UPDATE TypeTable
INNER JOIN ItemsTable ON
   TypeTable.TypeID = ItemsTable.TypeID
SET ItemsTable.NewItemType = TypeTable.TypeName
WHERE ((ItemsTable.State="Nevada"
   And TypeTable.TypeName="Mining"));
```

Although these examples left out the square brackets around the table and field names to keep the examples compact, using the square brackets is always safe, and the brackets are required if the table or field names include any spaces.

Making sure the right data is updated

In many cases the field names in the table you want to update and the table where the updates come from are the same. There's nothing wrong with this duplication, but it can cause confusion and that can lead to updating the data in the wrong table if you aren't careful. Generally this is less of a problem if you're working in Design view than in SQL view because in Design view the Table row clearly indicates which table to update.

Before you run a query that updates data in one table with data from another table, be sure to verify that the correct table is shown in the Table row of the column that includes the `Update To` expression. If you're working in SQL view, check to be sure that the table you want to update is on the left side of the equal sign following the `SET` keyword.

Chapter 17

Killer Ways to Improve Forms

*Y*ou need stronger tools than the Form Wizard to create great forms that reduce input errors and make users more efficient. You also need to know how to apply some special tricks and techniques that really take your forms up a step from the ordinary.

That's what this chapter is all about. Here you discover how to give users a clearly defined, limited set of choices so that you can be sure of getting good input. You see how to add macro buttons to automate certain tasks such as printing a report. And you find how to help your users by displaying text prompts to remove confusion they may feel about what sort of input is expected.

You know what they say about an ounce of prevention. . . . Keeping bad data out of the database is a whole lot easier than trying to find it after it gets buried in there.

Prequalifying the Data Entered

Let's face it — life would be a whole lot easier for you as an Access database developer if you didn't have to deal with all those darn users, wouldn't it? Imagine how sweet life would be if you never had to worry about someone making typing errors or coming up with yet another creative bit of data that might fit in the latest fantasy movie, but has no real relationship to reality. Well, that's the point of making sure that data is pre-qualified before it's entered into the database. *Prequalifying* requires setting up parameters that must be fulfilled before data is accepted into a form. If you give users a limited set of choices, you can be pretty sure that you'll end up with usable data. And you won't have to wonder what *maybe* means in the `Taxable` field, either! The two best ways of prequalifying data are to use lookup lists and to set default values.

Creating lookup lists

A *lookup list* is a wonderful invention. Lookup lists enable a user to choose from a set of existing values so that you can be sure that the data that's entered is one of those values.

A lookup list is a control that lists data options. The lookup list is typically added to a form by using a combo box, as shown in Figure 17-1; sometimes people use a list box (see Chapter 9 for a review of the differences between combo boxes and list boxes) for their lookup lists. The list of choices can come from a table, a query, or even be stored in the control itself.

Figure 17-1:
The
`TypeID`
field on this
form is a
lookup list
that's in a
combo box.

ItemID:	10930
TypeID:	

Archive
Art
Ashtrays
Autograph
Aviation
Banking
Billheads
Billiard

Record: |◄| ◄ | 1 | ... | of 6304

Regardless of the source of the list of values, users of the form can choose only one of those values, which is then typically stored in the field that's associated with the control.

It's also possible to store the selected value in a variable for use in an expression or a VBA procedure, but most of the time you simply store the value in the underlying table.

Choosing the source of lookup data

The list of values doesn't come from the table that's the form's record source. This concept can be one of the hardest to grasp because it seems so logical that you would get the data from that table; in reality, the list has to come from a different source. Part of the confusion probably arises from the way a combo box (or list box) works. When you move to a record that already contains data in the field that is the control source for the combo box, the combo box shows the existing value that's stored in the field. But even so, the combo box in the form also shows the other possible values that you can choose.

TIP

Here's a brush up on all the different kinds of sources you can set up as properties in the Properties dialog box:

✔ The *record source* is the table or query that feeds data to the form, and it's also where the data is stored as you enter or edit information on the form.

✔ The *control source* is the field where a control gets any existing value, and it's where data from the control is stored.

✔ The *row source* is where the combo box gets its list of choices to display.

Access offers a handy wizard that you can use to help you set up a lookup list when you add a combo box (or a list box) to a form. The following example shows you how to use the Combo Box Wizard to add a combo box:

1. **Open the form to which you want to add the combo box in Design view.**

2. **In the toolbox, click the Combo Box icon to select it.**

    Make certain that the Control Wizards button in the Toolbox is selected.

3. **Drag the field that you want to use as a lookup list onto the form.**

    The Combo Box Wizard dialog box opens, as shown in Figure 17-2, offering you three options.

Figure 17-2:
Choose
the type of
combo box
you want.

```
Combo Box Wizard

┌──────────────────┐   This wizard creates a combo box, which displays a list of values you
│  xxxxxx       ▼  │   can choose from.  How do you want your combo box to get its
│ xxxxxxxxxxx      │   values?
│ xxxxxxx          │
│ xxxxxxxx         │   ⦿ I want the combo box to look up the values in a table or query.
│                  │
│                  │   ○ I will type in the values that I want.
│                  │
│                  │   ○ Find a record on my form based on the value I selected in my
│                  │      combo box.
└──────────────────┘

              Cancel      < Back    Next >     Finish
```

4. **Choose the option that best suits your needs for the row source and click Next to continue.**

    In this example, I chose the first option. With this option, the lookup list displays values from a table or a query. With the second option, you need to enter a list of values that are stored in the control. With the third option, the control displays a list of values from the table so that users can look up specific records. The first option is the most commonly used (and useful) of the three options.

The row source options display, as shown in Figure 17-3.

Figure 17-3: Choose the row source for the combo box.

5. Select the table or query that you want to use as the row source and click Next to continue.

The tables must be joined in order to use a table as the row source. The field selection options appear, as shown in Figure 17-4.

Figure 17-4: Choose the row source fields you want to display in the combo box.

6. Add the fields that you want to appear in the combo box to the Selected Fields list with the > or >> buttons. Click Next to continue.

7. **If you want to sort the items that are displayed in the lookup list, select the sorting options. Click Next to continue.**

   The column display and width options appear, as shown in Figure 17-5. For information about sorting, see "Improving lookup lists with proper sorting," later in this chapter.

Figure 17-5: Adjust the column width if necessary.

8. **Adjust the column width by dragging the right side of the field name row. Click Next to continue.**

   You can also double-click the right edge of the field name row to automatically resize the column to fit the data.

   Leave the Hide key column check box selected so that users won't be confused by the extra, unnecessary column.

   The next dialog box gives you options for storing control source values, as shown in Figure 17-6.

Figure 17-6: Choose what you want Access to do with the value.

9. **From the Store That Value in This Field drop-down list, select the field where you want to store the data. Click Next to continue.**

10. **Enter the label you want to display next to the combo box and then click Finish.**

   The Combo Box Wizard dialog box closes and adds the control to your form.

Improving lookup lists with proper sorting

Although the Combo Box Wizard gives you the option to specify a sort order for the lookup list, you won't be given that option if you add a lookup list to a form by using the Form Wizard. In either event, you need to sort your lookup lists if you want to avoid the all-too-familiar out-of-sorts lookup list shown in Figure 17-7. Logically organized lists prevent users from making careless mistakes! If you've encountered unsorted lookup lists on your own forms and wondered how to fix them, this section shows you how.

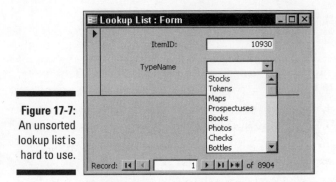

Figure 17-7: An unsorted lookup list is hard to use.

The key to fixing an unsorted lookup list is knowing where to look for the problem. When you create a lookup list that draws its values from a table, Access creates a `SQL SELECT` query statement in the control's `Row Source` property. You can modify that SQL statement to add an `ORDER BY` clause to specify a sort order for the value list.

You can modify the SQL statement in at least a couple of ways. Here's one that's easy and fast:

1. **Open the form in Design view and click the combo box to select it.**

2. **Choose View➪Properties or click the Properties button on the toolbar.**

   The Properties dialog box opens.

3. **On the Data tab, click the Row Source text box.**

4. **Press Shift+F2.**

   The Zoom dialog box appears, enabling you to view and edit the entire SQL statement.

5. **At the end of the SQL statement, move the insertion point just to the left of the semicolon, press the spacebar, and then enter** ORDER BY **and the name of the field you want to sort.**

   Figure 17-8 shows how the Zoom dialog box appears in my example.

Figure 17-8:
Use the
ORDER BY
clause to
sort the
lookup list.

```
Zoom                                                    ☒

SELECT [TypeTable].[TypeID],                    ▲    ┌──────────┐
[TypeTable].[TypeName] FROM [TypeTable] ORDER         │    OK    │
BY TypeName;                                          └──────────┘

                                                      ┌──────────┐
                                                      │  Cancel  │
                                                      └──────────┘




                                                ▼    ┌──────────┐
                                                      │  Font... │
                                                      └──────────┘
```

6. **Click OK.**

   The Zoom dialog box closes and your lookup list is now sorted in ascending order (from A to Z).

You can add DESC to the ORDER BY clause to sort the lookup list in descending order (Z to A) if you don't like the default setting of ascending order. In Step 5, simply type **ORDER BY TypeName DESC**.

If you prefer a more visual approach to setting the sort order, you can open the Query editor by clicking the Build button after you've selected the Row Source text box in Step 3. Make the changes in the Sort row and save your changes when you close the Query editor.

Setting default values

Setting a default value for a field automatically enters that value in the field when a new record is created. This simple technique can make a database more convenient to use because if the default value is also the most commonly entered value, users don't have to manually enter information in the field when they create a new record.

You can, of course, use the Default Value property in a table design to set up the table so the same value is always entered whenever a new record is created. In most cases, this is the best way to set a default value, because by setting the default value in the table's properties, the value is automatically entered, no matter how someone creates a new record.

In some cases, though, you should set the default value for a field by setting the Default Value property for a control on a form, as shown in Figure 17-9. If you set the default value for a control on a form, that value is only entered when a new record is created by using the form.

Figure 17-9:
Here the
`State` field
is set to a
default
value of `NV`.

> **Text Box: State**
>
> State
>
> | Format | Data | Event | Other | All |
>
> Control Source . . . . State
> Input Mask . . . .
> Default Value . . . . "NV"
> Validation Rule . . . .
> Validation Text . . . .
> Enabled . . . . Yes
> Locked . . . . No
> Filter Lookup . . . . Database Default
> Smart Tags . . . .

The real advantage to setting default values for controls on a form (when compared to setting the default value for the field in the table design) is that you can create different forms, each with its own default value settings. This can be very useful if you have a database that tracks orders. By setting up different copies of the order entry form for each order taker, you can set the default value for each of their individual forms to automatically enter the order taker's name. That way, you can make sure that every order is automatically credited to the correct person.

Crafting Forms That Are Easier to Use

You can easily create forms that do everything you want, but sometimes the downside of a form that does everything is that it isn't as easy to use as it should be. Making forms easier to use pays off in time saved and fewer errors, so after you have the basics down, putting in a little extra effort working on usability makes a lot of sense.

Making data appear in a logical order

People don't generally do very well when they're presented with a bunch of data that's in no logical order. That's why your telephone book is sorted by name and your calendar shows the dates in chronological order. You simply can understand and find information much easier if it's arranged logically.

Access likes order, too. Unfortunately, the sense of order that Access likes isn't always the same as the sense of order that makes sense to humans.

When you create an Access table, you almost always include a field that's used as a *primary key*. This key could be something like a customer ID number, a product identification number, or even a membership number. The values in key fields are unique, which makes keeping track of the records easier for Access to do.

The one little problem with most database keys, of course, is that they're pretty unintelligible to people. You probably wouldn't try to look up a customer named Fred Holabird by a number like 1079999.

When you enter information into a database, you probably do so in a random order. Unless you have a database that never changes, you aren't likely to add all of your customer records in alphabetical order. More likely, you will enter data as you receive it. For example, you may get an order from a new customer named Paul Johnson right after you finish entering one for John Mills. As a result, when Access creates the key values, Paul Johnson appears after John Mills. Sometimes (often, in fact) you may want to sort records by name. However, in general, you don't want to be stuck with a database that makes finding a specific customer's records awfully hard for the ordinary Joe.

Controlling the order for displaying records

You can easily control the order in which a form displays records by setting the Order By property for the form, as shown in Figure 17-10. In the figure, the OWNERLASTNAME field value is used for sorting the records. The Order By property appears on the Data tab of the Properties dialog box.

When you set a property such as the Order By property for a form, that setting has no effect outside of the form. Sorting in a form does not change the record sort order in the table.

Figure 17-10:
Use the
`Order By`
property of
the form to
set the sort
order for
the records
when
they're
displayed in
the form.

Form					
Form					
Format	Data	Event	Other	All	
Record Source			OWNERS		
Filter					
Order By			OWNERLASTNAME		
Allow Filters			Yes		
Allow Edits			Yes		
Allow Deletions			Yes		
Allow Additions			Yes		
Data Entry			No		
Recordset Type			Dynaset		
Record Locks			No Locks		
Fetch Defaults			Yes		

If you need to sort the records that are displayed in the form by more than one field, list the fields in the Order By text box separated by commas. Place the field names in order of importance. For example, if you want to sort by last name and then by first name, the Order By text box should look like this: `LastName, FirstName`.

Adding command buttons for common tasks

You do certain tasks quite often when you're working with your PC. Sometimes these are simple tasks, but you might have to press a half-dozen keys or click several times with your mouse to perform those tasks. Have you ever thought to yourself that you would like to just click once and have your computer take over and finish the job for you?

Setting a sort order for every occasion

Just as setting default values in forms sometimes makes using Access easier, setting the sort order in a form often makes more sense than trying to find a common sort order for every purpose. You may need to sometimes sort by customer name, sometimes by state, and maybe even by something like order size. By creating individual forms that each display the records in their own, unique arrangement, you give your Access users tools to make their work easier and more efficient without requiring them to master the mechanics of queries and sorting.

In Access you can use *command buttons* to run *macros* or VBA procedures that automate various tasks. (Macros are similar to VBA procedures, but not nearly as flexible or powerful. I discuss VBA procedures briefly in Chapter 7.)

Knowing what you can do with command buttons

Maybe the title of this section should really be "Is there anything you can't do with command buttons?" The answer would have to be yes, but you can still do an awful lot that might surprise you with command buttons.

Here are a few examples of things that you can do with command buttons:

- ✔ Print a report
- ✔ Open a form
- ✔ Exchange data between your Access database and another application such as Excel
- ✔ Run a mail merger to generate personalized form letters or e-mails
- ✔ Export information to an accounting system such as QuickBooks
- ✔ Save the world from the plague of (insert the name of your favorite villain here)

Okay, so maybe you'd need a really complex VBA procedure to make that last one work, but you get the picture. Command buttons are great tools that help make Access databases easier to use.

Creating your first command button

Access makes creating simple command buttons easy with the Command Button Wizard. This wizard offers a number of different common tasks that you can add to a command button.

Here's how to create a command button with the Command Button Wizard:

1. **Open the form on which you want to place a command button in Design view.**

   You might want to start with a new, blank form while you're experimenting with the Wizard.

2. **Click the Command Button icon in the Toolbox to select it and then click in your form where you want the button to appear.**

   The Command Button Wizard dialog box appears, as shown in Figure 17-11.

Figure 17-11:
Use the
Command
Button
Wizard to
create
simple
command
buttons.

3. **Choose the category of action you want the command button to perform.**

   As you select different categories, the Actions list displays the actions available in the selected category.

4. **Choose the action you want and click Next to continue.**

   The next screen of the Command Button Wizard appears, as shown in Figure 17-12. In this example, I selected the Mail Report action in the Report Operations category, so the wizard in Figure 17-13 displays e-mail options.

Figure 17-12:
If you select
the Mail
Report
action,
you must
choose
which
report you
want to
send.

5. **Select the report that you want the command button to e-mail and then click Next to continue.**

   The next Command Button Wizard screen appears, asking you to choose text or an image for the face of the button.

Figure 17-13: Choose the command button appearance you prefer.

6. **Enter a name for the command button and then click Finish to close the wizard.**

Getting up close and personal with the code behind your command button

Access actually goes to a lot of work when you create a command button. If you want to see how the command button works, right-click on the finished button and choose Build Event from the pop-up menu to display the VBA procedure that the Command Button Wizard created for your button. You can also click the Code or the Build button on the toolbar to display the code window. Here's the VBA code that resulted from the e-mail a report example:

```
Private Sub
    EmailSummaryButton_Click()

On Error GoTo
    Err_EmailSummaryButton_
    Click


    Dim stDocName As String


    stDocName = "Auction
Summary by State"

    DoCmd.SendObject acReport,
stDocName
```

```
Exit_EmailSummaryButton_Click:

    Exit Sub


Err_EmailSummaryButton_Click:

    MsgBox Err.Description

    Resume
    Exit_EmailSummaryButton_Cli
ck


End Sub
```

The `Dim` statement sets up a string variable named `stDocName` so that the variable can be used to store the name of the report you want to e-mail. The `DoCmd.SendObject` command sends an e-mail message and is actually a very versatile command. You can even modify the command by adding additional arguments such as the e-mail address of the recipient, a message subject, or message text to explain the purpose of the report. You can find out more about the `SendObject` action in the Access Help files by searching for `SendObject`.

Although giving the command button a descriptive name may not seem important right now, keeping track of the objects (like controls you've added to forms) is far easier if you give them a name that means something to you. Remembering the purpose of a button that has a name that Access assigned such as `Command0` can be pretty hard.

Creating command buttons that perform more than one task

If you're still wondering whether the Command Button Wizard is worth your trouble, consider how more useful our command button could be if, in addition to e-mailing a copy of a form to recipients outside of your office, a single click of the command button performed a second action, such as printing the copies of the form for distribution within your office. Experiment with creating a couple of different command buttons that perform related actions such as e-mailing and printing a report. After you do this, open the code window and see how similar the VBA procedures are for the different buttons. As long as the actions you've assigned are similar enough, your VBA code won't look too different, and you can easily modify one of the buttons to perform more than one action.

Take the case of e-mailing a report and printing the same report. Because these actions are so similar, only one line of the following VBA code differs from the previous example. You can easily add that single line from one button's code to the other button's code and build a button that does both tasks simultaneously.

Here's all you need to do to modify the earlier example and do both jobs:

```
Private Sub EmailSummaryButton_Click()
On Error GoTo Err_EmailSummaryButton_Click

    Dim stDocName As String

    stDocName = "Auction Summary by State"
    DoCmd.SendObject acReport, stDocName
    DoCmd.OpenReport stDocName, acViewNormal

Exit_EmailSummaryButton_Click:
    Exit Sub

Err_EmailSummaryButton_Click:
    MsgBox Err.Description
    Resume Exit_EmailSummaryButton_Click

End Sub
```

The only change here is the addition of the line:

```
DoCmd.OpenReport stDocName, acViewNormal
```

Now you have a button that performs two actions with one click. Amazing what a little ingenuity can do!

Creating a switchboard for better usability

If you're responsible for creating databases to be used by a variety of people, you probably want to make using the database as straightforward and obvious as possible. One thing that you certainly don't want is to have to explain how to perform basic tasks every time you get a new user (or when someone forgets for the 54th time how to print the same report). That's where a *switchboard* form comes in handy.

Switchboards are Access forms that aren't tied to a table, so they're not used to enter or edit any data. Rather, a switchboard is a form that contains a series of command buttons that open other forms, print reports, run queries, or do any other common task that you might want to automate.

In most cases you set up a switchboard so that it opens automatically whenever a user opens the database. One reason for this automated convenience, of course, is to keep you from repeatedly hearing (and answering) the question, "How do I open that switchboard thingy that lets me do stuff?"

Creating your own switchboard

The hardest part of the whole switchboard creation process is probably trying to decide which tasks you want to include on the switchboard.

Here's how to create a basic switchboard:

1. **Choose Tools⇨Database Utilities⇨Switchboard Manager.**

   In some versions of Access, you may see a message asking whether you'd like to create a switchboard (see Figure 17-14). If you do, click Yes to continue. If not, you're sent directly the Switchboard Manager dialog box.

Figure 17-14:
If you
see this
message,
click Yes
to create
a new
switchboard.

Switchboard Manager

The Switchboard Manager was unable to find a valid switchboard in this database. Would you like to create one?

Yes   No

 2. **Click Edit.**

    The Edit Switchboard Page dialog box appears, as shown in Figure 17-15, so that you can begin editing the switchboard.

Figure 17-15:
Begin adding items to your switchboard, using the Edit Switchboard Page dialog box.

Edit Switchboard Page

Switchboard Name:

Main Switchboard

Items on this Switchboard:

Close

New...

Edit...

Delete

Move Up

Move Down

 3. **Click New.**

    The Edit Switchboard Item dialog box appears, as shown in Figure 17-16.

Figure 17-16:
Select the items to appear on your switchboard.

Edit Switchboard Item

Text: New Switchboard Command

Command: Go to Switchboard

Switchboard:

OK

Cancel

 4. **Enter the text that you want to appear next to the first command button in the Text text box.**

 5. **Choose the action you want the command button to perform from the Command drop-down list.**

 6. **Select the corresponding switchboard, form, report, macro, or VBA function from the drop-down list closest to the bottom of the dialog box.**

    The name associated with the box changes depending on your selection in the Command list; the third box disappears if you choose the Design Application or Exit Application choices in the Command list.

7. **Click OK.**

   The Edit Switchboard Item dialog box closes and you return to the Edit Switchboard Page dialog box.

8. **Repeat Steps 4 through 8 for each command button that you want to add to the switchboard.**

9. **Click Close when you finish adding command buttons.**

   You return to the Switchboard Manager dialog box.

10. **If your switchboard does not show (Default) after its name, click the Make Default button.**

    This action makes your switchboard open automatically whenever a user opens the database.

11. **Click Close.**

    The Switchboard Manager dialog box closes.

Figure 17-17 shows a very simple switchboard I created for this example. You can get quite a bit fancier with your switchboard by opening it in Design view and editing the design just as you would modify the design of any other form. For example, you may want to add a company logo or some simple user instruction to the switchboard.

Figure 17-17:
The finished switchboard helps people use your database.

Presenting data for information only

Sometimes you need to protect people from themselves. Or maybe the more accurate way to say it is that sometimes you need to protect your data from meddlers who don't realize how much damage they can cause.

If you want to provide your users with a bit of extra information and still protect your data, you're well advised to follow some simple techniques to prevent people from changing certain information. For example, say you have a form that's used to enter the winning bids for items. You probably don't want anyone to change the descriptions of the items. Or, if you have a form that allows users to enter the descriptions of items you've recently logged into inventory, you aren't likely to want someone to change the item inventory numbers.

Making read-only fields

You can prevent someone from changing values that are displayed in a form by using a couple of different properties. In addition, there's one property that might fool you into thinking that it might help prevent changes, but which doesn't.

Found on the Other tab, the Tab Stop property may seem like it would prevent users from entering the field, but it really doesn't. You can simply click in the field and edit away even if you set the Tab Stop property to No. Don't even think about using this property to protect your data!

To prevent changes to values in a field, select the field in Design view and click the Properties button on the toolbar. Then consider the following property settings:

- ✔ **Enabled:** Found on the Data tab, setting the Enabled property to No prevents the field from being selected and grays out the field for users so that they know that they're being shut out. The values are still shown, but users can't change them in the form. This is the best way to present data in a form without allowing it to be modified.

- ✔ **Locked:** Also on the Data tab, setting the Locked property to Yes prevents changes to displayed values, but it doesn't prevent the field from being selected.

Setting this property to Yes is a sure way to confuse users because users see no indication that the field is locked (aside from the fact that nothing happens when you select the field and try to type in it). I recommend simply avoiding the Locked property for that reason.

Giving users help with text prompts

You can display text prompts to help users understand the purpose of a form control. These handy little messages save you all sorts of support calls, and because they're so seldom used, people will think you're an Access wizard if you add them to your forms.

You can choose from two flavors of text prompts:

 ✔ *Status bar text* is information that appears in the status bar at the lower-left corner of the Access window when the field is selected.

 ✔ *ControlTip text* is information that pops up when the mouse pointer is held over a control for a few seconds. Figure 17-18 shows examples of both types of text prompts.

Control tip text

Figure 17-18:
You can add text prompts to help users understand the controls on a form.

Status bar text

It may seem like a bit of overkill to use both Status bar text and ControlTip text, but if you're going to go to the trouble of adding one of them, you may as well add both of them. After all, some people navigate forms exclusively with the keyboard, so they never see the ControlTip text. And some people get so focused on the form that they ignore any messages that appear in the status bar. Unfortunately, this probably means that a certain percentage of your users won't really notice either of the efforts you put into adding text prompts, but you can't do anything about *those* people.

To add text prompts, follow these steps:

1. **Open the form in Design view and click the control that you want to modify to select it.**

2. **Click the Properties button on the toolbar to display the Properties dialog box for the control.**

3. **Click the Other tab to display it.**

   See Figure 17-19.

Figure 17-19:
Use the
Other tab
of the
Properties
dialog box
to add text
prompts.

Text Box: TITLE	☒

TITLE ▼

| Format | Data | Event | Other | All |

IME Mode	No Control
IME Sentence Mode	None
Status Bar Text	Enter the item title
Enter Key Behavior	New Line in Field
Allow AutoCorrect	Yes
Vertical	No
Auto Tab	No
Tab Stop	Yes
Tab Index	1
Shortcut Menu Bar	
ControlTip Text	Used for item descriptions

4. **Enter any text you want to appear in the status bar in the Status Bar Text box.**

   You can enter a prompt up to 255 characters, but depending on users' screen resolutions, only about 50 to 80 characters actually appear. This is not the place to draft the Great American Novel. Limit your remarks to a single, short sentence.

5. **Add any text you want in the pop-up list in the ControlTip Text box.**

   Here, too, you can enter up to 255 characters, but you should keep this even shorter than the Status bar text.

Chapter 18

Expert Methods for Sharing Reports

***

In This Chapter

▶ Sharing details of your report with Microsoft Excel

▶ Merging report data with Microsoft Word

▶ Incorporating OLE objects

***

*I*n a perfect world, you would never have to share your Access data with another application because Access would simply do everything you'd need to do without any outside help. But we don't live in a perfect world, and besides, the time is sure to come when you need to send Access data to someone who hasn't jumped on the Access bandwagon.

This chapter shows you methods that make sharing data with both Excel and Word simple and efficient. In addition, this chapter fearlessly takes on a topic that strikes terror into the souls of many Access users — using OLE *(Object Linking and Embedding)* objects in your reports. Okay, so maybe terror is a bit strong a word, but despite the fact that many Access users find them more than a bit intimidating, OLE objects are a type of shared data that can be awfully handy.

Sharing Report Data with Microsoft Excel

As powerful as Access is, an awful lot of people are simply more comfortable analyzing data in Excel when they have the option. Somehow that Excel spreadsheet just seems a bit more friendly and cozy than the various options in Access. Sure, the PivotTables and PivotCharts offer a glimpse of Excel's power in Access, but they're just not the same as truly moving over to Excel and mucking around with the data in that program.

Although you can exchange data between Access and Excel by using several different methods, this section concentrates on sending Access reports to Excel. Doing so offers several advantages compared to other options:

- ✔ When you send a report to Excel, you narrow down the data to a specific set of parameters that you want to analyze so that you aren't stuck with a bunch of irrelevant stuff in the Excel worksheet.

- ✔ Group levels in Access reports are conveniently saved as Excel outline levels, making data analysis much simpler.

- ✔ Most report formatting is preserved when you send an Access report to Excel, so if you want to generate a report in Excel, the formatting is already in place.

- ✔ Most of the sorting and layout work you put into your Access report remains intact in Excel, so you won't have to repeat the work you've done in Access after you transfer the report to Excel.

Laying out reports so that they work in Excel

You can export any Access report as an Excel worksheet, but you should keep a few things in mind to get the most from your report after it's in Excel. Although most data-related elements are exported, some report features, like report headers, report footers, page numbers, page footers, and all but the first page header aren't included in the Excel worksheet. If you need these types of elements in Excel, you have to add them there.

Because Access report grouping levels translate into Excel outline levels, reports that use grouping are especially useful in Excel. Figure 18-1 shows an Access report that groups items by type.

Figure 18-2 shows the same report that was shown in Figure 18-1 after it was exported to Excel and opened in Excel. Notice that the Excel Outlining bar along the left side of the window shows the grouping by type.

Finally, Figure 18-3 shows how the report appears after the outline is collapsed. Notice that the detail rows are hidden. Figure 18-3 does a great job of demonstrating how Access report grouping helps data analysis in Excel.

Figure 18-1: This Access report groups items by type.

You can, of course, expand any part of the outline to view the details. For details on using Excel, check out *Excel 2003 For Dummies* by Greg Harvey (Wiley).

Figure 18-2: This is the Access report after it was exported to Excel.

Figure 18-3:
The
collapsed
outline of
the report
shown in
Figures 18-1
and 18-2.

Exporting your report data to Excel

When you export a report to Excel, Access prints the report to a single-sheet Excel worksheet file. The report isn't actually printed, of course, but Access treats the process as if it were printing the report and it even reports the number of pages that have been printed as the report is being exported. This message might confuse you if you're not expecting it, but if you consider that Access has to assemble the report just as it does for printing, I guess the analogy is close enough. This Excel worksheet file is totally separate from your Access database file, of course, so any changes you later make in Access won't be reflected in the Excel file.

Follow these steps to export report data to Excel:

1. **Locate and select the report whose data you want to export.**

   You don't have to open the report (although doing so won't hurt anything if you want to verify the report's accuracy before you export it).

2. **Choose File⇨Export or right-click on the report and choose Export from the pop-up menu.**

   The Export Report dialog box appears, as shown in Figure 18-4.

Figure 18-4:
Use the
Export
Report
dialog box
to export a
report in
Excel
format.

3. **Select the latest Excel format that's available from the Save as Type drop-down list.**

   Your choices may vary depending on the version of Access you're using, but the latest Excel format is the best choice unless you're using a really old version of Excel (prior to Excel 97).

4. **If you want the worksheet to load automatically, select the Autostart check box.**

5. **Click Export to begin the export to Excel.**

   Access creates the Excel file in the current directory, using the existing report name as the name for the Excel file.

Another way to export your report to Excel is to open the report in Report view and then choose Tools⇨Office Links⇨Analyze It with Microsoft Office Excel. Alternatively, you can click the Office Links button on the toolbar and choose the Analyze It with Microsoft Office Excel option.

Sending Reports to Microsoft Word

As you can probably guess, you have a couple of choices for sharing Access data with Word. The method that you choose depends on what you want to do with the information after it is exported to Word:

✔ If you primarily want to make the data look a bit fancier or include it without too many changes in a Word document, you should probably send the output of an Access report to Word.

✔ If you want to create form letters or catalogs in Word, try the Mail Merge feature so that Word gets a table of data that it can draw from. Strictly speaking, you're not really sending a report to Word, but the process is important enough for you to understand that I discuss it anyway.

Access has great difficulty dealing with the OLE Object field type when sending data to another application such as Word. See "Using OLE Objects in Reports," later in this chapter, for a discussion of OLE Objects.

Sending report data to Word

Sending report data to Word is a process that's very similar to sending report data to Excel. Basically, you create your report, select it, and then choose Tools⇨Office Links⇨Publish It with Microsoft Office Word. Access then goes through the "printing" process that creates a Word document from your Access report.

The Word document you create by using the Tools⇨Office Links⇨Publish It with Microsoft Office Word command looks very much like the Access report itself — much more so than an Excel worksheet that is created from an Access report. That's because the Word document includes the report headers, report footers, the page headers, and the page footers from the Access report. Date fields and page numbering are also included (the Word document includes hard page breaks to make the document look even more like the Access report). Figure 18-5 shows how the report used in the earlier example looks after being sent to Word.

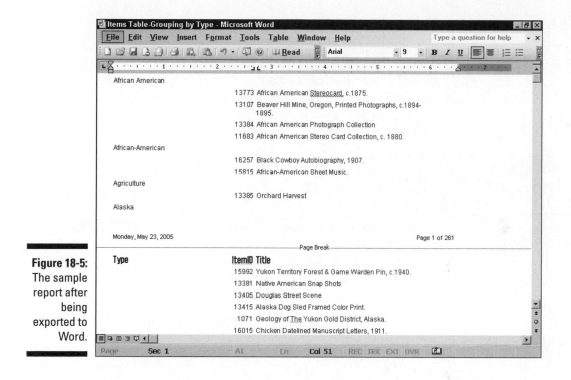

African American

	13773	African American Stereocard, c.1875.
	13107	Beaver Hill Mine, Oregon, Printed Photographs, c.1894-1895.
	13384	African American Photograph Collection
	11683	African American Stereo Card Collection, c. 1880.

African-American

| | 16257 | Black Cowboy Autobiography, 1907. |
| | 15815 | African-American Sheet Music. |

Agriculture

| | 13385 | Orchard Harvest |

Alaska

Monday, May 23, 2005   Page 1 of 261

——————————————————————Page Break—————————————————————

Type   **ItemID Title**
	15992	Yukon Territory Forest & Game Warden Pin, c.1940.
	13381	Native American Snap Shots
	13405	Douglas Street Scene
	13415	Alaska Dog Sled Framed Color Print.
	1071	Geology of The Yukon Gold District, Alaska.
	16015	Chicken Datelined Manuscript Letters, 1911.

Figure 18-5:
The sample report after being exported to Word.

Using the Word Mail Merge feature with Access

Word uses the term *mail merge* for any document that is automatically created from a data file, but that doesn't mean that you can only use this feature to create form letters. You can also use the Mail Merge feature to create personalized e-mail messages, various types of labels, and even catalogs.

You can't actually send an Access report to Word for use as a Mail Merge data source. Instead, you send the data as it exists in a table or you create a query to provide the data for the mail merge.

The basic idea here is that you need to provide Word with a table of the data for the merge, and the table must look similar to the Access Datasheet view. The first row of the table must contain the field names, each column must hold the data for a single field, and each row must contain the data for a single record.

You can choose one of two methods to create the Mail Merge file for Word.

✔ **Using Access features:** The first method works within Access and simply creates the Mail Merge file that you can use later in Word. That's the method I describe in this section.

✔ **Using Word features:** The second method creates the merge file and then immediately opens the Mail Merge Wizard in Word so that you can create your merged Word documents.

For information about using Word functions and features, take a look at *Word 2003 For Dummies* by Dan Gookin (Wiley).

Here's how to create the Word merge file in Access:

1. **Select the table or the query that you want to use as the data source for the merge file.**

2. **Choose File⇨Export to open the Export dialog box, as shown in Figure 18-6.**

Figure 18-6:
Use the Export dialog box to create a Word merge file.

3. **Select Microsoft Word Merge from the drop-down Save as Type dropdown list.**

4. **Click the Export button to export the data to the Word merge file.**

Access saves the Word file in the current directory, using the name of the table or query as the name of the Word file.

Word can use data from an Access table as the data source for a merge, but it can't use an Access query directly. That's one big advantage of creating the Word merge file in Access because selecting specific groups of records by using an Access query is much easier than limiting the records with the options that are available in Word.

Using OLE Objects in Reports

Most Access books either completely ignore OLE objects or they dismiss them with a few quick sentences. The general attitude seems to be something like "OLE objects are bad, bad, bad, and you should avoid using them." I have a different take on OLE objects, and that's simply that they're only useful to you if you understand them.

Understanding OLE objects

OLE stands for *Object Linking and Embedding* — one of those kind of nebulous terms that programmers seem to like to throw around when they're trying to snow everyone. *OLE objects* are simply documents that belong to another application that you use inside a document file. For example, you can embed a Word document into a field of an Access database. The Word document is the OLE object in this case.

You can use many different types of objects, from Adobe Acrobat documents to Excel worksheets, to Bitmap images, and even wav sound files. Exactly which objects you can use depends on whether the applications you have installed have registered themselves as OLE object sources.

Linking versus embedding

OLE objects can be *linked* or *embedded*. A linked object is actually just a reference to the filename and location of the foreign document. When you open a table, a form, or a report that contains a linked object, Access opens the linked document with the application that created the document and it appears as if it were really a part of the database. An embedded object is contained within the database. When you want to view the object in a table, a form, or a report, Access opens the embedded object by using the application that created it.

Understanding the merits of using OLE objects in your database

You're probably asking yourself why you'd even want to include a Word document in an Access database. Consider this. When you create a report in Access, everything that's in a field on the report has the same formatting. In a Word document, on the other hand, you can format the document as much as you want. If you include a Word document as an OLE object in your Access database, all the formatting that you applied in Word appears when that field is used in a report. Suddenly you aren't limited to the lame formatting choices offered by Access. You could, for example, place the title of a book within a description in italics — which is generally considered to be the "proper" way of formatting book titles.

The difference between linked and embedded OLE objects is very important in some cases, but it's pretty much a wash in others. Here are some things to know about linking and embedding:

- ✔ Linked and embedded objects look the same in Access. You can't easily tell by viewing a table, form, or report to know whether the object is linked or embedded.

- ✔ Linked objects are updated if the original document file is updated, but embedded objects aren't.

- ✔ If the source document for a linked object is moved or deleted, Access won't be able to locate it, and therefore won't be able to open the file.

- ✔ Because embedded objects are a part of the database file, moving or deleting the original source document has no effect on Access. The embedded object can still be used in a report no matter what happens to the original source document that's outside of Access.

- ✔ Embedded objects are often nearly impossible to export from Access to another application. As a result, that embedded Word document that so nicely gives you formatted text within a field in Access really isn't going to play nice if you want to use the Mail Merge feature in Word to produce a catalog.

- ✔ Linked OLE objects are slightly easier to export to another application, but you'd better be ready to study VBA programming pretty extensively if you want to get too fancy, because even though Access is more than happy to let you add OLE objects to a database, it's awfully stingy about giving them back!

There are many different types of OLE objects, and your success in using them depends heavily on how much work the programmers of your applications did to make objects (documents) sharable. You have no control over how well the programmers did their jobs, but you can lessen the potential for frustration by trying out a few OLE objects from your favorite applications before you commit to using them on a full-scale basis in your Access databases. I've found that sometimes just switching to a different source program for my OLE objects makes a major difference in how usable those objects end up being.

Adding your first OLE object to your Access database

Adding OLE objects to your database is the first step towards using OLE objects in reports. In this section I show you how to add a couple of different OLE objects to your Access database and then use them in reports.

You must begin by adding a field that has the OLE object data type to your table. For the purpose of these examples, I assume that you already have a table that has a field that is an OLE object type. In addition, I assume that you have created a form that has a box for the OLE object field.

Here's how to add OLE objects to your database:

1. **Open the form in Form view so that you can add items to the table.**

2. **Click the OLE object field to select it.**

3. **Choose Insert⇨Object or, right-click on the field and choose Insert Object from the pop-up menu.**

   The Microsoft Office Access dialog box appears, as shown in Figure 18-7.

Figure 18-7:
Use this dialog box to add new OLE objects to your database.

Microsoft Office Access	? ✕
⦿ Create New ○ Create from File	Object Type: Adobe Acrobat 7.0 Document Adobe Illustrator Artwork 12.0 Adobe Photoshop Elements Image Bitmap Image Image Document Media Clip Microsoft Clip Gallery Microsoft Excel Chart	OK Cancel ☐ Display as Icon
Result Inserts a new Adobe Acrobat 7.0 Document object into your document.	

4. **To create a new object to embed in the table, make sure that the Create New option button is selected and then choose the type of object you want to embed from the scrollable Object Type list. Click OK.**

   The dialog box closes and Access embeds the object. Access opens the selected application so that you can create the new OLE object.

5. **To add an existing object to the table, select the Create from File option.**

   The dialog box that appears (shown in Figure 18-8) enables you to browse your system to find the file you want to add.

Figure 18-8:
This dialog box helps you add existing objects to your database.

Microsoft Office Access	? X
○ Create New	File:
⊙ Create from File	C:\Documents and Settings\Brian\My Docume
	Browse... ☐ Link
	OK
	Cancel
	☐ Display as Icon
Result	
	Inserts the contents of the file as an object into your document so that you may activate it using the application which created it.

6. **Enter the filename of the existing document in the File text box or click the Browse button to browse for the document file to add.**

7. **To link the object instead of embedding it, select the Link check box.**

8. **Click OK to add the object to the table and close the dialog box.**

9. **Repeat Steps 2 through 7 for each OLE object you want to add to a record.**

If the object appears as an icon in the form instead of as the content of the object, make sure that the Display as Icon check box is not selected in the Microsoft Office Access dialog box.

Figure 18-9 shows an example of a Word document that has been added to the database as an OLE object. The Word document, which appears in the `DescriptionFormatted` field, utilizes a number of different formatting options (color, boldface, italics, and various fonts) that aren't usually available in Access.

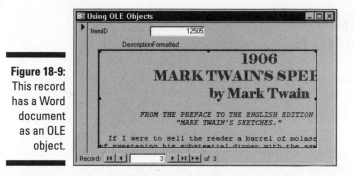

Figure 18-9:
This record
has a Word
document
as an OLE
object.

To control whether users can add linked, embedded, or both types of OLE objects, set the OLE Type Allowed property on the Data tab of the Properties dialog box for the OLE object field on the form.

Figure 18-10 shows how a report appears when you include multiple OLE objects in your database. In this case, the three visible records contain an embedded WordPad document, a linked bitmap image file, and a linked Word document file. Embedded and linked OLE objects look exactly the same, so you can choose the type of object that best suits your needs. You probably wouldn't use so many different options in your reports, but the figure does give you an idea of the possibilities.

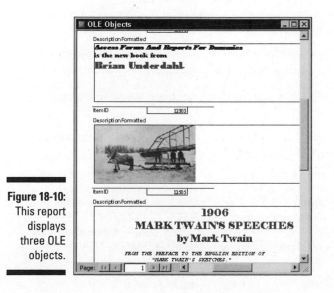

Figure 18-10:
This report
displays
three OLE
objects.

Troubleshooting OLE objects so that they actually work

Using OLE objects in an Access database is easy on the surface, but sometimes things don't go quite the way you planned. Here are some tricks that can help when things go wrong:

✔ **Problem:** You open a table that contains image files and you see the word `Package` in the OLE object field rather than `Bitmap Image`.

Explanation and Solution: This anomaly occurs in Access 2003 (but not earlier Access versions) because Office 2003 doesn't include the Microsoft Photo Editor program. As long as you have some sort of bitmap editing application installed (such as Photoshop), you can still edit the image file, but the image itself won't appear unless you convert the file to BMP or DIB *(Device Independent Bitmap)* format. You can use Windows Paint to convert many digital images to BMP.

✔ **Problem:** You see an icon that says `JPEG Image` instead of the actual image in a form or a report.

Explanation and Solution: Access doesn't like your choice of file type for some reason. You need to convert the image to BMP or DIB. This issue applies to several other types of image files, too, so if you can't see the image, try converting it to BMP or DIB before you do anything else.

✔ **Problem:** You try to open an OLE object but only see a message saying that the file can't be opened.

Explanation and Solution: Check to see whether the application that created the object is already open. If it is open and it's waiting for you to respond to a dialog box prompt, you won't be able to open a different object from that application until you respond to and close the dialog box.

✔ **Problem:** An OLE object appears as an icon and none of the earlier tricks in this list has solved the problem.

Explanation and Solution: Hmm . . . I don't know what's going on here. Try tinkering around in the Convert dialog box. Right-click on the object. In the context-sensitive menu that appears, choose the *source application name* Document Object item (where *source application name* is the name of the program that created the object). The Convert dialog box appears. Deselect the Display as Icon check box.

✔ **Problem:** You absolutely have to export OLE objects from Access.

Explanation and Solution: Truth? Access doesn't really give you a good option. But you can export OLE objects from Access if you're willing to be creative (and spend a little money). You need to install Adobe Acrobat (not the free reader) or another application that can create *PDF* — Portable Document Format — files. Then create an Access report that includes your OLE objects; convert the resulting output to PDF. You may have to then convert the PDF file into another format (such as Word), but at least can export the OLE object data and use it in another application. You're welcome.

✔ **Problem:** It still doesn't work.

Explanation and Solution: Sometimes stuff doesn't work, and all you can do is just move on. To be honest, just because an object type appears in the Object Type list in the Microsoft Office Access dialog box doesn't mean that it's going to work out well as an OLE object in your Access database. Access doesn't have any way to determine in advance whether objects that appear in the list are appropriate, so the only way to determine whether you really should insert the object is to try it and see what happens.

Chapter 19

Making Reports Look Better

*Y*ou want your reports to look good — otherwise, why even go to the trouble of creating a report? If appearance didn't matter, you could just hand everyone a copy of a datasheet printout and say, "The information you need is in there somewhere." No, that probably wouldn't cut it, now would it?

Improving the appearance of your reports actually involves using several subtle features that probably won't jump out and grab you individually; but these features are important if you want to make a good impression. That's why I've assembled these little items into this chapter to make it easier for you to pick up some final, finishing touches that make your reports stand out from the crowd.

Enhancing the Appearance of Important Information

Sure, all the information in a report is important, but some of it is more important than the rest. For example, you may want to be able to see at a glance the individual items that show profits; you probably also want to know which areas of your business aren't doing so well. In the end, that bottom line — how much you make (or lose) — is what you and the executives want to see.

Even though some information may be more important, the rest of a report should still be easy to understand and follow. Put some effort into making sure that your reports are clear and logical, adding emphasis to data that needs it.

Sorting report data for clarity

When you create an Access report from scratch, the report displays the records based on how those records are sorted in the underlying table or query — unless you specify a different sort order. Usually, reports that don't specify another organization order records based on the table's primary index. Although this sort order may be useful for helping organize items in a table initially, it may not be the order that you want in your final report. For example, instead of sorting a report that shows the items for an upcoming sale by ItemID, you may want to sort the items by state, by value, or maybe even by their discount percentage.

You can choose one of four methods to control the sort order for a report, in order of importance:

- ✔ Use the Sorting and Grouping dialog box to specify a sort order.
- ✔ Set the Order By property for the report.
- ✔ Base the report on a query that specifies a sort order for the records.
- ✔ Create an index for the underlying table.

Access doesn't stop you from specifying all four different sort orders (each with different parameters) for a single report. You can use all the methods mentioned without so much as a warning. Fortunately, Access does apply a pecking order to the methods so that you can be sure which of them wins out in the end. The Sorting and Grouping dialog box sort order is the most important, followed by the Order By property, using a query, and, finally, by creating a table index. If you want absolute control, use the Sorting and Grouping dialog box to set the report's sort order. Or, if you've tried to use one of the four methods to control the sort order and the report didn't sort the way you expected, check to see if one of the more dominant methods is controlling the sort order.

Using the Order By property

Even though a sort order specified in the Sorting and Grouping dialog box takes precedence over a sort order set using the Order By property, you may want to use the Order By property because removing a sort order that's shown in the Sorting and Grouping dialog box has the potential to really mess up your report if you're not careful. See the following section, "Understanding Sorting and Grouping dialog box caveats" for more information. Changing or removing the Order By property is always easy and safe.

To specify a sort order, using the Order By property, follow these steps:

1. **Open the report in Design view.**

2. **Open the report's Properties dialog box.**

   See Figure 19-1. You can click the Properties button on the toolbar to display this dialog box.

Figure 19-1:
Set the
Order By
property on
the Data
tab.

3. **Enter the field(s) you want to use to control the sort order in the OrderBy property text box on the Data tab, making sure to enclose the field names in square brackets.**

   You can specify multiple fields by separating them with commas, and you can specify a sort direction by adding ASC for ascending (the default) or DESC for descending after the brackets, like this [State] DESC.

Use the Order By property to temporarily override the default sort order for a report without making a permanent change. Simply set the Order By property, run your specially sorted report, and then delete the property setting to return the report to its original state (or set the Order By On property to No).

Understanding Sorting and Grouping dialog box caveats

Chapter 13 covers using the Sorting and Grouping dialog box, shown in Figure 19-2, in detail, so I don't spend a lot of time on the subject here.

Figure 19-2:
The sort order you specify in the Sorting and Grouping dialog box always takes precedence.

You need to be careful about using the Sorting and Grouping dialog box for temporary report sorting purposes. As Figure 19-3 shows, Access warns you about potential damage to your report if you attempt to remove any of the entries in this dialog box — even if they have nothing to do with grouping.

Figure 19-3:
Removing any entries from the Sorting and Grouping dialog box displays this message.

Of course, you can safely remove a line from the Sorting and Grouping dialog box if the line doesn't have any grouping associated with it. But if you accidentally delete a line that sets up a grouping level, everything in the group header and group footer for that level is also removed. To avoid this risk, I recommend using the Order By property to control report sort order instead of using the Sorting and Grouping dialog box.

Making data seem to jump out

Chapter 12 discusses a number of fancy tricks that you can use in a report, such as incorporating conditional formatting and applying different colors to alternate report records. These tricks do, indeed, make data stand out, but they're probably not techniques that you'll want to use on every report. This section takes a look at some other options that you can use to make the data on your reports look a bit more impressive.

When you add a text box to a report, the Format tab of the Properties dialog box for that text box provides a whole bunch of interesting options for changing the appearance of your data. Figure 19-4 shows the Format tab of the Properties dialog box for a text box that displays the State field.

Many of the properties, such as Format, Decimal Places, Visible, and so on are pretty easy to understand; if you're ever unsure about what a property does, watch the Access Status bar for an explanation of the property. Here's some information about some of the really useful properties you may not be aware of:

- **Hide Duplicates:** Use this property to prevent your reports from showing a value if it's the same as the previous record. This is handy if you group records but don't display the group header.

- **Back Style and Back Color:** You can set the background as transparent or change the background color.

- **Special Effect:** You can select an appearance such as raised or sunken to give text boxes a 3D effect.

- **Border Style, Border Color, and Border Width:** Use these properties to control the lines around the text box.

- **Fore Color and Font attributes:** You can change the text color, typeface, size, and so on of the fonts used to display the data.

- **Text Align:** You can set the alignment of the data within the text box.

- **Reading Order:** If necessary, you can change the order of the characters for languages that read right-to-left.

- **Scroll Bar Align:** You can set any scroll bars to the right or left side of the text box.

    This option is more useful in forms than it is in reports.

- **Numeral Shapes:** You can choose how numbers appear in the text box.

- **Margin attributes:** You can control how far the text is from the edges of the text box.

- **Line Spacing:** You can increase and decrease the space between lines of text to improve readability.

Text Box: State

State

| Format | Data | Event | Other | All |

Format	
Decimal Places	Auto
Visible	Yes
Hide Duplicates	No
Can Grow	No
Can Shrink	No
Left	0.2917"
Top	0.125"
Width	1"
Height	0.1667"
Back Style	Normal
Back Color	16777215
Special Effect	Flat
Border Style	Transparent
Border Color	0
Border Width	Hairline
Fore Color	0
Font Name	Arial
Font Size	8
Font Weight	Normal
Font Italic	No
Font Underline	No
Text Align	General
Reading Order	Context
Scroll Bar Align	System
Numeral Shapes	System
Left Margin	0"
Top Margin	0"
Right Margin	0"
Bottom Margin	0"
Line Spacing	0"
Is Hyperlink	No

Figure 19-4:
The Format tab of the Properties dialog box provides a wealth of appearance options.

Figure 19-5 demonstrates how some of the formatting options change the appearance of the data that's presented in a report. Notice that some of the options really need to be used with care because you can easily create an unreadable report. In this case the Fore Color example shows how a poor choice makes the data invisible.

Figure 19-5:
This report demon-strates how several of the formatting options change the appearance.

Text box formatting : Report

Arizona	Default settings
Arizona	Changed Back Color
Arizona	Raised Special Effect
Arizona	Short Dashes Border Style
Arizona	Changed Fore Color
Arizona	Changed Font Name and Font Size
Arizona	Changed Left Margin

Page: 1

Printing on Standard Labels

There's really only one practical way to create Access reports that print on standard labels such as mailing labels, and that's to use the Label Wizard. Sure, you can create this type of report from scratch, but doing so is an awful lot of work, and you won't end up with anything as good as what the Label Wizard can do, anyway.

People generally think of mailing labels when the idea of printing on labels comes up, but mailing labels are only a start. You could, for example, print out a set of labels, each containing an item number and brief item description for everything in your inventory.

You could use Avery 5385 Rotary Cards to print out a set of index cards for all your suppliers. From there, you can create a rotary file for a new employee. Or, maybe you want to create index tabs for the file folders you use to track each customer's orders.

To create a report designed to print on standard labels (or other related products like rotary index cards), follow these steps:

1. **In the Reports list, click the New button.**

   The New Report dialog box appears.

2. **Select the Label Wizard from the list of report design options.**

3. **Select the table (or query) that you want to use as the record source and then click OK to open the Label Wizard dialog box.**

   See Figure 19-6.

Figure 19-6:
Choose the label stock you want to use.

[Screenshot of the Label Wizard dialog box]

Label Wizard

This wizard creates standard labels or custom labels.

What label size would you like?

Product number:	Dimensions:	Number across:
5095	2 1/3" x 3 3/8"	2
5096	2 3/4" x 2 3/4"	3
5097	1 1/2" x 4"	2
5159	1 1/2" x 4"	2
5160	1" x 2 5/8"	3

Unit of Measure: ⦿ English ○ Metric

Label Type: ⦿ Sheet feed ○ Continuous

Filter by manufacturer: Avery

Customize...   ☐ Show custom label sizes

Cancel   < Back   Next >   Finish

4. Select the label type you want to use.

If you use a generic brand of labels, you may have to search the instructions that came with the labels to discover which standard label number they're equivalent to (virtually all labels use the same specs as one of the standard label types). You won't have to set up custom labels unless you have something really weird! Click Next to continue and display the font options as shown in Figure 19-7.

Figure 19-7:
Select the
font options
for your
labels.

5. Choose the font options that you want to use and click Next.

The layout options, shown in Figure 19-8, appear. Keep in mind that depending on the options you choose, some data might not fit the label and will be cut off.

Figure 19-8:
Add the
fields to
your labels.

6. **Add the fields to build the labels the way you want them.**

   Remember to leave spaces between fields and add any punctuation that you need. Click Next to continue.

7. **If you want to sort the labels, use the next screen of the Label Wizard to specify a sort order. Click Next to continue.**

   You can sort by using any combination of the fields you want even if you haven't used those fields on the labels.

8. **Enter a descriptive name for your labels and then click Finish to close the Label Wizard.**

If you have trouble making your data fit the labels, try using a smaller font size or a more compact font. You don't have to throw away the report you've just designed — simply open the report in Design view and make the necessary modifications.

Print a page or two of your report on plain paper to check the layout and alignment before you print the labels on expensive label stock.

Labels that have blank lines in the middle of the data look pretty unprofessional. Perhaps you have some customers who have a second address line that goes below the first address line and the line for city, state, and zip code, but you don't want that second address line to be a blank line for the majority of labels where the line isn't needed. The key to removing blank lines from your labels is to make certain that the Can Shrink property on the Format tab of the Properties dialog box for the text box is set to Yes. The Label Wizard automatically sets the Can Shrink property to Yes, so if you end up with blank lines in your labels, check to make sure this property wasn't somehow changed to No.

Keeping Related Data Together

Reports can be difficult to understand if related data doesn't appear together. Think about how confusing an address list would be if Fred Holabird's name appeared at the bottom of one page and his address and phone number appeared at the top of the next page. Now imagine how much more confusing a report broken like that might be to someone like your banker or that elderly client who was trying to understand the commissions on items they consigned to auction with you. Clearly, you want to avoid confusion whenever possible.

Understanding why Access splits records

Every report represents some sort of compromise. In order to make information fit right, you may have to limit the number of characters and thus cut off part of a long field entry. Or you may decide to allow a field to grow as much as necessary, only to have a very long entry split across a page boundary. If you want to limit the number of pages in a report so that you can complete the printing in a reasonable length of time and not have to spend a fortune on postage, you have to make difficult choices about what stays and what goes. Each of these compromises can work against you if you're trying to keep related data together.

In Chapter 13, you discover methods for grouping records in a report. Frankly, you're much more likely to have problems keeping related records together with grouped reports than you are with simple sorted, but ungrouped, reports. Not only do you have to cope with the variable number of records in each group, but also the group headers and footers tend to play havoc with your carefully designed page layouts.

Tricks you can use to avoid splitting grouped records

Although you simply can't keep related records together in every instance, Access offers some tricks you can use to minimize the problem as much as possible. If your report uses grouping, the Format tab of the Properties dialog box for the group header (or footer) has some useful properties relating to this task (see Figure 19-9).

Figure 19-9:
Use the
Format tab
to set group
properties
that help
keep groups
together.

Section: GroupHeader0				
GroupHeader0				

Format	Data	Event	Other	All
Force New Page	None			
New Row Or Col	None			
Keep Together	Yes			
Visible	Yes			
Can Grow	No			
Can Shrink	No			
Repeat Section	No			
Height	0.2396"			
Back Color	16777215			
Special Effect	Flat			

The properties that can help keep a group together include:

✔ **Force New Page:** Use this property to make Access start new groups at the top of a page.

✔ **Keep Together:** Use this property to make Access print each whole group on a single page if it fits.

✔ **Repeat Section:** Set this to Yes to print the group header at the top of each page.

You can use a combination of these properties to attempt to keep groups together, but keep in mind that the compromise for keeping records together is that you use more paper. That is, setting these properties to anything except No (or None for Force New Page) can use up a lot of paper when you print the report. Still, the compromise might be worth the paper if you can guarantee readability and eliminate confusion.

Tricks you can use to avoid splitting sorted records

If you aren't using grouping in a report, you aren't faced with quite as many layout variables, and keeping each individual record together on the same page is going to be a little easier. But you need to pick up a few tips and tricks:

✔ Make sure that the Can Grow and Can Shrink properties are both set to No for any fields that are in the Detail section of the report.

✔ Each report section has a Height property on the Format tab of its Properties dialog box. Add together the page margins (File➪Page Setup) and the heights of each report section to determine the total height of the report with one detail section. If the height of the detail section is set to an exact multiple of the difference between that total height and the height of the paper, records won't break across pages. You may have to shave a very small amount off the height of one or more sections to keep records in check.

✔ Make sure that everything on your report — including any horizontal lines, dates, and page numbers — can't spill over into the right margin on the printed report. This spillover can cause Access to get very confused about the page layout; the result is that your report ends up with a number of nearly blank pages.

Switching a report into Report view is an excellent way to determine whether your report layout modifications are doing what you expect them to without wasting a lot of paper printing samples.

Adding Your Logo to Reports

If you want to add a nice touch of class to your reports, why not add your own logo? Most companies and organizations have logos they use to add an official-looking appearance to letterheads, business cards, and so on, so why not use your logo on your reports, too?

Using a logo on an Access report is pretty easy, but there are a few little ways that Access might try to trip you up. Here's how to add a logo that you've stored in an image file:

1. **Open your report in Design view.**

2. **Click in the Report Header section of the report.**

   Make sure that you click the report section where you want to add the image before continuing; otherwise, Access adds the image in whichever report section was last selected (probably the Detail section) and expands the height of the section to fit the image size.

3. **Choose Insert⇨Picture to open the Insert Picture dialog box.**

4. **Select the image file you want to use and click OK to close the dialog box and insert the picture.**

5. **Make certain that the image is selected and click the Properties button to display the Properties dialog box for the image.**

6. **On the Format tab, select Stretch from the drop-down Size Mode list box.**

   This option enables you to resize the image without cropping it. The default setting for this property, Clip, crops the image when you attempt to resize it. The Zoom setting is similar to Stretch, but it's a little harder to control.

7. **Use the resizing handles along the sides and corners of the image to resize it as necessary.**

   You may also have to resize the Report Header to eliminate any extra height that Access added when you inserted the picture, and you may need to move some other objects, such as the report title, to get the appearance you desire.

Figure 19-10 shows an example of a report with an added logo. Doesn't it make you want to see the list of available products?

Figure 19-10: The logo makes this report look even more professional.

In most cases, the Report Header section is the appropriate place to add a logo because you use a logo for visual impact. Including a large logo on every page or alongside every record dilutes its impact. On the other hand, if you have a very small version of your logo, you could include that small version in the Page Header section.

Any image that you add to a report as a logo is an example of an *unbound control* because the image isn't associated with the data in one of the database tables. Images that are stored in fields as either linked or embedded objects can also appear in a report by including a bound control in the Detail section of the report. There's no special technique required to add these types of bound image controls to your reports, but the same Size Mode property considerations in Step 6 of the previous list apply to bound image controls, too.

Chapter 20

Adding Efficiency with Great Tools

In This Chapter

▶ Documenting your Access database

▶ Improving the performance of your database

▶ Sharing Access data

*A*ccess has an awful lot of powerful features — probably many more than most Access users will ever need. But you aren't the average Access user; you want to get more out of the application than the ordinary, everyday functions. You want power!

This chapter is about adding some real power tools to your Access toolbox. These aren't the wimpy little hand tools that ship with Access. No, we're talking supercharged add-ons that enable you to take control and show Access who's the boss! These are tools that help you document your Access applications, boost their performance, and share your data in ways you never dreamed possible.

Most of the tools I show you in this chapter are *third-party* add-ons for Access. Sure, you're going to have to pay a little extra if you decide that you want to add them to your toolkit, but you can use this chapter, along with the free trial version that most of these applications offer, to figure out which ones are right for your needs (and worth shelling out money for). You certainly won't need all these tools, but by the time you finish this chapter, you'll have a far better idea about what is out there to give you a bit of an Access boost. Obviously, I don't have room to show you all the ins and outs of these tools in a few pages, but that shouldn't prevent you from finding some real gems.

I encourage you to visit the Web sites that are shown for each of the items to find the most current pricing information, as well as any available options.

Using Cool Tools to Document Everything

Access databases can be awfully complex. If you've ever tried out the documentation tool that's built into Access (Tools➪Analyze➪Documenter), you know that getting useful information about your database can be a real struggle. And if you've ever had a database go belly up, you know even more clearly how important it is not only to know a lot about the structure of your database, but also to have some tools to help in the recovery process. The tools in the following sections provide that extra help you really need.

Comparing Access databases with CompareWiz

One of the most frustrating experiences for anyone who creates applications for other people is dealing with people who just can't help tinkering. Maybe a user thinks that changing this report or that form will somehow improve things, but often the tinkerer just creates a nightmare for you when someone else says, "It doesn't work," and you have to figure out what's wrong. No one, of course, will remember having made any changes, so it's up to you to try and determine what has been modified.

CompareWiz from Software Add-Ins, (www.softwareaddins.com) can come to your rescue when you find yourself in that sort of pickle. CompareWiz finds and documents the differences between two copies of an Access database. One copy, of course, may be your master copy and the other is the production copy that's used daily. By locating the differences between the two with this tool, you can cut short your troubleshooting by hours and concentrate on fixing the problem.

Figure 20-1 shows an example of how helpful CompareWiz can be. The AllowZeroLength property for the OwnerID field was changed from false (0) to true (-1) in the production copy of the database (the database listed in the left column in the figure). As a result of this change, users could skip over the OwnerID field without making an entry, and queries, forms, and reports that depend on that value would fail.

CompareWiz is available for all versions of Access going back to Access 97, so even if you don't have the most recent version of Access, you can use CompareWiz.

Unfortunately, CompareWiz can't tell you who made the change so that you can go and give the offender a dope slap! Well, maybe that's a good thing.

Object Name	Property Name	Value in First Database	Value in Second Database
First Database: C:\Documents and Settings\Brian\My Documents\Access Forms and Reports\Holabird Americar			Double-Click any Field to Zoom
Second Database: C:\Documents and Settings\Brian\My Documents\Access Forms and Reports\Holabird Consignr			
Table(Auction35Catalog)	-	-	<Not Found>
Table(Company List)	-	-	<Not Found>
Table(ItemsTable).Properties	LastUpdated	5/18/2005 9:38:39 AM	10/6/2004 12:44:47 PM
Table(ItemsTable).Properties	RecordCount	8299	11536
Table(ItemsTable).Field(ItemID)	ColumnWidth	690	-1
Table(ItemsTable).Field(TypeID)	ColumnWidth	1005	945
Table(ItemsTable).Field(OwnerID)	Attributes	2	1
Table(ItemsTable).Field(OwnerID)	Type	10	4
Table(ItemsTable).Field(OwnerID)	Size	50	4
Table(ItemsTable).Field(OwnerID)	AllowZeroLength	-1	0
Table(ItemsTable).Field(OwnerID)	UnicodeCompression	0	0
Table(ItemsTable).Field(NewDesc)	-	-	<Not Found In Second Datal
Table(ItemsTable).Field(NewItemType)	-	-	<Not Found In Second Datal
Table(ItemsTable).Indexes(ItemsTableOWNERID)	-	-	<Not Found In Second Datal
Table(ItemsTable).Indexes(ItemsTableTypeID)	-	-	<Not Found In Second Datal

Compare Differences

View differences for :

○ All Objects ○ Database ⦿ Tables ○ Queries ○ Forms ○ Reports ○ Pages ○ Macros ○ Modules

Record: ◄◄ ◄ 10 ► ►► ►＊ of 26

Figure 20-1: Someone made a change in a very important database property.

The OwnerID field was changed from required to optional.

Comparing the data in Access databases with CompareDataWiz

Even if you don't have to worry about someone changing the basic structure of your Access databases, you can easily end up with copies of the database that contain different sets of data. Perhaps someone took a copy of the database home over the weekend to do a report and decided to edit a customer's record because it needed corrections. Or perhaps you experienced a crash and need to figure out which of your backups contains the best set of records.

Access doesn't offer an easy way to compare the data in two different copies of a database. Sure, you could get fancy by linking or importing external data, but the complications that are likely to result are a recipe for confusion and disaster. I shudder to even think about the possible consequences of overwriting current data with outdated information.

CompareDataWiz, from Software Add-Ins, (www.softwareaddins.com), is the tool that you need to compare the data in two different Access databases. This excellent tool shows you which records have been changed, which ones have been added, and even which records were deleted in one copy of the databases. For example, Figure 20-2 shows that a record for someone named Brian Underdahl (funny, that name seems familiar) was added to one of the auction database copies.

CompareDataWiz is available for all versions of Access going back to Access 97, so even if you don't have the most recent version of Access, you can use CompareDataWiz.

When you know exactly how the copies of your databases differ, you can more easily develop a plan for either consolidating the information or for choosing the correct copy to keep. Even better, you can come up with a solution in a few minutes instead of spending hours making sure that you've made the correct choice on your own.

CompareDataWiz also offers you the option to print or export the results of the comparison. Using the export option is an excellent alternative to the somewhat complex Access database replication feature — especially if you don't need to constantly combine copies of the database on an ongoing basis.

Figure 20-2:
This figure
shows
that a new
record was
added to
one copy
of the
database.

CompareDataWiz2003 Compare Details

DB1 (Current): C:\Documents and Settings\Brian\My Documents\Access Forms and Reports\Holabird Americana.mdb
DB2 : C:\Documents and Settings\Brian\My Documents\Access Forms and Reports\Holabird Consignments.mc
Table Name : OWNERS

Identical Records | Different Records | Records in DB1 Only | Records in DB2 Only

DBOWNERID	OWNERID	OWNERFIRSTNAME	OWNERLASTNAME	OWNERMIDINT	COMPANYNAME	ADDRESS
327	Und1	Brian	Underdahl		Underdahl Computir	123 Dirt Road

Record: ◄ ◄ 1 ► ►► ►* of 1

Note: Only the First 20 fields will be displayed

Checking out your queries with Query Tree Editor

Query Tree Editor, from 4TOPS (www.4tops.com) may not be a tool that you need right now, but remember it for the future. Query Tree Editor helps you understand the extremely complex relationships that often occur in Access databases when one query builds on another, which, in turn, builds on another, and so on. With Query Tree Editor you can find the dependencies and successfully edit the related queries.

Programmers and developers are notoriously poor at explaining how the systems they develop function. A tool like Query Tree Editor can be a lifesaver if you've been asked to maintain or update an Access database application that someone else created, because your chances of finding understandable information about what's going on under the hood are probably somewhere between "not a chance" and none.

Query Tree Editor comes with its own SQL editor, as shown in Figure 20-3. In this figure, I've opened an order entry database created by one of the Access wizards to examine queries relating to the aging of receivables.

Even if you don't quite need the power of Query Tree Editor yet, 4TOPS offers some other excellent tools for importing and exporting data to Excel and Word. See "Bringing data from Excel with Excel Import Assistant" and "Merging data with Word by using Word Link for Access," later in this chapter for more details.

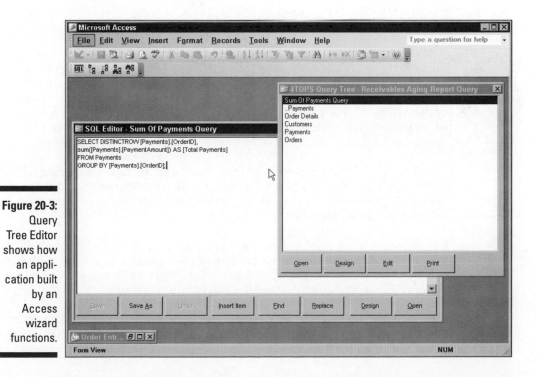

Figure 20-3:
Query Tree Editor shows how an application built by an Access wizard functions.

Fixing database corruption with AccessFIX

Can you imagine a worse feeling than the one that accompanies an Access warning that informs you that it can't open your company's most important database because the file is corrupt? Well, maybe there is something that could be worse — the feeling that comes over you when you remember that you haven't quite gotten around to backing up your files for a while, either. Somehow, I don't think this is going to be one of those days you look back on fondly.

Several things can go wrong with your Access databases. A power failure while the database is in use, a hard drive failure, or even a computer virus can all result in a database that won't open.

AccessFIX from Cimaware Software (www.cimaware.com) is an application that can save your bacon when Access decides to get uncooperative. In just a few minutes AccessFIX can recover the data you thought was lost and put you on the road to recovery. Cimaware also offers ExcelFIX for Excel files, WordFIX for Word files, and OfficeFIX to recover all three types of Microsoft Office files.

Cimaware offers a free downloadable demo version that you can use to determine whether your data can be recovered before you pay for a license.

The best thing you can do to avoid the panic and sense of loss that comes with a corrupt database is to use preventative measures. Never run an important Access database on a PC that isn't protected by an *uninterruptible power supply* — UPS. A UPS is cheap insurance against both power outages and power surges that can harm your computer and destroy your data. And always back up your files.

If you find yourself facing a corrupted Access database, nothing is going to be more comforting than a message like the one shown in Figure 20-4. In this case, 53,308 records were recovered. Just imagine how long reentering those records by hand would take!

In some cases, a database file may be so corrupted that AccessFIX won't be able to recover the complete structure of the database by looking at the damaged file. You can tell AccessFIX to get the structure information from another file, such as an out-of-date backup of your database.

After your file is recovered, AccessFIX saves the database in a new file with a different name. You can even choose to save the data in text files suitable for later importing back into Access.

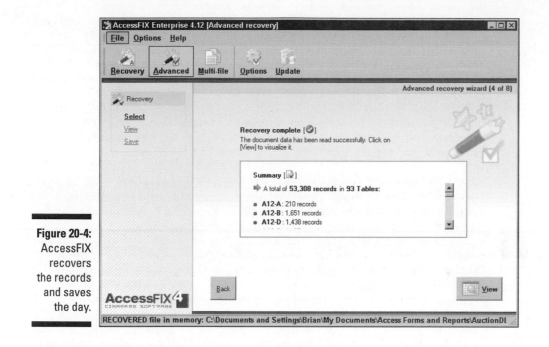

Figure 20-4:
AccessFIX
recovers
the records
and saves
the day.

Souping Up Your Database

Can you honestly say that your Access databases run as fast as you'd like
and that they're as easy to use as they should be? If not, have a look at
some tools that can help you add the extra zip and convenience your users
really want.

Optimizing your Access database with SSW Performance Pro!

Wouldn't it be great if you knew an Access expert who would be willing to sit
down and take the time to go over your Access databases with a fine-toothed
comb and then tell you exactly where you could make improvements? I'm not
talking about just any so-called expert, either. No, how about someone who
knows Access inside and out, who actually tests the performance and then
gives you specific recommendations about what you can do to get faster
performance?

Well, that's the idea behind SSW Performance Pro! from SSW (www.ssw.com.au). Instead of sending an expert Access developer to your office (which could be expensive, because SSW is in Australia), SSW created the SSW Performance Pro! tool that runs on your PC and then gives you a report about the results. (Besides, it might be a little less embarrassing to have a piece of software tell you which of your forms need a little extra work than to have a real person do it.)

Figure 20-5 shows an example of the type of summary report that SSW Performance Pro! produces. The program also provides more detailed information in another report.

SSW Performance Pro! can also check all the field names and table names to make certain that none of them contain characters that cause problems if you decide to split your database into *front-end* and *back-end* applications by using the Tools⇨Database Utilities⇨Database Splitter command.

Databases that are split into front-end and back-end applications store the tables in the back-end application and store the forms, reports, and queries in the front-end application by using table links. Splitting a database is often done to improve the performance of a multiuser database on a network, because each user can then have a local copy of the front-end part of the database and only the data has to be sent across the network. Unfortunately, splitting databases brings some additional considerations and complications that aren't covered in this book.

Figure 20-5:
Find out what's making your forms too slow to use.

Enhancing your Access forms with Selector

You simply can't plan for every possibility. When you create Access forms, you typically think about all the ways people want to use those forms and plan accordingly. For example, if you have a form that enables users to select customer orders, you probably choose between sorting the records by customer, by order number, or maybe by order date. The one thing you aren't likely to do is to figure out how to let users sort the records the way they want.

Selector from Peter's Software (www.peterssoftware.com) is one of a series of very useful tools offered by this company. Selector enables you to create forms that present users with a number of user-selectable sort options so that they can choose the method that best suits their needs. To change the sort order, users only need to click the column heading of the column they want to use for sorting — exactly the way they do when looking at files in Windows Explorer.

Figure 20-6 shows an example of how you might use Selector. In this case, users can click Order ID, Company Name, or Order Date to sort the list, and then select the order they want to see from the list.

Figure 20-6:
Selector
enables
users to
choose the
sort order
they want
to use for
selecting
records.

Creating better forms with ShrinkerStretcher

Have you ever spent a bunch of time carefully designing a form, only to discover that the form ended up partially off the screen when others try to use it? This ugly scene can result from designing forms with a higher screen resolution than your users are using. You might have a nice 1280-x-1024 (or even 1600-x-1200) resolution on your snazzy LCD flat-screen monitor (lucky!), but Fred back in Receiving might be stuck with that old system which maxes out at 800 x 600.

You could, of course, simply make small-sized forms that fit even the tiniest of screens, but ShrinkerStretcher, from Peter's Software (`www.peters software.com`), offers you another alternative you may find more acceptable. ShrinkerStretcher makes your forms and the controls on those forms resizable to fit any screen. Objects like labels, text boxes, combo boxes, and so on shrink or grow as necessary so that controls aren't hidden.

Figure 20-7 shows one of the example forms that are included in ShrinkerStretcher. Watching the controls resize is pretty amazing. Too bad you can't see the effect very easily in a screen shot.

Figure 20-7: Shrinker-Stretcher is the easy way to make forms that can be resized.

Creating forms from existing forms with OmniForm

One problem with Access forms that you aren't likely to resolve is the fact that they look like Access forms. Although this doesn't qualify as a serious issue for the vast majority of Access users, it can be a big problem if you work for an organization that has a whole bunch of "legacy" paper forms and a management team that insists that any electronic forms look exactly like the old forest killers.

If you find yourself in this type of situation, you have several options:

- ✔ You can keep on handing out the paper forms and then reenter all the data manually. Yippee.

- ✔ You can look for a job with an outfit that realizes that computers are here to stay.

- ✔ You can invest in OmniForm from ScanSoft (`www.scansoft.com`) so that you can create exact electronic duplicates of those old paper forms. Hubba hubba!

I really can't tell you which option to choose, but if you decide on OmniForm, you can scan existing paper forms to create forms that look just like the paper versions, but which enable users to fill out the forms on their PCs. You can create forms for use on Web sites or any other place where you might want people to fill in some information. OmniForm even includes Fillers, which are standalone data-gathering modules you can send to people so they can fill out the form without having OmniForm installed.

OmniForm doesn't actually create Access forms. Rather, OmniForm creates a rudimentary database of the form responses, which you then import into Access. Still, this process would certainly be a lot faster than reentering all the data from paper forms manually.

Using Software to Share Stuff

Information is generally far more useful when it can be shared. In the following sections I show you some ways that you can share your Access data both with people who don't have Access and with some of the other programs on your PC.

Using Snapshot Viewer for Access to send a report to non-Access users

Snapshot Viewer is a small application that enables people who don't have Access installed to view Access reports. Snapshot Viewer is available as a free download from the Microsoft Office Web site (`office.microsoft.com`). Figure 20-8 shows an example of an Access report viewed in the Snapshot Viewer.

You need to create a *report snapshot* by choosing File⇨Export and selecting Snapshot Format from the Save As Type drop-down list. This action creates the file that others can view with the Snapshot Viewer. As the name implies, the report snapshot is a static look at the report that doesn't change when the data in your database changes.

As an alternative to creating a report snapshot, you might want to consider creating a *data access page*. This is a Web page that links to your Access database and shows live (not static) data. A data access page is similar to an Access form, and you use similar techniques to create forms and data access pages. You can use the Page Wizard from the Pages list in the Objects list to create a data access page.

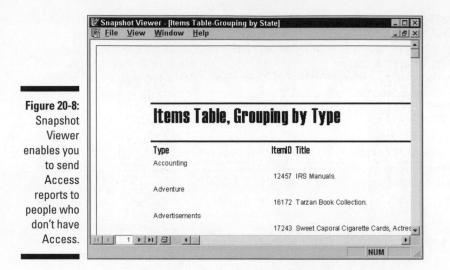

Figure 20-8:
Snapshot
Viewer
enables you
to send
Access
reports to
people who
don't have
Access.

Linking Access and PowerPoint by using Take-Off DATAPOINT

If you really need to share your Access data, nothing puts it up in front of a crowd quite like a PowerPoint slideshow. Of course, getting your Access data into a PowerPoint slideshow can be a real pain.

An excellent solution for this problem is DATAPOINT from Take-Off (www. presentationpoint.com). DATAPOINT is a PowerPoint add-on that enables you to create a slideshow using dynamic content from Excel worksheets, text files, or, you guessed it, Access databases.

Figure 20-9 shows a PowerPoint slideshow that is under construction, using DATAPOINT. The information in the slideshow is from an Access database. In this case, I'm building a slideshow to accompany an auction so that bidders see a description of each item as it comes up for bid.

Take-Off offers a free 30-day trial version of DATAPOINT that you can download. This company also has several other related products that you might want to consider.

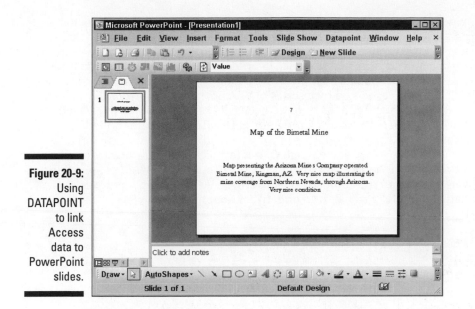

Figure 20-9:
Using
DATAPOINT
to link
Access
data to
PowerPoint
slides.

Sending data to QuickBooks with accessBooks Updater

If you use both Access and QuickBooks, you're probably already quite aware that QuickBooks doesn't really play well with the other kids in the sandbox. But if you're in a situation like one of my customers, you may have data in an Access database that would be awfully handy if it were also available in QuickBooks.

In this instance, the company has an Access application that tracks the bids for an auction, but the bookkeeping and invoicing are done with QuickBooks. Needless to say, reentering several hundred invoices into QuickBooks manually after an auction closes takes a lot of work and is prone to error; the situation is especially annoying because everyone knows that the information is already in the Access database, so close, and yet so far away.

Enter accessBooks Updater from Synergration (www.synergration.com). This program imports data from an Access database into a QuickBooks company file. Figure 20-10 shows you how accessBooks Updater appears just after making the connection between the Access database and QuickBooks.

You need to do some pretty fancy footwork to move data from Access to QuickBooks even with help from a third-party program like accessBooks Updater. I was hired to move data from Access to QuickBooks and to keep that data moving on a regular basis. In order to bring the auction data from Access into QuickBooks, I had to create a number of very sophisticated SQL queries that are executed by a series of VBA procedures in order to populate the tables that accessBooks Updater needs. When these tables were filled with the data from the auction program, accessBooks Updater added the information to the QuickBooks company file. Did getting this all set up take a lot of work? Yes, but the end result is that my client can now create several hundred invoices in QuickBooks in a couple of minutes instead of spending several days. And the company no longer worries about typing errors because the data is transferred directly without rekeying.

Figure 20-10:
The access-
Books
Updater
brings
Access
data into
QuickBooks.

AccessBooks Updater 4.0				
File Options Help				
Current Database: AccessToQB (Access)				
Table	**New**	**Mod**	**Status**	**Last Update**
Checks	0			
Credit Card Charges	0			
Credit Card Credits	0			
Credit Memos	0	0		
☑ Customers	200	0		5/27/2005 8:43:34 AM
Deposits	0			
Employees	0	0		
Estimates	0	0		
Inventory Adjustments	0	0		
☑ Invoices	123	0		5/27/2005 8:45:38 AM
➡ Update		🖳 View Error Log	🔃 Refresh	🔲 Exit

No database connection.
Connected to database: AccessToQB
Connecting to QuickBooks...
Successfully connected to C:\Documents and Settings\Brian\My Documents\Holabird \Auction2QBTest\A39\newamer2.QBW

Bringing QuickBooks data to Access with Digital Cows Deluxe Exporter

QuickBooks is just as difficult about letting any of its data escape as it is about allowing you to import data from another application. Sure, you can export a few of the lists to those almost incomprehensible (and virtually useless to anything except QuickBooks) IIF files, but you are really limited in exporting useful information. Well, it's your data, so I say that if you want to bring it into Access, you should be able to do so with minimal fuss and bother.

Deluxe Exporter from Digital Cows Technologies (www.digitalcows.com) gives you the freedom to export any of your QuickBooks data to Access, and a number of other formats. Figure 20-11 gives you an idea of the types of information you can easily export.

One way you might use Deluxe Exporter is to create a customer list in Access to use for advertising purposes. With all the QuickBooks data as fair game, you have the option to do an awful lot more in targeting your mailings to specific types of customers than you could with the simple customer address list that QuickBooks is willing to export on its own.

Figure 20-11: Digital Cows Deluxe Exporter brings QuickBooks data into Access.

Bringing data from Excel with Excel Import Assistant

Access can import data from an Excel worksheet, but you face some limitations to the process that aren't much fun. For one thing, Access really isn't very happy if you have anything in the worksheet that isn't part of the data — especially if that extra stuff is above or to the left of the data you want to import. And if your data contains any errors, well, guess where they end up?

Excel Import Assistant from 4TOPS (www.4tops.com) simply blows away the problems of importing data from Excel by providing you with tools and options for dealing with pretty much anything you might encounter. For example:

- You can easily import different parts of the worksheet to different tables.
- You can correct incorrect data on-the-fly.
- You can set up data mapping so that when you import the same type of data in the future, you won't have to specify what goes where.
- You can import data and automatically apply *autonumber* keys (unique values) to the records.
- You can automatically skip duplicated data.
- You can suppress error messages during the import process and automatically create an error log, electing to correct the problems after the import process is finished instead of dealing with each error in real time.
- You can automate the whole process of importing a bunch of Excel worksheets — which is especially handy if you have to import the data regularly.

Figure 20-12 shows an example of importing data from an Excel worksheet into an Access table, using the Excel Import Assistant. As the figure shows, you can control exactly how the data is imported by choosing from a variety of helpful options.

You can automate future imports by using the Save tab in Excel Import Assistant to save the settings of a complex Excel import session for later use.

Figure 20-12:
Excel Import
Assistant
gives you
full control
over the
data that is
imported
from Excel
into Access.

Merging data with Word by using Word Link for Access

In Chapter 18 I show you how to send Access data to Word by using the Tools⇨Office Links⇨Publish It with Microsoft Office Word command in a process known as mail merge. Although the Office Links tools are fairly handy, they're not all that flexible. If you really want your Access data to put Word through its paces, you need something like Word Link, from 4TOPS (www.4tops.com).

Word Link goes well beyond mere mail merge. By using the full power of the Office automation features, you can create documents in several different formats, add controls to Word documents, automatically reorient or resize Word documents that contain too much data, get data from users, and, oh yes, do a mail merge.

Figure 20-13 shows the dialog box where you begin creating a document with Word Link. Your first task is to decide which of the features you want to use — Word Link offers quite a selection!

Figure 20-13:
Word Link goes well beyond simple mail merges.

Dialog box contents:

4TOPS Word Link - Use Advanced Features

Welcome to the 4TOPS Office Link Wizard! This Add-In has many features, the more advanced ones are initially disabled to reduce the number of Wizard steps. To enable / display the advanced features check the 'Use Advanced Features' checkbox below this text.

☑ Use Advanced Features

Available Features - 19 of 19

- Adding checkboxes and radio buttons to documen
- Adding pictures to documents
- Automatic changing of documents page orientation
- Automatic naming of documents   A
- Automatic storing of documents   A
- Creating charts   A
- Creating multiple documents from selected records

Feature Description

Pictures from both OLE bound control and textboxes containing filenames supported

Help   Cancel   < Back   Next >   Finish

The A in the column to the right of the list of available Word Link features indicates one of the advanced features. You may want to hide these features by deselecting the Use Advanced Features check box while you're getting the basics of Word Link down.

Part VI
The Part of Tens

The 5th Wave   By Rich Tennant

I told Russell he should data model before we go any further.

Miss Claudia Schiffer, please.

In this part . . .

This final part helps you to find additional and very useful Access-related information on the Web. It finishes up by making sure you know some very important bits of information about queries so that your forms and reports are even more useful.

Chapter 21

Ten Great Access Sites Online

*T*he Internet has really changed the way people deal with the world. That's even more true for people who develop computer programs and Access databases, because you now have easy entry into a whole universe of other developers, tools, and samples just by visiting the right places on the Web.

Unfortunately, finding really good Access-related Web sites isn't always easy. The name Microsoft chose for its database software doesn't help because the word *access* is very common; any Web search turns up thousands of sites that have nothing to do with our favorite database, Microsoft Access. If you go searching, be sure to enter "Microsoft Access" in quotes to limit the results a bit.

In this chapter, I share some of the really good Web sites I've found that actually do have useful information on Microsoft Access. I couldn't fit them all in, and to be honest, I left out sites that I mention in Chapter 20 simply because I had to draw the line somewhere.

Oh, and don't try to draw any conclusions about the rankings of these sites based on where they appear in the chapter. I purposely list them in alphabetical order to avoid giving any clues to my personal rankings.

Access Database Tips

www.accessdatabasetips.com

The Access Database Tips site has many useful tips that can help you with tables, queries, forms, reports, and VBA modules. You can find a discussion of macros and VBA as well as various samples that are available for downloading. There's even an online newsletter that you can subscribe to if you want to keep up with the latest news from this site.

Access Monster

www.accessmonster.com

The Access Monster site has so many articles, tools, tips, and tutorials that you can probably spend days finding new things you didn't know about Access. There is also an extensive list of frequently asked questions. Because the resources are vast, you can probably find an answer for just about any problem because someone else has probably had the same question before.

Access Monster also offers a large number of online forums where you can ask questions or simply browse to see what other Access users are talking about.

Always read the information for new users before you post a question in an online forum. Barging right in with the attitude that you don't have the time to learn the ropes — you just need an answer NOW — is a sure way to ensure that you quickly become extremely unpopular!

Easy Access Database Directory

www.directory-base.com/access

The Easy Access Database Directory site offers tools, tips, downloadable samples, online magazines, and a whole lot more. Other Access users submitted many of the articles and samples and the Easy Access Database Directory welcomes your submissions, too.

The Easy Access Database Directory site also provides links and ratings for a large number of Access add-ins. As a user community, this site enables you to find out what the other members think about the various listings; community members often leave feedback.

Jamie's Software

```
www.jamiessoftware.tk/home.html
```

Jamie's Software is a site that might seem a bit sparse at first glance, but don't let that fool you. This site offers some free downloads that you won't find elsewhere, as well as a number of useful articles that can help you resolve some thorny Access issues.

Jamie's Software also has a message board that is sort of a free-form question and answer forum where users ask for help with various Access-related issues. This message board isn't really aimed at beginners, but if you've taken the time to gain an understanding of the issues, this site can be an excellent place to get just that little nudge you need to resolve your problem.

Lebans.com

```
www.lebans.com
```

Lebans.com is the personal Web site of an Access developer named Stephen Lebans. The site shares hints, tips, and source code that you can use in your own Access projects. The site owner does not respond to programming questions, but all the samples are provided with the complete source code so that you can adapt them as necessary for your needs.

To find the various files you can download from the Lebans.com site, there's a convenient <u>Contents</u> link. When you click the link you can find each of the available files listed in a handy tree-structured list. Talk about organized.

Microsoft Access Database Solutions

```
www.microsoft-accesssolutions.co.uk
```

The Microsoft Access Database Solutions site is another of those comprehensive sites that can keep you clicking and reading for hours. All versions of Access are included in the articles, tutorials, forums, and downloadable samples. This site is intended for Access users at all levels, so both beginners and more advanced users feel welcome here.

An interesting feature of the Microsoft Access Database Solutions site is the list of links to the latest news about Access and other database programs. In addition, this site sometimes has drawings for various free prizes that you might find interesting.

Microsoft Office Online Access

`office.microsoft.com/en-us/FX010857911033.aspx`

The Microsoft Office Online Access Web site is Microsoft's official Access user site. Here you can find various articles, downloads, tutorials, and other information — straight from the horse's mouth.

One very interesting feature of this site is that you can typically order a CD with a trial version of the latest Access release. This is especially useful if you're still using an older, out-of-date version of Access and want to see if the newer version offers enough new features to make an upgrade worthwhile, but you can order the CD even if you don't already have Access.

If you get to a point where you feel that you really need to get some professional help with your Access problems, this site could be a great place to start. It contains lots of links to both companies and individuals who know Access inside and out.

The main Microsoft Office Web site (`www.office.microsoft.com`) frequently offers updates for Microsoft Office. Many of these updates correct serious security issues, so check for the free updates often.

MSDN — Microsoft Developer Network

The Microsoft Developer Network is clearly aimed at professional application developers, but it also offers a wealth of extremely interesting and useful information for people who aren't quite pros yet. In fact, this site is so useful that I'm going to cheat a little and tell you about three interesting Access-related places at MSDN (but I'm only going to count them as one for the purpose of this chapter).

Although you can purchase a fairly expensive MSDN subscription, it's unnecessary to do so to gain entry to most of the useful Access info you can find here.

MSDN Access code samples

```
msdn.microsoft.com/office/understanding/access/codesamples
```

This arm of the MSDN site offers various code samples that you can use with Access. The samples are listed by the Access version they were developed for, but you can generally use the samples for older versions in a newer Access release.

MSDN Access site

```
msdn.microsoft.com/library/default.asp?url=/library/
          en-us/odc_2003_ta/html/odc_ancaccess.asp
```

At this area of the site, you can find technical articles, developer documentation, various downloads and code samples, and a link to *Smart Access,* a monthly newsletter aimed at Access developers and power users. You can also find some very handy links to things like the Microsoft Knowledge Base; the Knowledge Base offers incredibly useful and often esoteric answers to your problems with Access.

Office Solutions Development

```
msdn.microsoft.com/library/default.asp?url=/library/
          en-us/odc_2003_ta/html/odc_ancoffsol.asp
```

Here you can find links to a vast number of useful articles, code samples, and downloads. This particular site is especially useful if you need to expand your knowledge of Microsoft Office into the other applications beyond Access.

Roger's Access Library

```
www.rogersaccesslibrary.com/TableOfContents3.asp
```

The Roger's Access Library site contains a large number of Access samples that you can download and use for free. These samples are intended to show you how to solve various problems with Access, and you can build upon them to create your own solutions. All the samples are listed alphabetically along with a brief description of their purpose.

Seeing how someone else approached a problem can often steer you onto the path of figuring out a solution for another, similar problem. If you don't see an example that is exactly what you need, be open-minded and look through the list on this site to see whether you can find related information. You may be surprised at how much you discover!

The Access Web

www.mvps.org/access

The Access Web site is another FAQ *(Frequently Asked Questions)* site that is aimed at Access developers. As such, the topics tend to be quite technical, but also extremely useful. If you can't find the answer here, you probably aren't looking closely enough.

Chapter 22

Ten Things to Know About Queries (That Also Help You with Forms and Reports)

*Q*ueries are really important tools in your form and report toolkit. In this chapter, I give you a quick look at some important things you need to remember about queries.

Queries Act Like Tables

One of the most important things you need to know about queries is that they act like tables in many ways. True, you can't store data in queries, but you can use queries as record sources for both forms and reports. You can even use a query as the record source for another query. See Chapter 1 for more information.

Select Queries Are Always Safe

Select queries are always safe to run because they never modify any data. Instead, select queries return a record set, which is sort of like having a temporary table full of the results of the query. See Chapter 2 for more on the types of queries.

Do your experiments with select queries and change the query type only after you're satisfied that the query is returning the correct set of records.

All Queries Are SQL Queries

Every Access query is actually an SQL query. This means that you can always open a valid query in SQL view to examine or modify the query. The reverse does not hold true, however. SQL-specific queries generally cannot be opened in Design view because the Query editor has no way to represent some of the SQL-specific statements. See Chapter 7 for more on SQL.

Action Queries Can Harm Your Data

Action queries — make-table, update, append, and delete — actually make modifications to the data, which means that they can harm that data. Unless you've turned off the warning messages (which generally requires some VBA programming), Access warns you before you execute an action query. If you ignore the warnings, you have only yourself to blame for any damage that happens. See Chapter 6 for more on action queries.

You Need Joins to Use Multiple Tables in Queries

You can use fields from more than one table in a query, but only if you first create relationships *(joins)* between the tables. You can create those relationships in the Query editor or in the Relationships window, but there must be a valid relationship between the tables before you can run the query. See Chapter 5 for more on using multiple tables in queries.

Queries Select All Records Unless You Specify Criteria

If you don't want a query to return every record from the underlying table, you must specify criteria to narrow down the selection. Criteria you specify in a single row must all be satisfied (this is an AND condition). Criteria that are specified on separate rows only require that the conditions on a single row be satisfied (this is an OR condition). See Chapter 15 for more on specifying criteria.

Datasheet View Shows Results without Running the Query

Switching to Datasheet view displays the records that will be selected by the query without actually running the query. For action queries, this function safely shows you which records the query will act upon, but it won't show you how the records will appear after the query is executed. See Chapter 2 for more on query views.

Make-Table Queries Always Begin with an Empty Table

Make-table queries always create tables that only contain the records that are returned by the query. If you specify the name of an existing table as the target of a make-table query, any existing records in that table are wiped out before the new records are added. If you want to add additional records to an existing table without destroying what's already there, use the append query, not the make-table query. See Chapter 6 for more on make-table queries.

Queries Need a Record Source

Every query needs a record source — a table or another query — to supply the data for the query. In theory, you could create a single record table by using a make-table query that specifies each of the field values, but you'd be doing a lot of work for little purpose. See Chapter 2 for information on choosing a record source.

Delete Queries Are Forever

Access doesn't have a recycle bin. If you run a delete query and tell Access that you really do want to delete the records, those records disappear as surely as a July snowfall in Phoenix. If you're not absolutely sure that the records should be gone forever, make a copy of the records before you delete them. If you don't, how long do you think it will be before you realize that you shouldn't have deleted them? See Chapter 8 for tips on avoiding data destruction.

Index

• *M* •

Notes